AFTER THE FALL

Also by Suzanne Somers

Suzanne Somers

AFTER THE FALL

How I Picked Myself Up, Dusted Myself Off,

and Started All Over Again

Crown Publishers, Inc.
New York

A list of photograph credits begins on page 307.

Published by Crown Publishers, Inc., 201 East 50th Street, New York, New York 10022. Member of the Crown Publishing Group.

Random House, Inc. New York, Toronto, London, Sydney, Auckland
www.randomhouse.com

CROWN and colophon are trademarks of Crown Publishers, Inc.

Printed in the United States of America

Design by Karen Minster

Library of Congress Cataloging-in-Publication Data
Somers, Suzanne, 1946–
    After the fall : how I picked myself up, dusted myself off, and
started all over again / by Suzanne Somers. — 1st ed.
    1. Somers, Suzanne, 1946–   . 2. Television actors and actresses—
United States—Biography.
    PN2287.S63A3   1998
    791.45'028'092—dc21
    [B]   98-13230
                                                                              CIP

ISBN 0-609-60312-4

10 9 8 7 6 5 4 3 2 1

First Edition

On the eve of the publication of *After the Fall*, my mother died unexpectedly. I have always said that from death one can find meaning, but because my mother's passing is so new to me, I find myself only at the beginning of that journey. I'd like to think that she has now found everlasting peace with my father and that they are dancing and laughing in heaven as they watch over my family and me.

Mom, you were my guiding light on earth
and now you are the special star
that shines from above.

Dedication

⁂ After a grueling year of work, with way too many seven-day weeks, bordering on workaholism, I finally had the opportunity to take a much-needed vacation—six glorious weeks lazily roaming the Tuscan hillsides and the South of France.

On the second night of this restful romp, a fax from New York arrived at the bedroom door of our villa. It was from my lawyer, Marc Chamlin, congratulating me on the signed agreement with Crown Publishers for my next book. I smiled to myself, privileged to have an opportunity for the fifth time to devote three hundred or so pages to my point of view. Then I saw a startling sentence in the contract that I presumed must certainly be incorrect. I called Marc only to hear him say that, indeed, this next book was due in three months! How could I do that? I needed at least three months to gather my thoughts.

I called my agent, Al Lowman, literary's best, by the way. "Al, how can this be?" I asked.

"It's about momentum," Al explained. "Your last book *Eat Great, Lose Weight* was a winner and the publisher wants to follow immediately with *Think Great, Look Great*. You know what you want to say," Al continued. "We've talked about it so many times. It's the message in your lectures. It's the hope you offer in your video package. You can do it."

"What's the big deal?" my husband, Alan, interjected. "You know what to write. It's about uncovering the barriers from your past that keep you from being all that you can be."

My publisher, Chip Gibson, along with associate publisher Andy Martin and editorial director Steve Ross, all echoed the same sentiments. "People identify with you," they each said. "Your story offers hope. Coming from your background, you can show others that an abusive background doesn't have to imprison you."

For three days I sat in the plaza of our rented villa with a pen and a blank tablet in my lap. No matter how hard I tried, *Think Great, Look Great* wasn't coming to me. Then one day my darling friend, Nelson Davis, who was traveling with us along with his lady, Andrea, sat down next to me and said the following. "I remember hearing you speak at the Women, Inc., conference in Long Beach and I was impressed by your ability to create a linkage through all the events in your life that have brought you to this point. I was inspired by your positiveness and unwillingness to see yourself as a victim. Every bump in the road of your life's journey propelled you forward. The way you linked the events together made me see that each bump in the road was necessary and exactly the way it should be. When your speech concluded, I wanted more because through your words, I saw the possibilities in my own life. Continue that speech. Make the linkages and pass on the information so I can see that perhaps I, too, can have the same successes personally and professionally."

Suddenly it seemed easy. The words began pouring out of my head. My carpal tunnel syndrome painfully returned to my ring and baby fingers.

Six weeks and four hundred handwritten pages later, I called Al Lowman and said, "I have good news and bad news. The good news is I've finished the book. The bad news is it's not the book everyone thought I was writing. *Think Great, Look Great* will have to come after this. For some reason another autobiography poured out of me—a Part Two of sorts."

Al laughed hysterically. "I've never had a client like you. Send it to me. I've got to read it."

Well, Al called Chip Gibson, Chip called Steve Ross and Andy Martin. The Crown team then put the brakes on the original plan. Because these executives are young and enthusiastic visionaries, they were able to shift gears and map out a new plan.

So, thanks, Marc, Al, Nelson, Chip, Steve, and Andy for getting me off my butt. I like your style.

It takes so many people to produce a book. To my editor, Sue Carswell, thank you. She was a hoot to work with. "Just keep asking me questions as you read the manuscript," I told her. And she did. The pages were littered with remarks such as, "Whoa! Suddenly you're married to Alan and you haven't even explained there was a wedding. What was the wedding like? Who was there? What did you wear?" Or, she'd say, "This sounds a little too diva-ish." Or, "This must have been a very emotional moment. Tell us more." Sue made this a better book.

Thanks to Sue's assistant, Rachel Kahan.

To Wendy Schuman my publicist at Crown, thank you for your never-ending enthusiasm for this project.

Thanks to copy chief Andrea Peabbles and interior designer Karen Minster for their tireless work.

Thanks to Wendi Shapiro and Michelle Ong in my office.

Thanks to my personal publicist, Kelly Kimball.

And thanks to my dear friend Andrea Giambrone for her honesty and candor in reading this manuscript for me.

And a big thank-you to Marsha Yanchuck. She's been with me for almost the entire twenty-year span over which this book took place. She was my memory, my grammar consultant, my spell check, and my friend. Thanks, Marsha, for reading the man-uscript and galleys over and over checking for errors. You are the best!

But how do I thank my family? Alan, your trust astounds me. I am grateful for everything that you are to me in my life. Thank you for your bravery. At times these pages are not terribly flat-tering, but you urged me to keep going in order to flush it out. You've always known who you are and the judgment of others has never seemed to faze you. I admire you and love you deeply.

Leslie, ours is a triumphant relationship. Thank you for allow-ing me to explore all the depths of our stepdaughter/stepmother relationship. We've had rocky times, but now we have something so great together that everything that happened has shown its meaning. We had to work at love and today I couldn't love you more.

Stephen, I know how private you are, and I've tried my best to preserve your privacy while telling the story of our family struggle. Thank you. You are very dear to me.

And finally, Bruce. Now that you have your own child, you can truly understand the depth of my feelings for you. I chronicled your growth as a person through these pages. Out of the ashes you emerged strong, powerful, and a man. I am proud of you and love you with all my heart.

To all of you, I dedicate this book.

My goal in life is
to become the person
my dog thinks I am.

Introduction

What could be worse than losing the number one television show in America? Not losing it. Had I continued playing Chrissy Snow on *Three's Company*, the humongous hit TV show, I would not be the Suzanne I am today—a person I am happy to be.

I had been moving full speed in America's fast lane. Life was great. Nothing could stop me now, I thought. Money was plentiful; work was coming at me like bullets on an artillery range. I could pick and choose. I was dancing in the big time.

Then one day while my life was "speeding along that highway," someone opened the back door of the car and kicked me out. Suddenly I found myself sitting on the side of the road all alone, watching a cloud of dust as the car sped on without me.

Celebrity is an amazing gift, an opportunity of a lifetime. There's nothing like it. When fame came to me, it was like a drug, an ongoing incredible high. People called me "Miss Somers"; crowded restaurants magically had the best table available—"Come right this way, Miss Somers," I would hear; theater tickets were no problem, nor were hotel reservations or hair appointments. Crowded doctors' offices could always fit me in for an appointment when it was convenient for me. There was no waiting in lines for movies or sitting in crowded airport lounges. Pre-boarding was the new and luxurious experience—a chance to get settled in before the "civilians" were allowed on the plane. I no longer even needed to carry a purse. Somehow, somewhere, magically, someone would appear to take care of my needs. Runners, gofers were a new part of my life; "No problem, Miss Somers. I can get it for you." Anything—my favorite soup or the La Scala chopped salad, which I love—would be fetched and brought to me. Makeup people hovered to powder my nose, fix my lipstick, add more blush. Hairdressers—teasing, spraying, adjusting. Anything I wanted or needed was responded to with a resounding "Yes, Miss Somers! Yes! Yes! Yes!"

Nothing was a problem because I was earning money for the network, and lots of it. A hit TV show is big business with multimillion-dollar bonanzas. Keep the star happy. Don't mess with success. That's why studios would accommodate Elizabeth Taylor's demands for chili from Chasen's restaurant in L.A.—no matter where in the world she traveled. They'd march it up the Himalayas if that would keep her happy. Elizabeth Taylor sells tickets. Never say no to the star, because if the star walks, the project can fall apart. And the more popular the star, the more their demands are met.

I didn't ask for any of this special treatment. It just came to me and intensified with each new magazine cover or important television appearance. When you're hot in TV, your busiest times are "sweeps weeks." That's when the networks put out their best product because advertisers buy time according to Nielsen ratings, which are measured during sweeps. The higher the ratings, the higher the advertising revenues; and subsequently, there are more profits for the networks. When you are the hot star, everyone wants you to be on their show, because you will bring in viewers, which, in turn, brings in profits.

Once you are famous, you don't have to evolve as a person. It's not necessary or important that you read or think or make corrections in your personality. Nobody cares! Just keep the profits rolling in. There's no need to move yourself forward spiritually and emotionally.

But growth is the greatest gift we can give ourselves as human beings—to constantly evolve, to be the best person we can be, to tune in to our feelings and to face ourselves in all our nakedness and truly look at who we are. It is our opportunity to change and to grow.

If I hadn't been dumped off the number one show in America, I might have successfully continued doing sitcom after sitcom and being "Yessed" to death. Instead I was forced to come back to earth and look at myself from the vantage point of having "been there" and having lost my first huge professional opportunity.

As quickly as it all came, it was over. I was no longer America's darling. Suddenly I was no longer on the number one television show in the country, so I wasn't bringing in any profits; and when you don't bring in profits, the doors slam shut. The "friends" I had made along the way were suddenly too busy to see me. The open doors of the network executives closed in my face. The champagne and scripts stopped arriving. The party invitations dried up. I was moved way down the alphabet from the "A-list."

I felt ostracized, hurt, and shut out, disappointed that I believed I had been making "real" relationships. I had not understood that the invitations, the champagne, the scripts, the dinner invites, the open doors, and the friends were about business. This is the way it's done in Hollywood. The line between business and friendship is deliberately blurred. The pros, the ones who endure, understand this. It's the naive ones like myself, the new "hot" ones on the block, who get it confused and take it personally.

Today, twenty years later, I am grateful. If I hadn't lost every-thing, I never would have had to do the work to bring myself back. I'm not talking about success anymore, although that came with it. I'm talking about the emotional work that helped me find the self-esteem to be the person I am today. It's an ongo-ing journey that has brought, and continues to bring me, peace of mind, serenity, and happiness with myself and the new life I have created.

After the Fall is about the second part of my life's journey. This book picks up where my 1988 autobiography, *Keeping Secrets*, left off. *Keeping Secrets* helped me find clarity from a childhood of confusion, a childhood riddled with pain caused by living with a violent alcoholic father. I was severely affected by his disease simply by my proximity to it.

Alcoholism affected who I was, who I became, and who I am today, even though I never abused alcohol myself. This disease stripped away my self-esteem. When I was a child, my father told me over and over that I was "stupid, hopeless, worthless, nothin', a big zero!" Somewhere along the line, I began to believe him. My father was drunk while saying these things, but he was so much bigger than I was. He was my father; I had no choice but to believe him. He was the first teacher to whom I gave power over my life.

Then fame dropped in. Fame has a power of its own; it must never be abused. It must have meaning; otherwise, it is pur-poseless. Fame taught me a lot. I've learned and grown enor-mously since that imaginary car ride.

At this same period in my life, while I was trying to deal with my newfound celebrity, my personal life went into a tailspin. I was trying to blend my husband's children with my own child to make a real family. I had no idea the task we were undertaking when Alan Hamel and I said those words, "Till death do us part." As a result of my family's struggle to find peace, acceptance, and love, I learned that accomplishments are empty when you shut the door behind you at the end of the day and feel a thick, unhappy silence at home.

As always, to explain where I am today, it's necessary to tell you the story of where I've been.

Today I see all negatives as opportunities. Everything that has happened to me has been a lesson. A wasted life is one in which lessons go unheeded. People who live such lives are the people who give up, who choose to be victims.

I didn't give up. I am not a victim, and that is my proudest achievement.

Part One

THE LESSONS

ONE

"Put your heads between your knees," the pilot screamed. "We're going to try to make a landing in the water."

Two Island ladies sitting across from us started wailing, "Oh, Lord, we're gonna die; oh, Lord, we're gonna die."

I could see the black waters of the Caribbean approaching closer and closer out the window of our small twin-engine Fairchild. The engines labored against the hurricane-force winds. Bam! Another air pocket! We dropped hundreds of feet once again.

"Oh, God," I yelled. The screams of the eighteen petrified passengers pierced the blackness of the night. I don't want my life to be over, I thought. My poor little boy, Bruce, was expecting me to be home that night. He had been staying at my parents' house while Alan and I were on vacation. I knew Bruce was anxious to get back to his own room in our house and away from his grandfather's drunken, violent mood swings.

The cabin was illuminated once again. Lightning was all around us. I jumped in my seat as if that would protect me from the constant lightning flashes. Rain poured in slanted sheets against the flimsy windows of our small plane. I wondered how long the glass would hold from the force of the torrential waters. I held Alan's hand tightly.

"I love you, Alan," I said through tears. "I've never felt this way about anyone in my life. I don't want it to be over." It was as though Alan and I were in a capsule of quiet while the screaming and wailing of the passengers swirled around us.

"I love you, too, Suzanne," Alan said softly.

The plane jerked violently. Alan put his arm around my back protectively while our heads rested between our knees in crash position.

"We're going down! We're going down!" the pilot yelled through his microphone.

Oh, my God! I thought. I don't want to die like this, not in that water. I want to see Bruce; I want my life with Alan. I thought of my mother, my father, my brothers, and my dear sister. But mostly, I thought of Bruce. He was my life and the thought of him being motherless filled me with grief.

"By the way we're over the Bermuda Triangle," Alan said, trying to lighten the fear we both felt.

The plane was descending out of control, the winds bouncing our little craft like a kickball. I prepared for the worst. Alan's hand wrapped around mine, stopping the blood from flowing. The numbness in my fingers mirrored my fear. To believe you are about to die stops all feeling. You just wait for the inevitable. Then . . . Bang! Bong! We hit ground! Ground? Not water? We made it! We were alive! Bruce would have a mother. Alan and I would have a life together. We hugged each other tearfully. We had landed on a foamed runway in Miami. We had made it through one of the worst storms in the history of the Caribbean.

Alan and I grabbed our carry-on luggage and ran to the door of the plane. I wanted to put my feet on the ground and just kiss it. We had been spared.

———

The next day, January 2, 1977, exactly one day after surviving that near-fatal plane crash, I returned to Los Angeles, via San Francisco to get Bruce, and received a phone call from my manager, Bonnie. She said in her side-of-the-mouth, Runyonesque way, "Listen, I got a call from ABC for a new show they're doin' called *Three's Company*, and they seem really interested in you."

"I don't know," I said reluctantly. "I almost died last night, and I've been doing a lot of thinking. I just can't do this anymore."

"Whatta ya mean you almost died last night?"

"It was terrible," I told her. "It was the first time it had snowed in the Bahamas in fifty years. Our small plane was struck by lightning and was damaged. Alan and I said our last words to each other. I could see myself being eaten by sharks in the cold, black water. It was terrible.

"Coming that close to death got me thinking. I didn't sleep at all last night. I kept asking myself, What am I doing with my life? My career is stuck; I've done nine TV pilots over the last couple of years, and every one of them has failed. I'm weary from the constant rejection. They tell me I'm either too short, too tall, not funny enough, too busty, or not busty enough. All I hear is what I'm not. Let's just give it up. I'm not going to make it in this business. I've been going after an impossible dream. I don't know, Bonnie, perhaps I can teach cooking. I'd really enjoy that."

"Maybe you lived for a reason," Bonnie said thoughtfully. "Maybe God has big plans for you, Suzanne. Don't give up now. We've worked so hard, and I swear," Bonnie pleaded, "they seem really interested. Why don'tcha try one more time. Huh? Maybe this'll be the one. Maybe somethin'll happen."

I paused and thought for a moment. "All right," I sighed, "one last time, and then that's it."

I put the phone down and began the routine. Bruce was at school, so I had plenty of time to go to the interview and be back before he got home. I washed my long blond hair and put on a little makeup. I had been a pseudo–hippie flower child while living in San Francisco in the late '60s and makeup had not been part of the fashion. Miniskirts were now the style—the shorter, the better, worn with platform knee-high boots. To this ensemble I added a white cotton shirt with French cuffs. As I left my apartment, my hair danced in the beautiful afternoon sunshine—a typical day in southern California, and I was simply glad to be alive.

I jumped into my Chevy Vega and drove to Century City, the West Coast headquarters of ABC Television, to meet Bonnie. She was already there when I arrived and gave me a big hug. "You look good," she said as she surveyed my face and attire.

Still somewhat shaken, I replied, "Last night I didn't think I'd ever see you or anyone else again." We sat on one of the butter-soft leather sofas in the large and impressive lobby. The space had thirty-foot ceilings and enormous sheets of glass exposing an endless view of Los Angeles. In all the corners were large, beautiful live trees. I looked up and saw a well-dressed, attractive woman walking our way.

"Excuse me. Mr. Silverman will see you now, Miss Somers."

"Go get 'em," Bonnie said enthusiastically, and winked.

Normally I would have been extremely nervous walking into an intimidating situation like that, but compared with what I had experienced the night before, this was nothing. I felt a calm gratefulness.

Fred Silverman was a middle-aged guy with a round face and intense blue eyes. He gave off powerful and impatient vibes, kind of scary, but at the same time impressive. I could tell he was in charge and I found that trait appealing. He was sitting at a big desk in an even bigger windowed office that also overlooked Century City. The room was filled with what looked like a sea of gray suits; maybe twenty men, all seemingly dressed alike. A young brunette woman was sitting on the couch. She was dressed casually in contrast to the severity of the others. I wondered who she was. Fred was smiling; no one else was. This was serious business. A lot was at stake for the network. Their new show, *Three's Company*, had been given a green light if they could find the right blond to complete the trio. They had already hired Joyce DeWitt and John Ritter to star. Two pilots had been done with two other blond actresses, but the chemistry wasn't right.

"This is Joyce DeWitt," I was told. "She'll be playing Janet." So that's who she is, I thought. Joyce was very cute and not too tall, with big round expressive eyes, dark hair, and a serious demeanor. She was calm and had a lot of confidence, and I wondered how she had gotten like that. I was now feeling ill at ease in this setting. Something was making me feel intimidated all of a sudden. Joyce and I couldn't really talk to each other because of the peering eyes of the gray suits, but I felt comfortable in her presence. Somehow in this awkward environment her confidence made me feel more relaxed and that allowed whatever talent I had at that time to emerge.

"Would you mind sitting next to Joyce?" Fred asked. "We'd like to see how you look together." I wondered what they were looking for.

Something was different about this interview. Usually it was read a page or so, a "Thank you very much," and you never heard from them again. There was noticeable tension in this room. Whenever I get nervous, I try to make jokes, but this time my humor hung in the air like a bad smell.

Joyce and I read two pages, then another three pages. The room laughed, but only if Fred laughed. Fred would go, "Ha! Ha! Ha!," and then the sea of gray suits would go, "Ha! Ha! Ha!" This is weird, I thought. I had no experience in the business, so I didn't realize that millions of dollars were at stake.

"Well, thank you very much," Fred said to me, and I knew I was dismissed. I could feel all eyes burning through the back of me as I walked to the door. I felt like I had no underpants on. I had been through so many tryouts, seemingly hundreds over those last several years, that I never really expected to get the job. Today was probably no different, I thought, which was fine with me. I wanted to move on and make a change in my life. I hoped I could figure out how to develop a regular cooking school in my home that in time could work itself into something not only lucrative but enjoyable and creative as well. I actually felt great that I had something new to focus on. The constant rejection of auditions had become almost intolerable.

After the interview, I drove home to Santa Monica in my not-yet-paid-for Chevy thinking about how I could reconfigure my apartment kitchen to accommodate students, if I could find any. The advantage of so many years with so little work was that I had had time to teach myself to cook. I read cookbooks like novels, start to finish, trying every recipe I could afford. I had always loved cooking. When I was a little girl, I was given a book called *Susie's Cookbook,* and I thought it was written about me. On the nights when the house was quiet, my mom would read it to me at my request instead of nursery tales. It was filled with recipes, and I particularly liked Candle Salad.

"Read the Candle recipe again, Mommy," I would beg.

"Okay," she'd say. "You take a piece of lettuce and put it on the plate. Then a scoop of cottage cheese. On top of that, place a pineapple ring. Then you cut a banana in half and stand it inside the pineapple ring."

Then I would say proudly, "And you take a cherry and put it on top of the banana; and then you have Candle Salad! YEA!"

———

I was preoccupied when I walked in the front door of the apartment Alan and I shared.

I lived on Ocean Avenue with my then boyfriend, Alan Hamel, and my son, Bruce, who was now eleven years old. Alan and I had been in love for eight years. In 1974 I had moved to Los Angeles from Sausalito to be with him. There were no guarantees of marriage, but there was a sincere desire to try to make it as a couple. Times were tough. I was having financial difficulties from lack of work, and Alan was trying to bounce back financially from his divorce and dealing with all the confused feelings that came from sharing his life with my son, while his two children lived in his former home with his ex-wife. All three of our children were anxious and upset. My son did not like sharing me with Alan after having had me all to himself. Alan was having a hard time warming up to Bruce out of the guilt of not living with his own kids. I loved Alan and was willing to do whatever was necessary to spend my life with him, but I was aware we had a lot of problems to sort out if we were going to mend the hurt that swirled around us.

I had never in my life met a man like Alan. From that first moment in December 1968, at the KGO studios in San Francisco, it was as though an electric charge went through my body. I felt hot, then cold, with shivers. My eyes lost their ability to make contact. Looking into the deep pool of his blue eyes was too potent a connection. I had to look away, yet couldn't help looking back. He was hosting a national television show for ABC called *The Anniversary Game*, and I had been hired for a day as a prize model. In an instant I knew I had to be with Alan, if only one time, just to know I had experienced merging with another so completely. That is the power of kindred souls. It cannot be grabbed or analyzed or planned.

Alan couldn't know what emotional baggage I was bringing with me. Years of conversations were ahead of us, years of unraveling each other's tangled webs. We couldn't know the pain we would each bring to the table, nor would it matter. We were destined to work it out together.

As a person I felt emotionally supported by Alan in a way I had never experienced before. He became my lover and my mentor. His thinking was not clouded with limitations. Long before it was popular, he thought that anything in life is possible if you believe in yourself. Alan was somehow sent to teach me to believe in myself, which was no small achievement. My childhood had left me damaged, with no sense of self-worth. To have Alan say simple things such as, "Your poetry is good. You should find a publisher and make a book deal," was so foreign an experience for me, it caused my head to cock to the side in thoughtful bewilderment.

My love affair with Alan became the central focus of my life. I was constantly juggling my mothering of Bruce with my passion for Alan. I couldn't get enough of him. I would drop everything to be with him. There was always the emotional pull between my child and my lover. The few other men in my life prior to Alan always took a backseat to my mothering responsibilities. Except for one brief relationship when Bruce was a toddler, no man was ever asked to spend time in my home because of Bruce, nor did I ever date until after Bruce's bedtime. Our home belonged to Bruce and me. We were each other's worlds.

My childhood family did not fit into this life of my making, either. I felt judged by them, real or imagined, that they perceived my getting pregnant before marriage was a problem I had created for myself, which was true. Now I would have to live with the consequences and figure it out. I was lonely and frightened. The exception was my mother, who has always been my connection to safety. I have always been close to my mother, and during the difficult times, she held me to her with a loose tether, never quite letting me fall all the way down. But her life was overwhelming. She was enduring the burden of her drunken, violent husband, so she could not always be as available to me as I needed.

At that time, my family was in various stages of death by alcoholism. Sometimes my father would be so drunk he would not recognize me. My siblings—Maureen, Dan, and Michael—were dealing with their own problems with this insidious disease. Sometimes my sister could be emotionally present, but mostly her focus was staying sober to handle her daytime mothering responsibilities. Five o'clock was her magic hour—the reward for dealing with three screaming boys. Then the booze would come out and take away the pain.

I had moved away from my hometown of San Bruno, California, in 1964, mainly to stop feeling the judgment and the whispers of the locals. I had married my boyfriend, Bruce Somers, when I was eighteen and pregnant. In the two short years we were married, I was miserable and blamed him for our predicament. I had not yet learned the concept of "it takes two to tango." I felt that for both of us, youth had been cut short and our individual dreams would never be realized. What had been fun as girlfriend and boyfriend was now a new life of responsibility we were not ready to assume. We had no money, so paying the rent and putting food on the table kept us both in a constant state of panic, hardly conducive to starting a life together. The marriage was doomed from the start and our immaturity only fueled its demise. Bruce was a nice guy with an easy laugh. He excelled academically and had dreams of becoming a lawyer when he finished his studies at the University of San Francisco. He was two years older than me, but his twenty years were not sufficient to prepare him for fatherhood and marriage. We hardly knew each other. Our dating conversations had been about parties, sports, and the latest jokes. There had been no serious digging into our souls. I had no idea what he wanted out of life or where he wanted to live and in what manner. We had never discussed my love for performing or my dream of becoming an actress. In fact, it had been my success in high school in the lead role of Adelaide in *Guys and Dolls* that gave me the act-ing bug. Bruce was jealous of my interest in performing and the attention it took away from him. Soon after I'd graduated from high school, he gave me an engagement ring. I was not ready to be engaged, but I did not have the guts to tell him so. I didn't want to hurt his feelings because he had presented it to me so grandly in front of my entire family. I got caught up in the excite-ment of friends looking at my small but beautiful diamond and kept it on my finger to admire, always thinking that I'd give it back. With our engagement came new, special privileges. When it came to sex, the word "No" no longer held any impact.

"Why not? We're engaged to be married," he would insist. I felt obliged to allow him to "go further" than we had because of the ring. I would not let him "go all the way," but heavy petting has a way of getting out of hand, and before I knew it, I was preg-nant, even though I was still technically a virgin. I was devas-tated when the doctor told me "the happy news."

I didn't have the courage to tell my mother, so Bruce dutifully told her while I waited in my bedroom. My father was drunk, so telling him would have been a waste of time. He'd forget by the next morning anyway, and to tell him while he was "under the influence" was sure to create unnecessary violence. I felt badly enough already. I had disappointed my mother. Her eyes were watery and sad when I emerged after she heard the news, but she told me she loved me and that everything would be okay.

My teenage pregnancy was perfect fodder for gossip in my community. I was the shamed sinner. I had not been able to con-trol myself, so now I was getting what I deserved. My beautiful son was proof of my shame, and it was this that finally made me leave. I wanted to find a place where no one knew my history. I could reinvent myself and shed the dysfunction of alcoholism that had held me in a vise all my life. Two years after Bruce and I were married, we divorced. Once again, I was the subject of scandal, first having to get married because I was pregnant, and now getting divorced; but the union had been so wrong that we both felt it was better to get out now rather than later. I was the first person I knew who was divorced. It just wasn't done at that time. It was 1967, which is an eternity ago by today's behavioral standards, particularly by small-town standards. I walked away from the gossip and the judgment to begin again and moved with my son across the Bay to Sausalito.

Life is not easy for a young divorcée with a child and no support system, financial or emotional. At times I felt deep despair and loneliness, but every morning the shining face of my adorable child would look into mine and give me the strength to get through another day. I had never had a friend like my son. It was a relationship without complications, founded on unconditional love. Had I not been financially destitute, I truly would not have needed anything else in my life. We spent our days and nights together. Only food, shelter, and clothing forced me out of the house, like a mother lioness on the hunt. I foraged for work to pay for the necessities and somehow eked out a living by modeling for small-time accounts. Occasionally, a good job presented itself—ads for Chevrolet or Winston cigarettes. Those were the $500 ads, and one of them could get us through an entire month; but mostly it was $60 here and $60 there. Somehow we scraped by without the help of child support or state aid, but it was tough. Good jobs with opportunity, like my small but important role in *American Graffiti*, were in my future; but at the moment, work for me was bleak.

———

Then one day, without warning, I found myself locked eye to eye with Alan Hamel. Now my focus was divided between the two greatest love affairs imaginable. Both wanted all of me, and in that, the struggle began.

Alan was married, but the marriage was coming to an end. He and his wife had drifted apart over the years because of Alan's traveling and long absences. From the beginning, it had never been right, he told me. He had not been ready to settle down, but he had let life happen to him and now there were complications of routine and expectations that kept him from taking the painful steps of leaving. His children were a big part of his reason for staying. He had been able to coast in the relationship because he had never been seriously emotionally involved with another woman, and returning home to the excited faces of his kids, he said, made living this way worthwhile. I was not the first woman who had caught his eye, but I was the first woman with whom he had fallen in love. He loved his children dearly and did not want to cause them pain, so he tried to find a way to avoid being pulled back and forth between me and his family.

"Things are fine the way they are," he said. "It would be no different even if I were divorced," he kept explaining, hoping I would find this arrangement agreeable so he would not be forced to make difficult changes.

I was not evolved yet as a woman and had not even considered the immorality of my participation in this union with Alan. Had I been an accountable person at this time I would have insisted our relationship be put on hold until his marriage was officially over. But I didn't.

To avoid taking the next step, he protected his feelings by denying the fact that my life included my son. If he could deny Bruce's inconvenient existence, Alan could protect himself emotionally, so he had no interest in knowing Bruce on any level. I was sure I had no future with Alan, so I kept the two separate, never forcing them to acknowledge each other.

Alan was beyond handsome. He was a combination of cool, hip, fun-loving, smart, savvy, and sexy. Just the way he said "Hello there" with his deep voice would make my heart race. Because I saw no future with him, I treated each time as if it were our last. Every meal, every time we made love, we acted as though we would never see each other again. I would cling to him all the way down the stairs and out of my house and to his car, always one last long lingering kiss and a sense of profound emptiness as he drove away.

I loved him so much that to have him on these terms was better than not having him at all. In the darkness of my lonely nights I was filled with guilt. It was wrong, yet I couldn't stop. It was beyond sex; it was a sense of feeling comfortable with him, as though we had known each other all our lives. I couldn't and wouldn't ask him to change his life for fear I would drive him away. For three years we lived this way—Alan with his double life, Bruce and I with our private lives, and Alan and I with our love affair—three distinct and completely separate lives that never crossed over their invisible barriers. Then one day Alan told me he was ending his marriage officially. I had never asked him to and had not expected it. He wanted to be with me, he said, and was tired of keeping his lies straight. He didn't want to live dishonestly anymore.

Suddenly there was a future. I allowed myself to dream of Alan, Bruce, Alan's children Leslie and Stephen, and me as one big happy family. I knew this would take a lot of work, but we could do it. It was my dream.

In my naïveté, I thought we'd be able to smoothly roll over the next phase. I had not counted on the children's right to object. They didn't want new parents, nor could they see where they fit into our passionate twosome. We each threatened the other's children by our very existence. But relationships are about steps and this was the next inevitable step, like it or not. We were parents and our children were integral parts of our lives.

When I first met Alan's daughter, Leslie, who was four years older than my son, I felt as though I was being inspected at a meat market. She did not smile but instead looked at me warily and suspiciously. Somewhere in that moment, I imagine she must have decided that no one was going to make her feel any-thing she did not want to feel. I could sense her rebellion at being force-fed a new woman in her life. As Leslie's parents' mar-riage had disintegrated, she had taken the number one spot in her father's life. When he came home from a trip, she would greet him with the enthusiasm of an adoring wife. It was here that the competition began between Leslie and me. Maybe she fantasized that once I was out of the way, she could have her daddy all to herself. This is a common fantasy of most "Daddy's girls." I can imagine it is a wonderful fantasy to have, yet it was so far removed from the relationship I had with my own father that it was difficult to comprehend. But in Leslie's case, her father was extraordinarily handsome, powerful, sexy, and dot-ing. It would be hard for another to fill his shoes. Couple that with the fact that Leslie and her father are almost identical in spirit, and you have the makings of an extremely potent rela-tionship.

Leslie was born into an idyllic life. As a child, she was a free spirit, a very happy baby with a great sense of humor. She was very loving, always hugging and kissing everyone. She lived with her parents and her nanny in a beautiful old Victorian mansion in Rosedale, the best address in the heart of Toronto. Her bed-room was like a room in a fairy tale, complete with a canopy bed with a red-and-white candy-striped awning, and a large terrace overlooking the garden and coach house. In the winter the gar-den was a snow-filled wonderland, and the summers brought lush foliage in every shade of green. Most winters she went away with her parents and her nanny to Jamaica or the Bahamas or Acapulco, where for weeks she would warm up from the Canadian chill while playing on white sandy beaches.

It was a life surrounded by loving grandparents, aunts, uncles, and cousins, all of whom described her glowingly as "smart as a whip," unique, adorable, lovable, and incredibly artistic and cre-ative. How could she not feel safe surrounded by all the love and protection that comes from a functioning family system? Even her father's absences each week worked to her advantage. Daddy leaving was part of her routine and never ruffled her sense of confidence because he always came back; and when he did, it was with hugs, kisses, and presents! She was the apple of her father's eye; in her universe, she knew that she was number one.

When she was three, Leslie's brother, Stephen, was born and she had to work a little harder at being the center of attention. Stephen was an adorable baby with blond curly locks much like Alan's. He was a gentle child, much less outgoing than Leslie. But like his sister, he was artistically inclined, encouraged by their mother, herself an outstanding artist who paints, sculpts, writes books, and designs sets and toys. Stephen also had many of the qualities of his paternal grandfather, a gentle and dignified man, very private and fiercely loyal to his family. Stephen liked drawing and sculpting and even as a child was drawn to less conventional literature, like Greek mythology.

If Leslie was the instigator, Stephen was the mischievous one. As a child he would scurry around the mansion, playing games with his nanny, knowing instinctively which buttons to push to exasperate her. One time, at the age of five, Leslie waited in the family car with Stephen while their father went inside to get a forgotten item, leaving the car keys in the ignition. Leslie promptly put the car in reverse. As the car rolled down the long driveway backing out toward the street, Alan happened to look outside and he ran to the car in the nick of time to stop traffic and keep them from getting killed. Realizing their dad was upset, Leslie locked the doors. Furious, he ordered Leslie to open the window, but she convinced Stephen not to obey, somehow thinking they could stay in that car forever, avoiding punishment. Already, Leslie was strong-willed and had a mind of her own.

As Stephen grew older, he became more and more shy when he was in the presence of anyone other than his core family unit. Like his sister, he has a wonderful sense of humor, but only those he trusts get to see it. This gave him a mystique. Even as a child he had a mystery about him and an intense loyalty to those he loved. Blood connection was all-important. Without it, it was hard to penetrate the wall he constructed around his life.

When they were young, Alan's children attended the best private school in Toronto. Every day both of them dressed in their uniforms, a navy blue blazer with gray flannel trousers for Stephen and a gray flannel pleated skirt and navy kneesocks for Leslie. They walked the several blocks to school, accompanied for safety by their nanny. Leslie had an easy time with academics—nothing was difficult for her to grasp; Stephen struggled in a structured academic environment. On Friday nights there were pleasurable weekly dinners at Alan's parents. Alan's mother was a wonderful cook, and the reverence for the Sabbath was commemorated week after week with rich chicken soup in which kreplach floated delicately in the broth. Each yummy little "ravioli" was filled with a mixture of chopped chicken and onions made fresh by Alan's mother, Margaret. Crisp roasted chicken would follow, with potatoes and vegetables, and then Margaret's special honey cake. These dinners were part of the ritual of Leslie and Stephen's idyllic life. They could count on these occasions to further their rich cultural heritage. They were learning pride in their family, pride in their home, and feeling the safety a child feels when all is well.

This happy life continued until Stephen was six years old and Leslie was nine. It was then that Alan decided to move his family to California. He had been wanting to move to Los Angeles for several years. It was a choice that was to change his family dynamics forever. Los Angeles is so different from Toronto. For the same price as Alan's Rosedale mansion, he was able to find a typical California home in a middle-class neighborhood. Whereas his Toronto mansion had the trappings of quality— stained-glass windows, parquet floors, architectural detailing in the moldings, beautiful wood-framed beveled-glass windows—

the family's new house had none of these. It was a ranch-style home, with aluminum sliding windows laid out for the relaxed living of southern California, complete with a swimming pool. It was nice, but hardly comparable to the elegance and grandeur of the house they had left behind. Leslie's new room was too small to accommodate her beautiful canopy bed, and she no longer had her garden view and terrace.

Leslie and Stephen went to private schools, starting with the Lycée Français. Their new schoolmates were sons and daughters of the rich and famous. It takes a solid, strong family unit to keep kids on track in L.A. The fantasylike existence whittles away at everyone's grasp on reality. Children's birthday parties take on the proportions of weddings. Everything is overblown and overdone. The parents of this era in L.A. were hip, cool, and groovy. They smoked dope, took acid trips, and snorted cocaine. Many of the parents had completely lost touch with reality, and kids were spreading stories that their parents let them smoke dope as a family activity.

Alan and his wife were growing further and further apart, and Leslie and Stephen were feeling the tension in the house. They were starting to act out and rebel. When Daddy was home, there was the strained silence between their once-loving parents. Stephen and Leslie were too young to fathom the meaning of what was happening yet sensitive enough to know it wasn't something good. To confront their reality would bring about change, and change was overwhelming to entertain.

By the time I came into the picture in 1968, my impression of Alan's marriage was one of two people under one roof living separate lives. Knowing this helped to ease my guilt, but I was grateful when his marriage dissolved officially.

———

How naive of me to think that now everything was going to be great. Alan was dealing with his divorce and his guilt over what he was doing to his children. Bruce was horribly threatened by Alan's presence. He didn't remember ever seeing me in a love relationship with another man, and he felt competitive. When we had outings "as a family," they were anything but happy. All the kids were vying for total attention from their own parent. They would physically wiggle their way between us as if that separation would put them back into first place.

There were no talk shows in the early '70s that discussed family problems. There was no place to get information on this new phenomenon of blending families. My generation is the first who used divorce liberally. My parents stayed together for better or for worse (mostly worse) because the marriage vows were binding legally and morally. There was rarely an instance that justified divorce.

Our children no longer knew where they fit in. Our love threatened their imagined places in our hearts. (If he loves her, does that mean he loves us less?) Children of divorce develop a look on their faces that is unmistakable. It is a combination of desperation, neediness, and anger.

After I fell in love with Alan, Bruce's face conveyed "I'm-so-happy-everything-is-okay," but it was a mask he donned so as not to betray his real feelings. He did not like Alan or my involvement with him or his children; but he was powerless, so he pretended everything was okay.

Bruce was a darling, sweet boy with a shock of straight shiny light brown hair that hung over his eyes like a sheepdog's. He had expressive big blue eyes and a smattering of freckles over and around his nose. In all my years, I have never known Bruce to tell a lie. He is and was trustworthy to a fault. He has always been extremely sensitive, instantly able to pick up a mood in the room. Very little slipped by him. "Are you all right, Mommy?" he frequently asked. It always startled me, because I thought I was able to keep bad news from affecting him. He was worried from his birth. Even the way he looked at me when we first met as they pulled him from my body was with concern. "I promise I'm going to make a good life for you" were my exact words as I lay on the delivery table. It was an agreement I tried my best to keep; and for the most part, I did.

But single motherhood and my youth were frequently in conflict with my promise. When he was a little boy, I would assure Bruce I would be home from a work trip on a certain day. Often it would get extended for various reasons, mostly additional work; but there were the times that Alan would call me on location and say in his irresistible, deep voice, "Come visit me in New York," and I would fly there to have one stolen night of ecstasy. These times would be terribly disappointing to Bruce. He would cry when I called and told him, "Mommy's going to be one day later than she said." Today I wish I could undo these errors in my judgment, but it was my ongoing dilemma—caught between two great loves. Broken promises erode trust, and Bruce learned he couldn't count on me to be home when I said I would be. I felt badly about that. Luckily, I did not work that much, which created other problems; but when we were home together, it was wonderful. He was my best friend, and I tried very hard to be a mother and a father. I was his whole life, and sharing me was about to be a deeply troubling experience for him.

After Alan and I decided to try living together, our difficulties began. For the first time in our relationship, we were arguing a lot. We were used to the luxury of dating: long dinners sipping wine and holding hands; weekends of lovemaking. We weren't used to the daily drudgery of rent, bills, and groceries. Nor had we ever had to deal with school events, pickups and drop-offs for the children, the ex-wife, the ex-husband, and alimony and child support payments. The child support payments I needed to help support Bruce never came, and I received no alimony. I couldn't find work, and Alan was trying to start a new career in America.

We took out our frustration on each other. I guess you do always hurt the one you love. From observing Alan's behavior with others over the years, I knew he was a very controlling person, but I never realized just how controlling until we shared a home. He wanted me to do everything his way. I had recently ended three and a half years of lifesaving therapy sessions that had helped me understand my childhood and its effects on me. But now living with Alan and watching him ignore my son set me back emotionally. I didn't know how to deal with the situation. When Alan and I would fight, I would run to Bruce's room and sequester myself. Alan denied Bruce's existence to the degree that he rarely set foot in the door of Bruce's room unless Stephen was visiting and the two boys were playing together.

But running to Bruce as my confidant created a new dynamic for both of us. In my pain, Bruce became my protector, which was too much pressure for a small boy. I was lonely and needed his shoulder to cry on. Bruce felt happy to be able to provide that comfort, but it created false hopes for him. It opened up his thinking—Perhaps Mom will leave Alan and then we can go back to our previous normal lives.

Each time Alan and I made up became a disappointment for Bruce. But what could he say? He just stuffed the feeling down with all the rest of these new thoughts, presuming eventually it would all go away.

But our arguing escalated daily. Living together was such an intimate situation that those things that were bothering both of us could not stay swept under the rug for very long.

"It's not working," I finally said to Alan one day. "We're ruining what was the most beautiful relationship of my life. I think we should stop trying. Let's put our condo up for sale. I'll take my part and pay back my mother and maybe I'll have enough left over to buy something smaller for Bruce and me."

Alan sat in his chair looking at the floor. "It would work if you sent Bruce to live with his father," he said quietly.

"How could you even ask that of me? I can't choose between the two of you. I'd end up hating you!" I said exasperated.

"Well, I can't live with Bruce," Alan responded emphatically. "I feel too guilty not living with my own son."

There was a long silence between us while we both gathered our thoughts. Finally, I sadly said, "Well, I guess that's that. Let's call a Realtor."

Two days later a local real estate agent arrived at our home to prepare the listing. "Where are you moving to next?" she asked innocently.

"I really don't know," I said, sounding upset. "You see, we're splitting up. We have irreconcilable differences."

"Oh," the Realtor responded uncomfortably.

"It's not really about us," Alan told her. "I love Suzanne. I want us to be together. We just have some serious problems we can't resolve."

"Well, if he could just put himself in my place and not be so selfish, we *could* work it out," I told the stunned woman. She was nervously looking back and forth between Alan and me.

"Suzanne thinks I'm selfish, but she hasn't tried to understand my point of view."

"Yes I have," I said angrily. "But what he wants from me is impossible. I want to be with him. I love him deeply."

"And I love her, too," Alan told the agent.

"Then maybe we should try a little harder," I told the agent. "It seems a shame to walk away after all this time," I said, now crying.

"Then why are we doing this?" Alan asked me.

"I don't know," I said emotionally. "I'd miss you terribly. I don't want to live without you."

Alan came over to where I was standing and put his arms around me. I began to sob uncontrollably. "I'm sorry; it's been so crazy," I said through my tears.

"Me, too," Alan said sincerely. "I'm sorry, too. I love you."

We held each other tightly for a long time. Finally we broke our embrace. I wiped my eyes and looked around the room for the Realtor. "Where'd she go?" I asked.

"I don't know," Alan said. "I guess she left."

We both stood in the middle of the room, confused. Then we looked at each other and started laughing hysterically at the absurdity of the whole experience.

The roller coaster of our relationship was now in place. We loved each other and we were going to have to try to find a way to deal with our problems.

———

From the perspective I have today, I realize Alan was and is the perfect choice for me in so many ways. Subliminally I needed him to be controlling so I could find the power I was never able to have with my father. When I was a child, my dad had been in control of everything—what the night would be like, what the day would be like, our happiness quotient. If he was happy (which was almost never), we were happy. If he was unhappy, the whole house shuddered. So much of my therapy was about learning to take control of my life and my happiness, taking responsibility for myself, training myself to demand that others treat me with respect and that my happiness and opinions counted.

Now I found myself living with an Alan who was very different than he had been when he was my weekend lover. His guilt over his children made him moody. My son's presence made him angry. I felt guilty about Alan's treatment of Bruce, so I overindulged Bruce by agreeing to activities that involved "just the two of us, not them." This made unifying all of us even more difficult. All three of our children were learning to divide and conquer. Unconsciously, they were trying to split us in two. In turn, Alan overindulged his children—dinners that didn't include

Bruce and me, weekends without us. His kids acted as if everything was okay, that having Daddy all to themselves was "more
fun than before." They would have fabulous weekends of amuse-
ment parks and fishing trips, all the french fries they could eat
at McDonald's, and countless stops at Baskin-Robbins for ice
cream. Alan was a guilty dad.

I was experiencing familiar feelings and depression. I had
allowed the chaos of my childhood to follow me into my adult
life. If Alan was happy, I was happy. If Alan was upset, I was
upset. If Bruce was sad, so was I. If Leslie and Stephen felt
threatened, so did I. Leslie and Stephen were in uncharted
waters. The safety of their idyllic lives had vanished. Their faces
showed anger, but they were too young to understand their
feelings. Neither Alan nor I grasped the validity of our children's
feelings at this time. We were all awash in misunderstanding and
our mutual inability to confront each other and our reality.

It was 1974. I thought I had entered this part of my life "well."
I thought I was all healed. Why did I feel like such a mess? I was
losing "me" again. I had come so far in my emotional development through my therapy; but obviously not far enough. Even
though I didn't understand what was happening, there was a
familiarity in my feelings. In this new situation I would find
myself lifting up and roaring like a wounded animal. What were
my outbursts about? What was this incredible frustration? I
would throw things at Alan; I would kick and scratch and act
crazy. He would look at me like I was sick and storm out of the
house. Later in the night he would come back and get into our
bed. I was never asleep; and like a bad little girl, I would reach
over and make him love me. Over and over the roller-coaster
scenario repeated itself. The next day, like an alcoholic, I would
apologize and promise never to lose control like that again. But
I did. One day after a huge argument over Bruce, I was so frustrated, I tried to kick the windshield out of our moving car.

"I hate the way you treat Bruce," I screamed.

Several times I tried jumping out of the passenger door while Alan was driving at full speed. He would grab my arm and the car would swerve dangerously until he could find a place to stop and calm me down. I was out of control. I loved him; I hated him; I loved him. . . .

I was frustrated because I couldn't make him feel about Bruce the way I wanted him to feel. I was trying to control him. My craziness gave Alan the upper hand. He lost respect for me when I was like this and then I was rendered powerless.

I didn't realize that control was the issue. I wanted equality, equally shared power in my relationship with him. It is so easy to look back and see it with clarity today. But when you are living inside the vortex of a storm, it's very difficult to find your way out. It was going to take a lot of work from both of us and a willingness to take the necessary steps if we were to have a successful relationship.

It's very tough to find balance between emotions and intellect. Intellectually, I understood the difficulty of blending families, but that didn't make it any easier. I was still immature and fragile. I was also battling my own jealousy and resentment at having to share my life with Alan's children and the guilt that accompanied these feelings. If I had been older or maybe more mature, perhaps I could have handled things better.

After growing up in the grip and control of my dad, I was feeling resentful of Alan's controlling nature. Therapy had taught me to understand my value as a person. I had gone from being told by my therapist that I had the lowest self-esteem of anyone she had ever met to becoming confident enough to demand of Alan that after five and a half years, we take the next step of living together or I would go my own way. I meant it, too. He continued his long holdout; so, sadly, I decided I had to move on without him. I knew I needed to be in Los Angeles to pursue a career in show business, and I took the steps to make that happen. Ultimatums are interesting. They work only if you mean them. They can't be about manipulation, and they can't be empty threats. I wasn't willing to stay in a static relationship. Either he needed to commit and accept Bruce, or I needed to move on. I've always believed in marriage, even though my first one was disastrous. I've always wanted to marry and have a settled life and a family. We were still a long way from marriage, but we had taken the next step. Neither of us wanted to fail again, so living together gave us an opportunity to move forward slowly, but it wasn't easy.

———

While visiting Alan on the set of his talk show, called *Mantrap*, in Vancouver, British Columbia, I had met my manager, Bonnie. Alan occasionally hired me as one of the "three charming and articulate females interviewing one male celebrity guest." It was the dawn of women's liberation. I was clearly in over my head on the show, but I now understand that I was meant to provide what Alan calls "eye candy." I didn't have the confidence to add anything intellectual at that time, but I'd always had a quick wit, often at my own expense. Also, Alan paid each guest nine hundred dollars for each appearance, and to me, it was like finding a gold mine.

Bonnie was a fast-talking New Yorker who booked Alan's show. One day she took me aside and said, "Listen, I'm going into personal management, and I think you could be a big star. I'd like you to be my first client." I had nothing to lose, so I agreed.

After seven years of knocking my head against walls in San Francisco with bit parts, catalog work for Sears and JCPenney, and jobs so unimportant that film companies referred to them as "picking up something local," I was finally going to get some help in jump-starting my career.

Bonnie was about forty years old at the time, attractive, and a tough cookie. She had frosted brownish blond hair that she wore in a short, curly style. The women I had known so far in my life were not like her. I was raised with small-town women who deferred to men of social standing as if they were gods.

Bonnie was assertive, aggressive, and sometimes crude. Her attire was almost gaudy and she had a tough outer shell. This aggressiveness was what I needed around me if I was to move forward in male-dominated show business. I liked Bonnie. She was a worker, and every once in a while, she would let down her guard and allow me to see a softer side of her personality. But that was rare. Once she cried with me because she had never been able to find the right guy to settle down with and have a family. She had to be tough, she told me, because she realized early on that no one was going to take care of her. She always had to do it herself. I related to that. That's probably why we found each other. Even though we were completely different types, we were two women who had to figure out how to survive by ourselves. Bonnie tried hard. She'd have me fly down from San Francisco using my only legitimate credit to get me in the casting door. "Yeah, she's the blond in the '57 T-Bird from *American Graffiti*," she'd tell them. And curiosity opened some doors.

"So, you're the girl," I'd hear on interviews. I was always embarrassed, because to me *American Graffiti* was just one night's work on a low-budget film with a bunch of unknowns, directed by a guy I'd never heard of named George Lucas. I had no idea of the impact *American Graffiti* had made. I didn't understand the chord it had touched in America.

One day it paid off. After hundreds of contacts and as many turndowns, Bonnie got me an audition to guest star on a new sitcom called *Lotsa Luck,* starring Dom DeLuise, which aired in 1973. I was asked to read with the producer to play a new blond in town upon whom Dom would develop a big crush. After my reading, the producer said, "Very good. Could you come back in two hours?"

As Bonnie and I waited in the NBC commissary, sipping our Coca-Colas at a lunch table, Johnny Carson and his producer, Fred De Cordova, walked in. "Hey, girls, whatcha doin' here?" Johnny asked.

I gulped.

"Uh, I'm waiting to hear if I got a part on Dom DeLuise's show."

"Well, if they're looking for a great-looking blond, you'll get it. Good luck," Johnny said, and they left with their coffee.

What an incredible day that turned out to be! I not only got the guest starring part on *Lotsa Luck*, but three days later I found myself walking out from behind that famous curtain on *The Tonight Show*. I had given a copy of my poetry book, *Touch Me*, to the producer. After reading on the flap of the book that I was *the* blond in the T-Bird, Johnny asked me to read a selection of poems from my book. I became known as the *Touch Me* Lady and from that day on was frequently asked to appear on Johnny's show.

But that wasn't the best part. Years later I learned from Fred Silverman, who was the president of ABC Television at that time, that he was watching Johnny that night and was so charmed by my sweetness and naïveté, he decided that one day he would find the right show for me on his network.

———

These thoughts ran through my mind like a movie on fast-forward that day in January 1977 as I washed the makeup from my "interview face," back to my usual everyday shiny, clean skin. I put on my favorite faded Levi's and a T-shirt. Bruce would be home from school soon, and I was looking forward to walking down to the beach with him.

I had almost forgotten about the audition at ABC, but as I was hanging up the blouse I had worn to the audition, the phone started ringing. "Hello," I said calmly.

"OMYGOD! OMYGOD!" Bonnie screamed through the receiver. "You got it! You got it!"

For a moment I couldn't figure out what she was talking about. Then comprehension sank in. I was speechless. It was beyond my wildest dreams, and there was no way at that moment I could ever have known that the course of my life would be changed forever.

TWO

﷼ I was in a daze. The oncoming weeks were a frenzy of publicity photos, wardrobe fittings, interviews, and rehearsals. There was a buzz in the TV industry about *Three's Company*. For the era this program was considered racy. The show was about two girls and a guy sharing an apartment. Joyce DeWitt played Janet Wood, who worked in a florist shop, and I played Chrissy Snow, an office typist/secretary. The two girls shared an apartment together until they had a party one night; upon awakening the next morning, they found Jack Tripper, a student chef (played by John Ritter), asleep in the bathtub. Because they had an extra bedroom they weren't using, and they liked the idea of additional help with the rent, they agreed to let Jack move in. The girls told the landlord that Jack was gay so the landlord wouldn't be upset. Therein lay the premise for *Three's Company*.

I was starting to understand why everyone had been so nervous that day in Fred Silverman's office. The show was due to start production, and they had been short one "star." STAR! What a strange new identity. I had done nothing to deserve it, yet all the magazines were asking my opinion and calling me "Miss

Somers." It was pretty hard to feel worthy of all the attention. But this new life was a great distraction from the personal problems Alan and I were having with blending our families.

Alan was genuinely happy for me. Jealousy is not one of his traits. "You are going to be so great in this part," he kept saying. He had been in the entertainment business for many years and continually encouraged me in the beginning weeks to calm my overworked nerves. "Just relax," he said over and over. On the night of the first airing, he called everyone we knew to remind them not to miss the premiere.

In retrospect I can see that this new development in my life was very hard on Bruce. Not only was he having to share me with Alan, but now he would also have to share me with my new active career. Being my darling boy, he kept his happy face and pretended everything was okay in order to make it easier for me. The price for pretending would have to be paid later; but for now, I thought things for him were good.

Celebrity comes in an instant, ready or not. There is no way to prepare for it. I was stunned the entire first season.

The first pickup for *Three's Company* was only six episodes, because it was a midseason replacement, but we were practically assured of a full pickup of twenty-four episodes starting in the fall of 1977 because of our sensational ratings. Nevertheless, I worried that if somehow, something went wrong, I would lose this incredible momentum. I had been paying attention to the successes of Jay Bernstein, the famed publicist-turned-manager who had catapulted Farrah Fawcett from a spokeswoman for toothpaste into an icon adored by fans all over the world. I felt that if I could hire Jay to be my publicist, he could use the success of *Three's Company* to get me publicity. The only problem was that Jay's fee was $2,500 a month. And I really couldn't afford it.

"I'll make you a deal," I said nervously to Jay at our first meeting in his office; framed magazine covers of Farrah covered his walls, including that famous poster of her in a bathing suit with her nipples showing. "I'll give you all the money I am making for this series, which is $2,750 a week," I said, "for the entire first six weeks of the series, except for my manager's fee, which goes to Bonnie. In return, I want you to make sure that people know who I am. If for some reason this show doesn't make it, I want to be visible enough to use this opportunity to get my next job."

It meant Jay would begin working for me during the summer months that bridged the gap between the first six episodes and the start of the fall season. I turned over all six paychecks to him, knowing I was gambling with the only big money (by my financial standards at that time) I had ever made. But it was worth it to me. It was my first (and maybe only) big chance.

Jay had magic. He was a publicity genius. In retrospect, a big part of my splash onto the scene was Jay's ability to manipulate the media. He knew everyone on a first-name basis. He would use Farrah as his poker chip. "You can have Farrah for your cover if you'll do an article on this unknown, Suzanne Somers." It worked in my favor.

"By the way," he'd say, "she's the beautiful blond in the T-Bird."

Jay later told me he didn't find me all that great looking and he didn't know if I was talented. "You had a raw beauty," he said, "but you hadn't developed a 'look' yet. But I had not seen this kind of tenacity since I handled publicity for Sammy Davis, Jr.; so I decided to take a chance with you."

On the show Joyce and I found instant camaraderie in our insecurities. John somehow seemed to take the flow of fame more easily. I guess being the son of Tex Ritter, the famous singing cowboy of my parents' time, left him better equipped to handle the craziness of launching *Three's Company*. Besides, this was not his first job. He had been in the movie *Nickelodeon*, with Cybill Shepherd, and had played the minister on the TV series *The Waltons*. But *Three's Company* was his first "hit."

Three's Company went on the air Tuesday night, March 15, 1977, and on its first outing was the number three show in America. *Happy Days* was number one and *Laverne and Shirley* was number two. This was a time when there was no cable TV to speak of and no video rentals. In fact, no one I knew even owned a VCR. Being the number-three-rated show in all of TV then was much more meaningful than it is today. The viewers could only choose from ABC, CBS, or NBC. We were getting a forty-six share, which means that almost half of the entire population watching TV that night during our time slot was watching our show. And America instantly took to my character, Chrissy Snow. She was a lovable, ditzy blond with a heart of gold and a circuitous route to logic. Somehow Chrissy always figured it out in her own convoluted way. The reaction was instant. The day after the first show aired, I was flabbergasted by the recognition. Everywhere I went—the supermarket, in my car at a traffic light, the dry cleaners—people would say, "Hey, you're the girl from that new show about three people in an apartment."

It was an incredible rush. I couldn't believe my good fortune. During that first short season I'd wake up every morning pinching myself to make sure it wasn't all an unbelievable dream. I worried constantly that somehow I'd lose it.

Chrissy Snow became a living, breathing person to me. I understood her soul, her moral code. In many ways she was the child I'd never gotten to be. Suddenly I understood what being a happy child could be like, and it was wonderful. In analyzing the show, I now see that Jack and Janet represented the parents, and Chrissy was the child. Chrissy was safe, nurtured, and protected as if she were in a normal healthy family, with all the decisions revolving around what's best for the child.

———

In the dysfunctional home of the alcoholic, like the one I came from, or in an abusive environment, everything revolves around the addict or abuser. The needs and feelings of the rest of the family don't count. The family is as strong as its weakest link. This was my childhood scenario, which accounted for my feelings of inadequacy that had plagued me thus far. I had never felt important as a child. I had always felt less than other people, other children. I took on the shame of my father's disease as though it were my own.

I remember, as a little girl, my older brother, Dan, telling me that before I was born, it hadn't always been like this. He said, "We used to have friends over, we had parties. Everyone liked to be around Dad." My sweet brother Danny was telling me this to make me feel better. We had just experienced another horrible, violent night hiding in the closet from our dad. I was crying and scared, and Dan was trying to comfort me the way he always did, even though he was only four years older than I. But I didn't understand. I misconstrued his comfort and only heard that my birth, my arrival into this family, had ruined everything.

I spent my early life trying to figure out how to be a better daughter so Daddy would love me enough to stop drinking. Of course, I was never able to be as good as I needed to be, because my father drank alcoholically for thirty-five years. I tried to be perfect. I tried to excel at everything. Dad once told me that if I got straight A's, he would give me five dollars. I came home with A's and one A–, and he wouldn't pay me. It wasn't good enough. Perfectionism takes its toll. Human beings are never perfect. We are always in a state of learning and, hopefully, correcting our imperfections.

So Chrissy was a chance to do my childhood over. I lived out my real child self for five years in front of America. And they got her. They understood her thought process. She would never tell a lie and possessed a soul so pure, so innocent, like that of a dar-ling puppy, that everyone wanted to take care of her.

So here I was, costarring in *Three's Company*, loved, nur-tured, safe, successful. Finally I was accepted. I was as worthy as other people.

But something felt wrong. Deep down in my gut, where we all really live, I didn't feel deserving. It all came so fast, so suddenly. Too much attention; too much adulation. I thought my years in therapy had unraveled my confusion. Little did I know that the bulk of the "work" lay ahead of me.

THREE

From the beginning of my relationship with Alan, I wanted to marry him. In fact, it had become one of those subjects of conversation that could easily ruin the evening. I loved him enough to commit; why couldn't he? The reasons, of course, were evident. We had a lot to work out between us; namely, our children. But I was naive and talked myself into believing that marriage would solve all our problems. All along, Alan was adamant that he was never getting married again, nor did he want any more children.

"Why?" I would ask, frustrated.

"Because marriage made me feel trapped," he told me. "I'd feel like I'd have to be home rather than want to be home."

"Well," I announced dramatically, "I plan to be married. I hope it's to you; but if not, I'll find someone else!"

"Fine," Alan answered, exhausted.

We had been through this same discussion so many times. If one of us didn't end it, we'd wind up in a huge argument.

As I look back, I am astounded by my immaturity. I should have been more evolved in my thinking. I knew better. I was taking several emotional steps backward. My prior therapy had taught me I had a right to what I needed, what I felt, what I wanted; but now I was using ultimatums as a weapon without substance. We both knew I'd be there forever. Because of my empty threats, Alan continued to hold the power in our relationship and this made me feel crazy. I wasn't able to step back and look at our relationship with maturity. It's not the accumulation of years together that makes it the right time to marry. When the time is right, there is a feeling you both have. There is an awareness that the obstacles are now moved aside to allow commitment. We still had too many obstacles. There was too much intractability, an unwillingness to work on what was wrong.

Landing the part on *Three's Company* gave me confidence. It took away my desperation. It refocused me. I was no longer destitute. I could live without Alan. I didn't want to, but I knew I could.

Somehow my lack of desperation allowed Alan to relax. I stopped pushing the issue. I began to be comfortable with living together. Financial independence transformed me. In the '70s, it was very difficult for women to live safely and comfortably because we normally didn't have much earning power. Couple this with supporting a child, or children, and it appeared clear why so many women were willing to accept marriage on less than ideal terms just to get the financial monkey off their backs. My lack of money before the *Three's Company* years beat me down. The simple provisions of life—food, shelter, and clothing—took an enormous amount of planning and energy. Extras were out of the question. For example, I have only a handful of pictures of Bruce growing up because photographs were an expense I could not afford. I did not own a camera.

Now, with a little money in my pocket, I became more rational about marriage. "When the time is right," I told Alan. "In the meantime, it's better like this." I meant it. The big rush was off. We started getting along better. We were enjoying each other

again. The fear of pushing emotional buttons that would provoke an argument had dissipated in this one area, lightening the
load of emotional baggage somewhat.

Discussions about our children were still very flammable. We
walked on eggshells in this area and spoke cautiously, but we
were moving forward as a couple. We were trying to find peace
together in these new and uncharted waters. We were doing the
best we could with the information we had at that time.

In July 1977, John, Joyce, and I were asked to guest on *The
Dinah Shore Show*. Dinah's show was the hot talk show of the
'70s and was watched daily by most Americans who were home
in the afternoons. Dinah was romantically involved with Burt
Reynolds at that time and the media wrote incessantly about
them because she was much older than he. John and I joked easily with her about her love affair. Because Dinah and I were both
avid cooks, we did a cooking segment where we made a great
chocolate cake. I honestly don't remember what I said to Dinah
about Burt to provoke her to push a piece of cake in my face,
but it was done in fun and the audience laughed uproariously.
We were those madcap kids from the apartment and could get
away with almost anything.

After the show, Alan and I went to our favorite restaurant, Le
Restaurant on Melrose Place, to have a romantic dinner. I was
on cloud nine. *The Dinah Shore Show* had been great. *Three's
Company* was great. My life felt great. It was one of those perfect nights where problems took a backseat and a pervading
sense of joy took over.

Alan and I ordered a bottle of red wine, and as we waited for
our medallions of lamb to arrive, we sipped the delicious nectar
out of large crystal goblets. The candles on the table were
encased in pink glass, which cast a golden pink glow on the rose-

colored velvet walls. We snuggled on the cozy satin banquette, and for that moment, all the world seemed shining and soft.

Alan took my hand and said, "I love you, Suzanne. Will you be my wife?"

It came so easily; it felt so right. It was time! I wasn't surprised as much as I felt settled, content.

"I love you, too," I answered. "I would love to have you as my husband."

We decided to have a relatively small wedding that autumn in our newly purchased home, a beautiful glass house that sat right on the sand, overlooking the blue waters of the Pacific Ocean. The house would be ready about the first of November and we could easily get married on November 19, which just happened to be one month and three days after my thirty-first birthday.

It had been a phenomenal period for me. I was marrying the love of my life and my career had skyrocketed beyond my wildest expectations. So far that year I had been on the covers of fifty-five national magazines, including one of the highest-selling covers of *Newsweek* to that date. The same week I planned to marry Alan, *60 Minutes*, the most popular newsmagazine show on television, came to my home to do a feature on me as the next Farrah, the next blond. I was so busy with personal and professional obligations, I came home on Friday afternoon, November 18, and found Morley Safer sitting in my living room, waiting to interview me. The morning had been so busy that I was running late. Imagine . . . late for *60 Minutes;* but this was my new reality.

The next day, I married Alan in the living room of our beautiful new beach house, the same home we live in today.

I wanted a perfect wedding, and mostly it was. We invited eighty people, mainly family, with a few business friends. John Ritter, Joyce DeWitt, Norman Fell, and Mickey Ross and Bernie West, who were two of the show's three producers, all attended. Joyce looked beautiful in a green silk brocade Chinese tunic with black silk pants. I was limited by space and a desire to keep it small, so I did not invite everyone from the show, which created a little negativity on the set, but nothing insurmountable. I invited only the people to whom I was closest.

My mother and father; my sister, Maureen, her husband, Bill, and their children; my brother Dan and his wife, Mardi, and their children were all in attendance.

My brother Michael had had a slip in his recovery from drug addiction, so he was not in an open state of mind to attend a wedding. I didn't know if I could count on him. Michael could maintain sobriety for months, even years, but then he might go on a binge of drinking and using and wouldn't remember where he had been. It was sad because underneath he had such a sweet nature. In many ways binge drinkers and users have the most difficult time with recovery because they are able to go for long periods of time without using.

The wedding was to be held upstairs in our living room overlooking the ocean. We constructed a lovely *huppa*, a gorgeous canopy of flowers under which the rabbi conducted the ceremony. Above the living room on the balcony, three sopranos sang Gregorian chants counterpoint to our friend Allen Blye singing cantorial music downstairs. The music was beautiful and conveyed the message that with understanding, cultures can meld and coexist in love. I wore an antique lace Victorian top with an off-white silk floor-length soft skirt. Bruce and Stephen wore brown pin-striped wool suits and Leslie was lovely in lilac matte jersey. It was a stormy beach day, but by the time of our ceremony, the sun had broken through and decided to give one of God's great shows. As I walked down the aisle of our living room toward my husband-to-be, the sky turned a magnificent fiery orange of every imaginable shade, which contrasted with the midnight blue of the ocean. Between the golden sunset, the howling winds, the rich sounds of cantorial music and Gregorian chant, it was the perfect moment I had waited for all my life. For that brief time, all problems ceased and only deep love and com-

mitment to my new life consumed my thoughts. I shook with
nervousness all through the ceremony, as did Alan. Marriage
cannot be taken lightly, and it was the seriousness of the commitment we were making to each other that caused us to trem-
ble with sincerity.

After taking our vows, Alan crushed a glass on the floor
(which is customary in Jewish marriages), and then our guests
applauded as we kissed as husband and wife for the first time.

The girls singing Gregorian chant were replaced by a small
jazz band and the dancing began.

My family loves to dance, and immediately my sister and
brother were on the dance floor, which got everything going. My
father was newly sober and not used to socializing without
booze. But I was proud of him and he was bursting with pride
over me. I had "done good." I was famous and no one in our family or my hometown had ever succeeded on this level.

Alan and my dad were awkward with each other. My father's
usual icebreaker with men was to talk sports, but Alan had no
interest in sports. Also, my father was used to charming a group
with jokes, but it was not until I had become involved with Alan
that I truly became aware of my dad's tendency toward racism.
He loved jokes with racist punch lines. I was afraid one of his
jokes would end with "kike" or "Jew," and because of this, I felt
nervous when Alan and my dad were together. My dad's ethnic
humor made me cringe. Prior to the wedding I told him these
jokes were in bad taste. He felt embarrassed and uncomfortable.
Still, I could see my father was attempting to change his behavior and I loved him for that.

Alan and my mother got along great. He understood her sweet
nonjudgmental nature and felt protective of her. She looked
radiant and beautiful in a blue floral silk dress.

My sister was also newly sober along with her husband, Bill,
and they found comfort in each other's sobriety, which allowed

them to reenter social occasions with strength between them. My sister looked stunning at my wedding. She was calm, relaxed, and proud of herself.

Almost everyone came to our celebration with joy—my parents, Alan's parents, our friends, and the *Three's Company* gang. They all recognized that Alan and I truly loved each other and came to wish us well.

Our children, on the other hand, were not so happy. None of them smiled during the ceremony. In fact, they all looked glum. I'm sure this was not a good day for any of them. Each one had tried so hard to divide and conquer and they lost the battle. They felt threatened by our union and didn't know where they fit in with Alan and me now being a united front.

We should have talked it out with all of them. The wisdom of this escaped me at the time. I should have let them express their feelings and fears. I should have let them air their anger. It was ignorance, or maybe deep down I didn't really want to know how they felt. Perhaps, as with so many other issues in my life, I felt time would heal the situation on its own.

———

I remember that as a child I would ask my mother, "Why did you marry Dad?" I knew he had been a heavy drinker before they were married.

"Well," she sighed, "I thought after we got married he would change." Now I could truly understand her answer. I presumed after Alan and I married, he would suddenly love Bruce, and I would magically find the love I was searching for with my stepchildren. It was this lack of reality with which I entered my marriage. The headiness of my career allowed me to pretend to myself that everything would be okay personally.

When Alan and I were alone, everything *was* like magic. Our lives were filled with the intensity of our dating period. The magazines and tabloids declared ours "TV's Wedding of the Year" and us "The Most Happy Couple." I didn't want to think of the flip side. Everything was perfect except for the fact that our children were miserable.

We honeymooned in Paris and stayed in Oscar Wilde's suite at L'Hôtel. By day we roamed the art galleries on the Left Bank; and by night, we held hands, drank wine by candlelight at little bistros, and kissed while walking along the Seine River. I wanted it to stay like this forever.

———

Returning home brought reality. Our children needed us and that need broke the spell of the intensity that had surrounded our marrying.

Before long, we were arguing again. We had taken a drive with the kids to apple country outside of Los Angeles, and Bruce had been giving us his views on life, in particular that he was anti-guns.

"What? Are you crazy?" Alan asked irritated. "You live in some kind of Pollyanna world? It's tough out there. You've got to be able to defend yourself. You and Stephen both should know how to properly handle a gun. It could be the difference between life and death."

As we were standing outside in the apple orchard, Alan put two fingers to Bruce's temple. "You mean to tell me that if I was a criminal and pulled the trigger right now, you wouldn't believe in guns? You'd just let yourself get killed?"

I was horrified by Alan's brutal example. Bruce was upset. "Just because I don't agree with him, he tries to make me feel like a fool," Bruce whispered to me angrily.

"Well, he's not always right," I answered, trying to be consoling. But I was angry. I seethed all the way home. I didn't want to argue in front of the kids, so I said nothing.

That night we slept in the same bed, but like two continents, not touching. When morning came, I was ready to explode. The kids had left for school. I faced Alan angrily. "How dare you talk to Bruce like that. How dare you use that crude demonstration. What was that about? Do you hate him that much?" I screamed at him.

"I have a right to my opinion," Alan shot back. "You two trust everybody. You're small-town people living in the big city. I'm just trying to get him to face reality."

"Well, this is not the kind of parenting I want from you," I shot back. "Why don't you just try telling him he's a good kid?"

"Why don't you quit trying to make me into something I'm not?" Alan answered angrily. "I'm sick of walking on eggshells in my own house." At that, he threw his cup of coffee into the air, and as I walked toward our bedroom, the hot coffee accidentally hit my chest. I had been dressed and ready to appear on Regis Philbin's *A.M. Los Angeles* show that morning. I stopped and watched the coffee drip down my dress. I was horrified, beyond anger.

"This is not working," I said, furious. "I don't want to live like this, either. It's over, Alan. We've gone too far. I can't take it."

I walked upstairs to change my clothes. Alan followed me. "Get away," I said. "I mean it. It's over." I walked past him and out the front door to the waiting limousine sent from Regis's show. I didn't look back as I got into the car. As we drove away, I knew we were beyond repair.

FOUR

I always loved doing Regis's show and had become one of his frequent guests since my star had risen. This morning, though, I was terribly preoccupied. I was overwhelmed by sadness that after all Alan and I had been through, it was now going to be over. Just last week it had been so perfect. Paris had been our playground. But that was our addiction to each other. The highest highs to the lowest lows. I remembered what my therapist had once told me: "Fleeing from a fight does not help matters. You've got to hear what each other is saying. It's rarely about the matter at hand. Hear the message behind the words." What had we really been saying to each other? I wondered. I felt so confused.

During this time, Regis was asking me questions about my "big wedding." "What did you do? Did you dance? Where did you go on your honeymoon?" As I blankly answered the questions, I spotted Alan standing at the back of the studio. He had followed me there. I wanted to run to him and tell him I loved him, that we could work it out. Alan looked at me and nodded his head. He wanted to work it out also.

52

By now, John Ritter, Joyce DeWitt, and I were having the time of our lives. The success of the show was heady. By our second season (technically our first season had been only six weeks long), we were the number one show on American television, leaving all others in the dust. No other program could get close to our unbelievable success. The three of us were like children, bouncing around the set, laughing, joking, acting like kindergartners. It was conducive to the chemistry. It was what was appealing to viewers: three kids living in their own apartment—two girls and a guy—and it was nonsexual, but at the same time very sexual. John's character was constantly groping at Joyce and me, though never actually making any contact. That would have changed the dynamics. There was an innocence about all of us, yet also a naughtiness. "Oh, those kids," people would say. We were the "kids." The producers even referred to us as the "kids."

"Go get the kids," they'd tell the production assistant.

"Tell the kids to meet us in the conference room."

"How're you kids doing today?"

"Hi, kids. Did you see the ratings?" We loved being the "kids," even though we really were grown-up. I was thirty-one, John was twenty-nine, and Joyce was twenty-eight. In some weird place in my mind, I finally had a safe family. I loved going to work; I loved being a "hit"; and I loved being Chrissy.

———

Several weeks later, Alan called me at the studio. "Guess what?" he asked. "You've won a People's Choice Award for Favorite Actress in a New Series. The awards ceremony is in two weeks, so get yourself a fancy dress."

"Really!" I said, flabbergasted. It was all too much. A People's Choice Award is immensely meaningful because it is voted for by the people in a national poll. I was very excited. I had grown up watching famous people receive awards on these types of shows, but I never dreamed I would be one of them.

Lenny, the wardrober on *Three's Company,* designed a pink silk charmeuse slip of a dress with a pleated, floor-length cape of the same silk, fastened by a brocade frog at the neck. It was glamorous and beautiful. I couldn't wait to wear it.

The big night came, and I felt like a princess stepping out of my limousine. Flashbulbs popped in my face. "Chrissy! Chrissy! We love you," I heard coming in waves from the throngs of people standing behind the red velvet ropes. I floated down the red-carpeted entrance in a state of disbelief. How my life had changed. Inside was more glitter and glamour. Jane Fonda, Mary Tyler Moore, Angie Dickinson, Warren Beatty—everywhere I looked, there was another famous face.

And then I heard the magical words . . . "And the winner is . . . Suzanne Somers, Favorite Actress in a New Television Series." I kissed Alan, John, and Joyce and then floated up to the stage. The award was very heavy crystal and I almost dropped it. The audience laughed.

"Thank you very much," I said emotionally to the audience. "This means so much. My dad always said, 'Get yourself in the middle, Suzanne! Get noticed.' Well, I can't do much better than this. Thanks, Dad. I love you all." And I walked off the stage.

For all the bad and bitter times, it was my dad from whom I wanted approval. In my moment of triumph, it was my dad who came to my mind. Blood connection is more potent than we can know, and the child within is forever looking for that little pat on the head.

"I was damn proud of you," my dad said on the phone the next day. His voice was trembling.

"That's all I've ever wanted to hear from you, Dad," I replied. "I love you."

———

The People's Choice Award propelled me further forward. The only glitch was that John and I were getting the bulk of the publicity. All the pictures were of John or me or of John grabbing after me. Joyce had initially shunned publicity, saying she was an "actress," not a "celebrity"; so most of the magazines passed her over. Nevertheless, bits of resentment were brewing. Joyce is an incredibly learned and gifted actress. She had been at the top of her class at UCLA. The network plucked her out of school with a contract after having seen her in a play put on by the respected UCLA Drama School. I felt that Joyce resented my success; and I felt badly, because I liked her. I had taken very few acting lessons; what I didn't know about acting I learned by watching my two talented colleagues. I was like a sponge; I learned instantly. For example, John knew how to mug for the camera. I would watch him, and then a light would go off in my head. I can do that, I'd say to myself. I realized I was working with two skilled professionals, and I used the first full year as a crash course. As I became more confident, I barreled onto the set like a bull. I had figured it out. I found comedy easy. I'd always had a natural wit, and that worked in my favor.

In many ways, my lack of knowledge worked for me. Joyce was a serious actress and would come to work with pages of subtext written opposite every line she had to say. Her approach was to break down each line to discover its real meaning and back it up with intent. My approach was simpler. I had studied briefly with Charles Conrad, one of the premier acting teachers, and he had taught me to believe what I was saying. It made sense to me. I didn't need to do homework or study on weekends. Chrissy just "was." She came from the most wounded part of my soul. She was the good girl. She was pure and I protected her, nurtured her, and cared for her deeply. There was no drama class that could teach me that. I knew how Chrissy worked. "Chrissy wouldn't say this," I would hear myself saying to the writers. I knew her moral code and I would not allow her to do or say anything that was not vintage "Chrissy." The writers and producers would respect my objections. I was teaching them who Chrissy was. Originally, she had been written as a stupid blond. I gave her a heart, and everyone fell in love with her.

If you're lucky, maybe once in a successful career you get a character who lives and breathes and gets into the consciousness of the country. It's a creative thrill. Jean Stapleton had it with Edith Bunker, Carroll O'Connor had it with Archie Bunker, Lucille Ball had it with Lucy, and now I had Chrissy. It's more than having good writers, although they are integral and important. It's something that clicks in your brain. You know this person better than anyone. In a way, it's like giving birth. The only negative is that sometimes the character can imprison you. An actor can be so identified and beloved in one role that the public doesn't want to see him or her in any other form. Carroll O'Connor has never had the same degree of success with any other character as he had with Archie, nor has Jean Stapleton been able to be anyone we loved as much as Edith.

Lucy remained beloved because she always gave us Lucy, right up to the end. Even with her boozy voice and the garish eyelashes, she was still Lucy. She didn't disappoint.

But I wasn't concerned with this at that time. I would have been happy to play Chrissy the rest of my life. I was curious to see how she turned out. What did life experiences do to her? Did she grow and change, or did she remain the same wide-eyed, trusting virgin that she was?

Mickey Ross, one of the producers of the show, was my comedy mentor. He was a former Broadway actor who had had moderate success onstage. As the producer/head writer on *Three's Company*, he finally hit the jackpot.

Mickey was extremely talented. To this day, he is probably the best comic talent with whom I have ever worked. At the time he was sixtyish, tanned, and great looking, with wavy silver hair and Mel Gibson blue eyes. To stay in shape, every day he found time to drive to the ocean from the studio and swim vigorously in the salt water for at least a half hour.

Mickey was not a materialistic guy. I was never aware of any particular car that he drove. I imagine it must have been nondescript. The rest of us were experiencing the financial rewards that accompany a show this successful, and we were acquiring "things." John got a new silver BMW, Joyce bought a fabulous house in the Malibu Colony, and I was sporting a new gold Rolex watch, which I still wear every day. But Mickey seemed to remain the same. He was interested in the work only. He and his wife lived in the same small rented apartment that they'd lived in for years, and he seemed to wear the same clothes every day. They were clean and pressed, but it was as though he had five white short-sleeved cotton shirts, five pairs of tan khaki pants, a brown cotton windbreaker, brown belt, and soft brown leather loafers. I admired that quality in him and I admired his dedication to his craft. He was an excellent writer, actor, and director. It was the producer part of his role that was not his forte. Producing requires business sense. He was strictly creative. He had a soothing sound to his voice and, when he was calm, an engaging laugh that was regularly interrupted for a puff on his cigarette. He did have a short fuse, though, and I instinctively knew to avoid provoking him.

Mickey understood what I was creating with Chrissy, and he also became protective of the character. "She's right," he'd say when I would protest a line. He was my ally. Mickey gave me more kudos than he did the others because in his mind, I was his creation, which eventually contributed to an atmosphere of resentment. Sometimes the air would get thick with tension and unsaid feelings. This was my new and subliminally dysfunctional family. We could never put our feelings on the table, because in reality, we weren't a real family. We were a bunch of people thrown together, having incredible success, and the stakes were high. None of us were going to mess with that.

Mickey would work with me between scenes, during lunch, and even after work. I listened; I learned; I watched. He became like a father to me. I wanted to please him. He was very controlling. If I didn't do a line or a scene perfectly, he'd scold me, or he'd look disappointed. I would apologize and then make sure to dig deeper into my soul and feelings to further purify this character. Chrissy walked differently than I did, without any awareness of her body and sexuality. She was a woman/child. Men wanted to both protect her and have sex with her; women loved her purity and innocence and knew they could trust her.

I lived and breathed this character. When in public, I was confused about who the people wanted me to be. I thought they could never love the real me the way they loved Chrissy. And I loved being loved. I wanted to please everyone.

Mickey was cool and distant around Alan. Maybe they were too similar. Alan liked Mickey because he understood him. He respected Mickey's talent and appreciated the energy Mickey put into my instant training as a comedic actress. They both had been raised in Eastern European Jewish immigrant households, so they were simpatico, understood each other and what they were about. Still, even though Alan and Mickey seemed to be cut from the same cloth, I always sensed an underlying struggle between them.

Alan was the only person who had more control over me than Mickey did. The line between me and Chrissy was becoming blurred for Mickey. There was a strange sexual tension between us, like a father who desires his daughter but knows it's wrong. Alan had what I think Mickey thought he wanted: the woman, the character, and control.

Alan would get perturbed with me in the early days of my success when I would forget to leave my professional persona at the studio. He liked the small-town simplicity that he'd fallen in love with, but sometimes the headiness of newfound fame threw our relationship off-balance. It's the pampering that goes along with success in my business. It's the "Yes, Miss Somers," "I'll get it for you, Miss Somers," "No problem, Miss Somers." In the beginning I liked it. I had never been treated like that before. I started to believe the "star" image, which was dangerous. It was Alan who grounded me, brought me back to reality. "You are not the star at home," he would say when I expected the same treatment I received at the studio. I knew he was right, but sometimes the line was blurred for me. The character was under my skin. She had acceptance, which was what I'd always wanted. It was hard to leave her at the studio at the end of the day.

———

More magazine covers. I was actually getting impatient with shooting magazine covers. It wasn't the magazine covers themselves I was tiring of; being featured on the cover of a magazine is a thrill and a privilege. But the extra work outside of the show swallowed up the time I needed to be with my family, especially Bruce. He never complained, but I could see in his eyes that he wanted more of my time. He wanted to hang out, or to have our long talks. Bruce and I had always had abundant time together and wonderful discussions. One of his favorite topics was God, because I had chosen not to raise him Catholic like his cousins. I would tell him that God is of every individual's understanding, but that to me, all living things make up the energy that collectively is "God." That is why, I would tell him, it is important to respect all life in every form, even the teeniest bug, because it too is part of the energy. Every person should be treated with love because they are part of "God," or "the force." Each person has something to teach and something to learn. Bruce loved the hours we spent on this particular subject. But lately we hadn't had much time to have our talks.

I would shoot magazine layouts after work and on weekends. A magazine cover is big business. Nothing about it is haphazard. The editor would usually fly to Los Angeles from New York, bringing the hottest New York photographer and her team with her. There were photo stylists to make sure the colors, the outfit, the perfect ring or flower were present in the composition. Wardrobe assistants would bring racks of the latest fashions from the hottest designers, and they would spend hours choosing what I would wear, while I waited. The hairdresser of the moment would perfect my coif. Nobody wanted me to wear the ponytail-on-the-side-of-the-head that had become my trademark. They all wanted to change me, present me in a "new way." I was so overworked, I just let them sculpt and mold and move me around and create a look. I loved having my makeup applied professionally. I now had my favorite makeup artist. His name was Bjorn, and he used to call me "Baby Doll." He was the one who urged me to color my hair whiter and whiter. He gave me pink cheeks, a big pink mouth, and big round dark eyes. The "look," I called it. Chrissy was now complete. I still didn't know where Suzanne, the person, fit in. On weekends I didn't feel secure in public without "her" makeup on.

One of my photo shoots was for *Harper's Bazaar*, a four-page spread shot by the renowned photographer Bill King. Bill was a strange kind of guy. He didn't talk much and he didn't like static shots. For his pictures you had to jump and leap and hop—over and over, jumping, leaping, hopping. The layout of me lying across two pages on my stomach, wearing only lace dance pants, was the only time during the fourteen-hour shoot that I was still. But there was something glamorous about New York and all those women wearing black suits with men's shoes, making editorial decisions—"Have her wear a sleeping bag in this setup. It will be fa-a-abulous!"; about makeup artists painting not only my face but my body also. I felt like I was watching a movie, except I was in it.

With my life suddenly turning topsy-turvy with career demands, I was finding Bonnie, who had been so instrumental in getting me there, now creating an atmosphere of chaos I couldn't deal with. Several times a day she'd call the rehearsal hall and scream through the phone, "They want you on *Hollywood Squares.*"

"You can't do *Hollywood Squares*," Alan would say later that night. "She should be reading scripts and making an overall network deal for specials, movies, and an ongoing series after *Three's Company.* If you start showing up on game shows, you're going to lose your specialness. You're the star of the number one show in America. Use it as a springboard!"

But Bonnie came from the world of daytime television, and that is where she had her contacts. She was floundering in prime time. "Tell 'em to go fuck themselves," she'd say when she didn't get the kind of reception she was used to in daytime TV. I needed someone stronger for a manager, someone with finesse, someone who knew their way around the nighttime big-deal world of prime time, someone like Jay Bernstein. I kept thinking to myself, Look what he has done for Farrah Fawcett. I wished I had someone like him advising me. I spent so much of my energy calming Bonnie down. "Try to relax," I'd tell her. I needed someone to take this incredible heat off my shoulders.

Maybe it was time. We weren't too far into the series yet, and Bonnie was commissionable for the entire five years of my contract. Bonnie deserved her commission. It was because of her urging that I had auditioned for the series. Because of her original tenacity, I had landed on prime-time television. But I knew she would be devastated, and I didn't want to hurt her.

"As long as you take care of her financially, she'll be okay," Alan said. "This is business. This is your one big chance. You have to do what is right for your career. If she isn't right for you, it will drag you down."

It was my first tough decision. The kind of situation that creates enemies. Bonnie had to go.

"I'll call her for you," Alan said. "I've known her longer. This way there'll be a buffer so she won't dump all over you. Give her a couple of days to digest the information, then you can call her. She's smart; she'll understand."

I appreciated Alan for absorbing the initial reaction from her. I've always hated hurting people, and I knew delivering this news was not going to make her happy. It was the "chicken" way to handle it, but that was who I was back then.

"I'm really sorry," I told her when I finally talked to her shortly thereafter. "Please understand." I felt awful and sad. I liked Bonnie, and she was actually gracious about it. Disappointed, but gracious.

"I knew Alan would ace me out," she said. But in reality, Alan was not part of my plan at that time. I felt if I could get Jay Bernstein to manage me, along with benefiting from his publicity skills, I would be on track for the future. Somewhere deep in my heart I knew that one day Alan would take over as my manager. But it was too soon right then. Alan and I were still dealing with control issues, my need to feel equal, and the continuing problem of blending our families. Every argument we had (and there were still a lot of them) was about control and our respective children. It always ended with one of us storming off like a child.

There were big explosions coming down the road and we both knew it. We were two warriors, Alan being Goliath and I, David. At some point I was going to bring out my slingshot and go to battle with him. Yet I never wanted to win. I just wanted equality, a respectful partnership on every level, and I wanted a peaceful marriage. I'm not sure I had that clarity at that time, but, subliminally, peace and equality were my goals. I knew one day I would take my power, and each argument was bringing us closer to that goal. The danger was not going beyond the point of no return. Sometimes arguments can get so destructive, so ugly, that you can't recover. I know we were both cognizant of this; yet, being so close, we knew each other's buttons. When one of these was pushed, a blackness shrouded the house and we knew we had gone too far.

Jay took over as my manager midway in the second season of *Three's Company* in 1978. That's when the "action" really began to go into that "phenomenal state." It's what Jay wanted. He had continually been telling me, "Get rid of Bonnie; she's a lightweight."

———

Jay Bernstein was a Hollywood success story. Handsome and ageless, he had grown up in Oklahoma City, where he idolized stars such as Errol Flynn, John Wayne, and Marilyn Monroe. In his mind he saw himself as one of them—glamorous and carefree. He came to Hollywood and got a job in the mailroom at the William Morris Agency, working from 9:45 A.M. to 6:45 P.M. every day, six days a week, and also worked nights at the Burbank Ball Bearing Factory. On weekends he parked cars at Lawry's Restaurant on La Cienega, and one time as he parked Clark Gable's car, for a moment he imagined it was his car, his life. He wanted the big time and was willing to work for it. He didn't know if he was as smart as all the others, but he did know he would work harder. Before long Jay started his own public relations company. He never stopped pushing forward. When his employees went home to their kids, he shifted into high gear. He made sure he finagled invitations to premiere parties and social gatherings. He went out every single night, dressed to the nines in custom suits bought on credit, and courted new clients. Before long he was in charge of publicity for Sammy Davis, Jr., Frank Sinatra, the 5th Dimension, Red Buttons, William Holden, and others. He was on the map and moving up.

Jay was young, eager, and dynamic. He wanted to own the town. By the time I met him, he was at his peak.

Because Jay received no commission on *Three's Company*, he was motivated to drum up as much extra work as possible. Now I was busier than ever. He soon put together future deals for me to star in three feature films and two TV movies of the week for my first hiatus, *Happily Ever After* and *Zuma Beach*. Every time he had the chance, he talked me up with reporters. "She's the next Farrah," he would tell them. Jay was flamboyant, a showman. He loved excitement and drama. He proudly proclaimed he was not saving any money, but spending it all because he planned to be dead of a heart attack by the age of fifty. He was thin and of average height, sported a goatee, and always wore thin gold-rimmed yellow sunglasses. His clothes were expensive—soft suede jackets, Brioni suits, Gucci loafers in suede and velvet. Always present was one of his canes from his antique collection.

He never hung up his clothes; he threw them on the floor after wearing them, and it was his valet's job to collect them and take them to the dry cleaners. His dry cleaning bill ran over $1,500 a month. If he tried on a suit or a shirt and then decided to wear something else, that too was dropped on the floor and sent to the cleaners.

Jay wore tons of jewelry—a large solid-gold Rolex watch with a tiger's eye face, large gold or sterling belt buckles, gold chains around his neck heavily laden with medallions of different sizes, and rings on several fingers. He clanked when he walked; security-checking devices rang like fire trucks when he went through. He was a character; he was eccentric. I enjoyed that about him.

He also had a great sense of humor. Jay and Alan and I would laugh all the time. We were having fun. We had the pulse and we were enjoying it.

But Jay also knew how to manipulate me by pressing my insecurity buttons. By our second year together, he'd call me at night and say, "You're slipping! Farrah's got four covers, Cheryl's got three covers, and you only have two." I'd buy into it and get off the phone biting my nails, thinking I was about to fall from grace. Again, I still didn't have any sense of "me" and how much I was worth emotionally or in the marketplace.

The momentum around my career took its toll on the set. John Ritter and I had now risen up and above the show itself. During our summer break in 1978, John was doing two motion pictures, and I was scheduled to star in two TV movies. Our outside careers caused tension with Joyce and also made the producers feel insecure about their ability to control me. Somehow they didn't see it in the same way where John was concerned. They also did not like that Jay and Alan had so much influence over me. They didn't trust Jay. He had advised Farrah to leave *Charlie's Angels* after one year to do features, and they were afraid I'd be influenced to jump ship, too. They were also nervous about Alan. They knew he was smart and savvy and that he recognized that *Three's Company* was more than a good time. It was a huge business opportunity. They felt threatened by Jay and by Alan and me as a couple. Rather than seeing my rising fame as an opportunity to soar for everyone, they felt backed into a corner like scared snakes. They coiled, ready to strike at all times, which created an unspoken adversarial feeling on the set. My happy TV family was quietly becoming more and more dysfunctional. For me it was a familiar scenario.

From the perspective I have today, coupled with my present maturity, I realize I could have tried harder to create a peaceful coexistence. But at that time I didn't understand I had that power. I was in the middle. Like a child of divorce, I was running back and forth trying to keep peace on all sides and not accomplishing the task. I was trusting Jay; I couldn't alienate Alan; I wanted to be Chrissy, "the good girl," for the producers; and I didn't want to upset John and Joyce. I wasn't savvy enough to understand that I held the cards. I had no concept of my value. I didn't question Jay; at home I feared upsetting Alan, so I said nothing when I was angry or upset; and at work I couldn't speak up to the producers about anything that was bothering me.

———

Every day something amazing was happening. Steven Spielberg called me at the show (I didn't have an office or an assistant yet) and asked if he could meet with me regarding a new movie called *1941* with John Belushi. I didn't find this remarkable or out of the ordinary. Even though I had never met Steven and I was excited, I was getting calls similar to this every day. I invited him to my beach house for lunch so we could talk without being disturbed by fans at a restaurant.

That weekend, Alan was in Vancouver doing his network television talk show for CTV (Canadian Television Network). Bruce, now thirteen, dreamed of being a director when he grew up and was in awe of Steven Spielberg and the fact that he had directed his first feature film when he was twenty-six years old, called *Sugarland Express*. In fact, it was Bruce who filled me in on Steven's history. He was the "boy wonder" of new films and had been taken under the wing of Lew Wasserman, the genius who had propelled Universal Studios into rarefied air with a string of successful films. Sid Sheinberg was the heir apparent to Lou Wasserman, the day-to-day guy who coddled, protected, and nurtured Spielberg into becoming the hottest director in the business.

"Can I meet him? Please, Mom?" Bruce pleaded.

"Of course," I told him. "We'll all have lunch together. Just be polite; don't interrupt and don't bug him."

"I promise," Bruce said.

I greeted Steven at the front door on Saturday afternoon. I was wearing a baby pink bathing suit because it was a scorching ninety-nine degrees that day. He was young and cool, and immediately I found it easy to talk with him. I felt like I had known him for some time. He wore jeans and a short-sleeved Hawaiian shirt and told me that until recently he had lived down the street from me. His attractiveness came from his focus. He had a power about him, yet it was cushioned with a gentle quality. I liked him immediately. It was a beautiful sunny day, and we sat on the roof, which was under construction for a new deck, munching on salads and talking for about four hours. I was just happy to be sitting still for a spell, and I presumed he was getting a sense of me; watching for personality quirks, vulnerabilities, insecurities . . . those character traits a great director tucks away but can pull out of a hat when he needs them by pushing the actor's emotional buttons. I'm sure he came to see if I truly was the ditzy blond on the show or if there was more to me. We laughed a lot; and when he left, he said he'd like me to be in his movie. It meant moving the *Three's Company* shooting schedule by two weeks, but I said I was sure that wouldn't be a problem. After all, ABC and my producers would recognize the great promotional benefits of having their star in a big, fat, expensive Spielberg movie along with John Belushi, who was huge box office at that time from his *Saturday Night Live* fame.

Wrong! My producers refused to budge. They weren't going to relinquish their power. "No? They said no?" I asked Alan incredulously. "Why? What could possibly be the reason?"

Alan put it to me bluntly. "Well, Mickey already had the schedule laid out and thought it would inconvenience the rest of the group to move things around." He added, "Pretty stupid and shortsighted!"

This now created new feelings of resentment inside me toward Mickey. He didn't want me to get too big for my britches. I had a contract with *Three's Company*, and they exercised their control, so I lost this great opportunity.

With maturity, I've found it to be a waste of time to worry about what I didn't get. It's the glass half empty, glass half full syndrome. But at that time, I saw the missed chance of working with Spielberg as the half-empty glass. In the words of Kurt Vonnegut, "shoulda, woulda, coulda" means you didn't. *1941* turned out to be the one movie of Spielberg's that flopped. But working with Steven was the missed opportunity. How did this missed chance change my life? I'll never know. I do know that my life wouldn't be what it is today, because every experience is life-changing. Maybe it would have sent me on a different course, but maybe not. I have to believe it was meant to be; yet it was a tough nut to swallow.

FIVE

 That summer of 1978, Paul Anka asked me to come to Monte Carlo to guest star on his TV special extravaganza *Paul Anka in Monte Carlo*. It was fabulous. Prince Rainier virtually turned the city over to us. I did a musical number dancing down the village streets of Monte Carlo singing "Gee, How Lucky Can You Get?" How apropos! The song finished with a montage of me going from one fabulous boutique to another, modeling and hamming it up for the cameras in one incredible couture fashion after another.

Donna Summer, the worldwide disco sensation with the incredible voice, was also on the show. We did a piece together at Jimmy's Disco about sisters. You know, Somers and Summer. After we finished, we stayed to have even more fun.

Jimmy's Disco was the most famous disco in the world in the '70s. It was the playhouse for the rich and famous, sprinkled with European royals. Roaming about were Arab sheiks, Princess Caroline of Monaco, Princess Yasmin of Jordan, and other royals, whose names I didn't know. Strobe lights and crystal balls created an atmosphere of fantasy and illusion. Beautiful models in slinky gowns lounged on the banquettes sipping

champagne and smoking cigarettes dramatically, like movie
queens. All the women were dressed in couture fashions—silks,
satins, bare midriffs, smooth shoulders. There were couples
kissing in the corners. Many of the men were in white dinner
jackets or black custom-made tuxedos. Those who were not
wore the leather look of the Rolling Stones—black leather pants
and bare chests peeking out from Italian silk shirts. Everyone
pretended to be unimpressed, but it was not so. Everyone was
looking at everyone else. It was the most incredible show I had
ever seen or been a part of. All the while "Love to Love You,
Baby" blared from hidden speakers so loud you had to yell to be
heard. It was a beautiful mélange of swaying bodies and lights
reflecting off diamonds. The famous, the royals, the phonies all
mingled together, creating an atmosphere of unbelievable glamour and excitement.

Jimmy's Disco was owned by Régine, the disco queen and
most famous hostess in all of France, perhaps in all the world.
She danced and drank champagne all night, every night,
whether she was in Paris, Morocco, or Rio, where she had her
other clubs. She said she slept all day and awoke at 6:00 P.M.
when her live-in facialist and masseuse rubbed her face and
body with oils and creams to bring her back to life for that
night's fete.

Régine was great at making sure the "right" people met one
another. I was standing on the top stair at the entrance talking
with Donna Summer when Régine came up to me and said,
"Suzanne, dahling," in her thick French accent, "you have to
meet Stavros Niarchos. He thinks you are fabulous!"

Stavros Niarchos was a famed billionaire shipping magnate,
and he took a liking to me. I was young, blond, and American.
Stavros was used to having anything he wanted. And he decided
he wanted me. Stavros was a little man, Napoleonic in his
demeanor, and I'm sure women were merchandise to him. In his

heavy Greek accent over the loud disco music he said, "Suzanne, you are so beautiful. I want to give you a party."

I yelled back over the music, "Okay, but I'm bringing my husband."

Stavros didn't miss a beat. A husband was no obstacle to him. I'm sure he thought, If this works out, I'll buy him.

"Whatever!" Stavros said. "Bring whoever you want."

"There are a lot of us," I told him.

Stavros couldn't know that no amount of money or power in the world could interfere with my feelings for Alan.

I called Stavros the next morning from our fabulous waterfront suite at the Loew's Hotel, with Alan's urging. "It will be an incredible experience for you and the whole group," Alan said.

"Bonjour, *Atlantis*," the butler answered.

"Stavros, please."

"Hello, Suzanne," Stavros said brightly when he came on the line. "Will you come to my yacht tonight?"

"I'd love to, Stavros, but there are sixty people in my group, including Paul Anka, Donna Summer, and Ringo Starr."

I thought this might put him off, but he said, "Good, bring them all. We'll have a big party!"

Europeans; they love to have a good time.

Gathering sixty people that night took some doing. The job of arranging cars and meeting times was given to the production assistant on the show. Nevertheless, by the time everyone was there, we were running forty-five minutes late.

Alan, Jay, and I pulled up in front of Stavros's magnificent yacht. It was breathtaking. At the bottom of the gangplank were two white-jacketed and -gloved men of his senior crew. It was more military in feeling than a pleasure yacht, but that was how Stavros liked it. The whole package was impressive. Did they salute? I wondered to myself. Again, it was like a dream. My whole new life was a dream. The small-town girl rubbing elbows with the big time. I remembered my dad's violent rages, my crying mother, the fistfights, the craziness, the shame, the guilt, and it seemed like another world—a time long ago. I had been given a new chance at life, and I was grabbing it.

I walked up the gangplank with Alan and Jay directly behind me. I was wearing a yellow Laura Biagiotti gauze dress, the same color as my hair. The skirt blew in the wind. I saw Stavros as soon as I reached the top. He was wearing white linen pants and a navy blue blazer with a gold silk ascot, which looked great with his silver hair. He had a powerful demeanor, yet tonight he looked nervous, as though he was worried we wouldn't show.

"Ah, Suzanne, you look beautiful."

"Thank you, Stavros. This is my husband, Alan Hamel, and my manager, Jay Bernstein."

Stavros was charming to Alan and Jay. "Ah, you are lucky men," he said. Stavros started most sentences in English with "Ah."

I laughed. Stavros was no threat to Alan and he knew it. We were there to enjoy ourselves, and we did. Stavros was a fabulous host. The evening was incredible from beginning to end. White-gloved waiters walked around with huge bowls of caviar and chilled bottles of Dom Pérignon. While Jay "worked the room," Alan and I drank champagne and nibbled on caviar, standing on the top deck of *Atlantis* with a view of the beautiful city of Monte Carlo on one side and the Mediterranean Sea on the other. The sumptuous yacht had a swimming pool and thirty-two staterooms, each named for the artist whose original works of art hung in the room—the Renoir room, the Picasso room, the Chagall room, and so on. It also had a helicopter and a state-of-the-art communications room that appeared as if it could have rivaled the U.S. Navy's.

"Call whoever you want," Stavros said to me grandly while taking Alan, me, Paul Anka, and King Hussein's sister, Yasmin, on a tour. I couldn't think of anyone to call. I didn't know what I would say with everyone listening. "Hello, guess where I am"? I'd sound like a yokel.

During cocktails Stavros came up to me and swatted me on the arm. I was a little startled at this. "Suzanne," he said, "you sit next to me. You can bring with you whoever you want to sit next to you." Europeans do not sit with their spouses or escorts at dinner parties, but since I was American, I knew this meant I would be able to have Alan sit next to me. I needed Alan for protection, because this little guy was scary.

During dinner the strap of my dress kept slipping off. Stavros said gruffly, "What's wrong with your dress?" A subtle little indicator that this guy liked to have everything his way. But what did I care. He wasn't my husband. Other than that, the evening was the stuff novels are written about, only this time I was in the story.

"Call me when you get back to America," Stavros said when we were leaving; but I never did. It would have sent the wrong message. For one night Alan was amused by Stavros's blatant overtures, but to continue the relationship with Stavros would have invited trouble. It was what it was. As I flew home to Los Angeles, I snuggled in the cozy blanket provided by Air France's first-class service and relived the previous several days. Who would have thought, I pondered, that Suzanne Mahoney from San Bruno, California, would one day be dancing with princes and billionaires, nibbling on caviar toasts while sipping $200-a-bottle champagne . . . then I fell into a dreamy sleep.

SIX

The fame machine moved forward without my help. It now had a life of its own. Every move I made was recorded. Photographers waited as I got off the plane. Snap! Flash! Ready or not, I was theirs. Alan hated this invasion of our privacy. I enjoyed it but felt badly that Alan didn't. I was afraid that if we pushed the attention away, I would lose all that I had gained. My nature is to be nice. I am a pleaser. When you're a celebrity, those who take from you know no boundaries. Photographers will have you stand and pose for them forever, so it became Alan's job to be the bad guy. "Come on, we've gotta go," he'd say.

"Aw, just one more," they'd yell.

"I said no," he would say firmly. Then he'd grab my arm and move me away from them.

I would feel embarrassed. I was afraid not to be the nice girl. Unfortunately, what you fear is what you draw to you. I was afraid of losing my fame. I believed I was my accomplishments. There would be lessons to be learned down the road. But I was living in a state of mild panic. If they knew who I really was, I was afraid they wouldn't be interested. I had a lot to learn and a lot of growing to do.

Notice how often I've used the word "afraid"? My new life was an enviable one; yet rather than enjoying the moment, the present, I was driven by fear.

Picasso said, "Youth is wasted on the young." Sometimes I think back and wish I could do parts of my life over. It seems that so many of my opportunities were missed, misused, or wasted. But as my wisdom increases, I realize that age is a gift we are given for surviving. Every event is just as it should be. I had to experience the lowest sense of who I believed I was before I could pursue my highest vision of who I really am.

I knew from the healing I had had so far, which was the understanding and forgiveness of my father's disease, that I had moved forward and evolved into a person I was no longer ashamed of. In my mid-twenties, my therapist had helped me grow far beyond my childhood vision of myself, far enough to get me to this moment in my life. She had helped me to believe in myself, to believe that I wasn't worthless, hopeless, and stupid, as I had thought. She helped me to realize that I had talent, that I counted, and that with hard work, dreams could be realized. She was rebuilding my spirit, repairing the damage that had left me like a broken little bird. Her work was fixing the human condition. I thought this was all I needed to do, but I could feel an inner struggle. I knew I had more emotional work to do. I just wasn't ready to dig inside and feel the pain again. But pain doesn't go away. It waits patiently to be healed. The deeper the wound, the more work it takes. I didn't realize what lessons lay ahead of me. I thought when I was completely healed emotionally, the "work" would be finished. I had no comprehension at that time of the spiritual work that would continue the ongoing evolution of my inner self. I didn't know that forgiveness was not something I required only between my father and me, but that my father had been, in essence, my teacher of compassion and forgiveness with others. But it wasn't time yet. Life unfolds slowly.

———

At home things were schizophrenic—wonderful and terrible. Alan and I were more in love than ever and angrier than ever. It was a passionate love, and I believe our passion kept us together during these rough times.

In the spring of 1978, Alan suggested private boarding schools for all three children. The Ojai Valley School was a wonderful environment and challenging intellectually. Removing them from the Los Angeles area, where drugs and addicted parents seemed the norm, was a sensible idea. Drugs were rampant in the Los Angeles schools in the '70s, and one of Bruce's friends at the Santa Monica school had already been caught several times with drugs in the schoolyard.

Part of me felt that Alan also saw this as an opportunity to avoid having to spend every waking hour with my child. I felt torn emotionally. It did make sense; it would be beneficial for all three children; but it also felt to me as though we were farming out our problems. Yet Bruce craved normalcy. He wanted order and routine, and at this time, I was not able to give it to him. I would cry into my pillow each night at the thought of sending him away five days a week. When Alan would try to comfort me, my body would become frozen. In my mind I blamed him for the dilemma. I lost sight of the positives associated with this school. It had the potential to be a real opportunity.

In the end I decided to give it a try. Bruce and I talked about it for a long time. He was not anxious to go away, but we reached a decision together. He would try it for two weeks. If he didn't like it, he could come home immediately. If he was scared or lonely, I told him, I would drop anything I was doing and drive the two hours to Ojai and get him. He would come home every weekend, and he could use our credit card to call me anytime and as often as he wanted. I told him I would go with him and stay as long as he needed me while he adjusted.

Since Stephen and Leslie were living at their mother's house, it was not for us to decide where they went to school. Alan suggested to his ex-wife that this might be beneficial; but at the time, she had a wait-and-see attitude.

In the fall of 1978, Bruce and I packed the car to go to his new school. The drive to Ojai seemed to take an eternity. We held hands in the front seat and his palms were wet with worry.

"I love you, sweetheart," I told him over and over.

Bruce and I arrived at the school and were directed to his room by a really pleasant and kind-looking young man who would be one of his teachers.

"Hi, Bruce," he said good-naturedly. "We've been looking forward to meeting you." Bruce liked him immediately.

Bruce's new room was simple and had huge windows overlooking a beautiful big tree with stables in the background. We unpacked his things—new sheets, blankets, his favorite pillow, his baseball glove and balls, jeans, T-shirts, his good sports jacket, posters, and other special things from his room to make him feel at home. His roommate came in around this time and Bruce and his new friend found instant camaraderie. Two hours later Bruce was settled in and was being called to his first school assembly.

He looked at me and said, "Why don't you go, Mom? I like it here. I think it's going to be fun."

My sweet darling Bruce, I thought. "Are you sure, honey?" I asked. "I'd planned on staying a few days."

"But there's nothing for you to do," he said, "and it looks like I'm going to be busy. It's okay. I'll see you when I come home this weekend."

"Okay, darling, if you're sure you're okay," I said hesitantly. "Remember, whenever you need me, I'll be here. I want you to be happy. If you find you aren't, we'll change things."

I kissed him good-bye and hugged him at least ten times.

"Mom, I've got to go," he said, smiling; and then he and his new friend ran off to their first assembly.

As I drove through the village of Ojai toward the ocean, I felt hollow inside, like my guts had fallen out. I pulled into the parking lot at the public beach and got out to take a deep breath of ocean air. I needed to fill myself with something to remove the emptiness I felt inside.

I sat at the water's edge with my head in my hands and sobbed. Tears and salt air mixed together and stung my eyes. Through the heaving of my aching chest I asked the God of my understanding to help me to know if I was doing the right thing and to please take care of Bruce and his pure, beautiful soul during this time.

Things eased up a bit between Alan and Bruce. School gave them both space from each other during the week. Bruce came home on weekends, and I would try to keep my schedule clear to be with him, although it wasn't always possible. I knew enrolling him in this school was a positive move, maybe even an essential one. Yet I missed being with Bruce every day. He was my pal. I felt guilty sending him to boarding school, but he was flourishing as the school year moved on. His grades were great and he liked the routine and the kids. In my childhood family system, we couldn't afford luxuries like boarding school. Perhaps, had such a school been available and affordable, I might have missed the bulk of our family dysfunction, but then I also would have missed learning important lessons. This school provided a protective shield from Alan's coldness. Sometimes it was as though Bruce was invisible to Alan. That way Alan could deny that he was sharing his life with someone else's son and not his own.

Weekends, when Bruce was home, were especially hard times for him. He is a sensitive person and unused to having anyone dislike him. The more Bruce tried to connect with Alan, the more Alan retreated. Then I would get angry. I didn't understand my feelings, so I would bury them inside until the anger would erupt into one of my inappropriate explosions. I couldn't deal with the reality that I was letting someone hurt my child's feelings, because then I would have to insist Alan change his behavior. If he would not, or was unable to, I would then have to make the choice to leave him. And I couldn't do that. He was my husband. I loved him, but I was not evolved enough to demand life on my terms . . . yet.

Again, we choose what we need to learn, and both Bruce and I would learn later on, through this experience, to demand to be treated the way we deserved. If you allow someone to push you around, they will. The way Alan was acting was unfair. He married me, and that included the whole package. I was Bruce's life. His world was with me. I could not, would not, abandon him, ever. If it came down to a choice, there was no decision. A mother has an unspoken agreement with her child: I will keep you safe; I will never abandon you; I will guide and nurture you throughout your life.

But as time went by, I began to realize that boarding school gave me some space also. I needed to find the courage to stand up to Alan, not as the out-of-control, roaring lioness (which showed my extraordinary immaturity), but with the same strength I had shown several years earlier when I'd forced the issue of the two of us living together.

Once I could do that, once I could demand that we do the work to heal ourselves individually and as a family, then not only would I grow, but we would all benefit and move forward. I was willing. If that meant family counseling together or individually, I wanted it. But Alan said, "You're the one with the problems, Suzanne; I'm fine with our life. So if you want to go see someone, do it." I'd want to kick him when he said this, but this was his way. He was afraid to explore his real feelings. It would make me feel crazy inside. Yet every once in a while he would let me in. One night in the dark, he whispered, "I know you feel hurt.

I'm trying to figure it out. I don't want to make either of you feel bad." It was a start, and I loved him for that.

At other times, though, Alan would shut me out, which made me feel like a yo-yo. My emotions were out of control. In my fantasies I wished I could just drive the car like a maniac, crash, die, and end the pain. But who would take care of Bruce? From the time of his birth, Bruce was my gift and I was protective of him. He was responsible for keeping me sane and on track, just by being alive. I needed to do more emotional work to find relief from my up-and-down moods.

———

I believe we seriously underestimate the severity of damage done to children of divorce. There is such pain involved when parents split up. Suddenly the children no longer feel safe. The rug of security is pulled out from under them. Adults protect their children from the truth to keep them from getting hurt; but in reality, the situation becomes more difficult because the children do not know where they stand.

Alan's children felt tremendous loyalty to their mother. They probably thought Daddy had left their mother for me. Why would they want to forgive me? They couldn't blame their father, because then they would have to face their feelings of anger and abandonment. It was easier to direct that anger toward a stranger, the new woman. There was nothing to lose, and it did provide a vent for their pent-up feelings.

My behavior didn't help much. I tried to connect with Alan's children by being so-o-o nice and so-o-o kind. I'm sure my sugary sweetness made them sick. I thought I was doing everything I could, but in reality, my behavior was false and his kids knew it. I was afraid to act the way I really felt. I was trying to be some kind of parent to them, but they didn't want another mother. Who could blame them? I hadn't even come close to earning their friendship yet. My thinking was all mixed up. I didn't know what I was feeling. I wanted to do the right thing, but Stephen and Leslie's rejection was hurtful; and that hurt would then turn into anger.

Feelings are our own truth. If only we were able to know the value of facing them. Even the Bible says it: "The truth shall set you free." But none of us were smart enough at that time.

SEVEN

When Stephen came over on weekends, it was obvious he was not happy. He was usually sullen and brooding. By contrast, Bruce acted like a happy puppy (guess where he learned that), so everyone outside of our family would remark at how nice a kid Bruce was. This, in turn, would make Stephen recoil even more. Sadly, in reality Stephen was being honest. It had to be threatening having his father living with my son. He wore his anger on his face. It was never necessary to ask if he was okay. You could tell by looking at him that he was not. There was intense but unspoken jealousy between the two boys— like Cain and Abel. It was simply that their insecurities were misunderstood. Sometimes they'd forget their circumstances and just be boys, and from downstairs I'd hear them laugh and play. But most of the time there was a thick quiet between them. I believe they each wished the other would disappear . . . forever.

Alan added fuel to this fire by treating Stephen like a prince. It's how he dealt with his guilt. We were all doing the best we could. No one was deliberately trying to hurt anyone; but I could tell Bruce felt left out at these times.

Boarding school was having a positive effect on Bruce. He started to test Alan by instigating little arguments. Bruce knew Alan's stand on most political issues, so he would make statements to Alan that were in opposition to his thinking. "I don't believe in capital punishment," Bruce said, for example, knowing it would irk Alan. I would get nervous that the two of them might allow their mutual annoyance to get out of control. I was afraid of the consequences. I felt an emotional tug between these two men in my life, and I never knew whose side to take.

Whenever I wasn't working, Alan's children would be at our house. Most weekends, holidays, and vacations were with the kids. My neck ached from the constant tension. I needed to talk with someone, but there never seemed to be time to start the process. My *Three's Company* schedule was full-time, and all the extracurricular work was scheduled on weeknights and around the kids' weekend visits and activities. Finding a good therapist is not easy. You are lucky if you find the right one on the first try. Usually you have to go through three or four, sometimes more, to find the right one.

It became obvious to us that Stephen must have felt threatened that Bruce lived with us and he did not. I discussed the situation with Alan, and we decided to invite Stephen to live with us permanently. At that time he was living between his mother's house and ours, whoever was serving the best dinner. It was annoying. He needed to choose to stay at one house or the other.

After thinking about it, he chose to live with us. It was time to be with his father. It was a difficult transition for all of us, but it was the first step toward finding peace in our marriage. Now Alan had his own son living with him. I hoped he would no longer hold on to his anger at Bruce. What's fair is fair. Now we each had our sons with us living under the same roof, and Alan loved having Stephen with him full-time.

Then there was Leslie. Children will act out until they are understood, and Leslie seemed angry from a place so deep that even she couldn't understand it. She was angry with me, her father, and her mother; she seemed angry at the world. If facing feelings were easy, we could have cleared this up over time. But none of us understood. I only knew that whenever Alan and I were having a quiet dinner or dancing to a tape of Tony Bennett in the living room, the phone would ring and the mood in our house would instantly go to black.

Usually it was Leslie's mother who called, exasperated. It was always something. Leslie was smoking dope; Leslie had snuck out of the house; or Leslie's school had called about her absences. Whatever it was, it would shatter our good time, and somehow Alan and I would end up fighting. I didn't know how to deal with Leslie. There was something powerful about her and it made me afraid to demand she treat me the way I wanted to be treated. Instead, I took out my anger at Leslie through Alan, in the same way Alan took out his anger over living with Bruce on me. Leslie seemed determined to destroy herself and to take us with her if she had to. What a mess.

Every time I tried to connect with Stephen, he retreated, which added to my hurt and confusion. It was sad. Alan and I had so much going for us as a couple, but our inability to understand our feelings was threatening our ability to successfully blend all of us as a family.

I don't think having a stepmother called "Chrissy Snow," the sweetest woman/child character on television, helped matters. I wish at the time I had had the wisdom and the insight I now have. I would have been able to see her pain. I would have had compassion. I would have allowed her, encouraged her, to express her true feelings. She probably needed to tell us that she hated us, that she felt betrayed by all of us. Instead she acted as if everything was fine, but her self-destructive behavior said otherwise. I was only fifteen years older than she was and still battling my

Alan and me on the island of Eleuthera the night before our plane almost crashed.

My makeup artist Bjorn, who gave me my '70s "look."

My short but memorable role as *American Graffiti*'s blonde in the T-Bird.

Chrissy.

Clockwise from left: Don Knotts, Richard Kline, me, Ann Wedgeworth, Joyce DeWitt, John Ritter—the cast of *Three's Company* in season number three.

The first Chrissy poster.

John Ritter, Joyce DeWitt and me.

Our wedding day, in 1977—
Leslie, Stephen, Alan,
me, and Bruce.

My sister, Maureen,
and I share a dance.

Mom and Dad.

Alan and me.

Crowds, bodyguards, and police protection were a new fact of my life.

Barry Manilow,
Fred Astaire,
and me at a
Hollywood gala.

Alan and me
photographed at
the Regency Hotel
in Manhattan
the week I was
cohosting "Dick
Clark's Rockin'
New Year's Eve."

Elliott Kastner gave me his '57 Silver Wraith Rolls-Royce.

I gave Jay my first
six weeks' salary
to make me a star.

Jay Bernstein with
his famous cane.

Jay Bernstein, the starmaker.

Donald Sutherland and me
in *Nothing Personal*.

The Sands Hotel, Las Vegas.

Stephen, Bruce, and me
on New Year's Eve
in New York City.

My "Suzanne Somers
and 6,000 Sailors"
special.

The pink gown made
by Ret Turner for the
"6,000 Sailors" special.

Nominated
for my first
Golden Globe,
in 1979.

Chrissy in action . . .
Jack asks if she has eaten
his prize pie.

Ret Turner adjusting the
concertinas on my costume
for "Suzanne Somers and
50,000 G.I.s" at Ramstein
Air Force Base in Germany.

Entertaining
American soldiers
in Germany.

own immaturity. I could only see what was wrong. I had no insight into how to correct the situation. We didn't know the war going on inside Leslie was to be our greatest battle as a family.

Frankly, I don't know how our marriage survived dealing with Leslie, and I don't know how Leslie survived us. I had never imagined myself to be a "wicked stepmother," but that was now my casting. Leslie thought I was a "bitch" because I was the one who did all the yelling and screaming. At times I would explode with frustration and rage, especially when Leslie would take things from my closet. I would yell at Alan, "Why don't you do something?" And the kids would hear us.

Yet it was not all bad. There have to be some redeeming factors in every situation; otherwise you wouldn't put yourself through it. Every once in a while we'd all let down our guard and, for a moment, see one another differently. We'd laugh together at Sunday dinners. Bruce and Leslie always really liked each other and that helped all of us. My cooking brought pleasure to the family, and I would go out of my way to prepare everyone's favorites. I made Sunday dinners as often as possible, and I'd prepare wonderful things—roast duckling with maple syrup and vanilla, plum tarts for dessert. Cooking was all I could do for them. It was the only gift my stepchildren would accept from me. And it worked. They would come hungrily awaiting the feast.

On nights like these, Alan and I were able to relax, to relinquish our positions. Occasionally he would do something really nice for Bruce, like take him on an outing or help him with schoolwork, and each time he did that, our defensive walls would come down a little bit more.

———

Blending families is incredibly hard work. No one enters a blended family willingly. We all come kicking and screaming.

During this time I ran into the mother of a friend of Leslie's at a clothing store. "How's Leslie?" she asked.

"Fine," I said tightly.

"I just love her. She is so sweet, so bright, so funny."

It was an insight. Leslie had another side she refused to show me. I could tell by the woman's tone that her affection for Leslie was genuine. How I wished I could know the Leslie she knew. That one sounded easy to love. Maybe one day I will, I thought. I can't give up hope. I must keep trying any way I know how.

———

Bruce continued to excel at Ojai Valley, not only intellectually but emotionally as well. The faculty was extremely nurturing and created an atmosphere in which he flourished. And the school was more than academic; the students also enjoyed overnight hiking trips in the Ojai mountains, cookouts, sing-alongs, science trips, and coed dances. Bruce would talk excitedly with me each night about the day's activities. It was an incredible relief to me that he was happy.

Over the summer, Bruce told me one day, "I have an A average, so I think I could get into the Thacher High School for this fall if we enroll me right away." Thacher was the other private boarding high school in Ojai and required a high academic standing for entrance.

Stephen had seen how much Bruce was enjoying the environment at Ojai, so he asked if he could go there when school commenced in the fall. Both Alan and I were thrilled by his enthusiasm.

Leslie was still not doing well in the Los Angeles school system and had been sneaking out of school with her friends. One day the principal called Alan and told him marijuana had been found in her friend's purse and that all the kids seemed stoned. When questioned, Leslie was defiant and insisted she didn't know anything about drugs. But Alan was worried about her. It was the third time she had been caught leaving school, and Alan told her he wanted to change her environment. He felt Ojai would be a great change for both Leslie and Stephen.

That next semester, all three kids would be enrolled in the Ojai schools—Bruce at Thacher and Leslie and Stephen at Ojai Valley.

EIGHT

$\mathcal{J}_{c\odot}$ That same year, 1979, I was a nominee for a Golden Globe as Best Actress in a Television Series, along with Jean Stapleton and Linda Lavin. I didn't prepare anything as an acceptance speech, because I was sure Jean Stapleton would win. *All In The Family* was such a popular show and Jean won Best Actress every year. But it was fabulous just to be in such illustrious company. I chose a Jean Harlow–like, pink satin Nolan Miller gown that was strapless and shirred at the bust and had a fitted waist and a slit that showed a lot of leg. The arrival was dazzling. Our long black stretch limousine pulled up in front of the hotel. The customary red carpet was beautiful and seemed to stretch for a mile. As Alan, Jay, and I emerged, flashbulbs popped like rockets all around us. It felt surreal. As my eyes adjusted, I saw many other stars who made up the parade into the Beverly Hilton. Jaclyn Smith looked gorgeous, as did Cheryl Ladd, Chevy Chase, Robin Williams, John Travolta (who was with Marilu Henner), Jane Fonda, and so many others. I felt like a starstruck fan. I forgot people were watching me; I was so busy watching the other stars.

Then Jay chose this opportunity to mess with my mind again. We were walking into the auditorium, with flashbulbs going off all over the place, when he said, "I don't think we can sell you as the next Marilyn Monroe anymore. You're getting too old. I think we have to think of you more as a Judy Holiday type."

Well, that's a great bomb to drop, I thought as I walked inside. It wasn't the Marilyn Monroe or Judy Holiday part, it was the "too old" part. Jay didn't see this statement as mean-spirited. "You have to imagine we're in a war," he told me often. "You spent almost your first thirty years with nothing to show for it. Now you're in the big time. Think of it as boot camp. You don't have time for emotions. I have to keep pushing your ass over the fence no matter how difficult, because you didn't come to me already trained to comprehend what I have planned for your career. I told you all along you were going to be a big star. My job is to make people love you, and if it means changing tactics or repositioning, that's what we are going to have to do."

But Jay didn't understand timing. He never took time off. He thought about his clients every waking hour, probably also in his sleep. He had no family, no children, no relatives I ever met, no parents that he communicated with, and no real friends. Just his clients—me, Farrah, as well as Kristy McNichol. It didn't enter his mind that walking into the Golden Globe Awards was an inappropriate time to lay strategy on me. It just happened to be the moment the idea came into his head. Jay had a way of pulling my confidence out from under me. Thank God, I didn't win. I couldn't have walked onto that stage; my ego was so shattered. I was feeling ugly and old, and I was only thirty-two. To my surprise, Jean was not the winner. That night belonged to Linda Lavin.

Celebrities are a pretty insecure lot. The more I read about them and the more I meet them, the more I am constantly surprised by their defensiveness, which is just a mask for their lack of confidence. One of the most nervous people I have ever met is a famous actress who has won several Academy Awards. She

seems all fidgety and unable to connect. From outward appearances, she has it all—beauty, intelligence, talent, a happy marriage, and megabucks. What is it about? Maybe she is just shy,
but I think it's more than that. I think so much is expected of us.
Each new facial line is noticed and dissected. Show business
requires a perfection that is unnatural, unattainable. I'm sure the
continuing trend toward plastic surgery is the result of the press
and media expecting their celebrities to defy nature.

In Jay's case, it was not only career strategy, it was also control coupled with manipulation. If he could keep me scared, I
wouldn't leave him. He could feel it coming. Alan and I were
becoming a united front. More and more we were doing it our
way. I trusted Alan's instincts personally and professionally. He
was smart and he was making an effort to try to change things
at home, even though they were baby steps. I believed we would
work out our problems and in time he would take over the reins
of management. And I was sure Jay was smart enough to know
this.

One evening, Michael Eisner, then head of Paramount (now
head of the Disney empire), asked Alan, Jay, and me to dinner at
La Scala Boutique in Beverly Hills. He offered me a three-picture
movie deal.

Jay said, "Turn it down. They aren't offering you enough. You
can do much better. You're on every magazine cover in the country. Everyone knows who you are. America loves you. You'll
bring enormous visibility to their projects. That translates into
money; you deserve to be paid well. They'll get their money's
worth."

I had no idea if he was right or not. I had to trust him. He was
my adviser. I didn't accept Eisner's offer. I look back now and
think, Pretty stupid of me! I didn't understand that if my pictures
succeeded, I could name my price, so it didn't matter what I
earned on these three movies. The important thing was to break

into feature films, which is a difficult crossover for a TV actor. But Jay was not interested in long-range thinking. He knew his days were numbered.

That's the way the game is played in Hollywood. It's safer to think short-term—take the money and run. Jay always told me, "I know what's going to happen . . . I'll get you up where the air is rarefied, you'll become deified, then I'll become nullified."

"No! No!" I would protest. "It won't be like that."

I really wasn't thinking about leaving Jay at this time. He was doing a stellar job. Somehow, though, Jay's and Alan's egos were on a collision course. Jay's plan was to make me the biggest movie star in the business. I didn't truly believe in myself yet, so I had a difficult time taking him seriously. But it was Jay's constant and subtle attempts to come between Alan and me that became destructive. He knew that whatever he and I discussed, I would then discuss it with Alan as we lay in the dark at night. Pillow talk is one of the most potent forces in the world. Defenses are down; there's a relaxation and a softness to the discussion—and Jay could not participate in this. It frustrated him. So he'd push my insecurity buttons on the phone each night. It was a subtle undermining of Alan; and if Jay caught me on a night when Alan and I were having trouble, it affected me.

Sometimes Jay's emotional level was like that of an eight-year-old. It was this immature part of him that liked upsetting things between my husband and me. In some strange way, when this happened, he would feel he had won that round.

I believe Jay cared about me. To this day, he tells me that he loved me then and loves me today, not in a sexual way, of course. I was a piece of what he considered his family. His life was primarily Farrah and me. He didn't need or want our men around. Jay said he saw himself as John Wayne running to protect me.

"I would have done anything to protect you," he said. "If I couldn't help you by jumping over the fence, I'd go under it. If that didn't work, I'd go to either side. If the obstacle persisted, I'd tell them I ain't gonna move this fence, I'm just gonna blow it up." This is how he talked. He saw himself as a savior. In Jay's mind he was my ultimate superhero, and there are very few managers who truly shape and mold a career.

How can you know anything when you first get into this business? There is no school to teach stardom. If you're lucky enough to grab the brass ring, you get thrown into the business with no expertise. Without protection, the vultures hover, knowing you will not have any idea of what to do with your new visibility. They pick and pluck at your flesh. It is pure luck if you choose advisers correctly for yourself.

There is also no training for handling money. During those years it was coming at me by the truckload from endorsements, salaries, and movies. It became meaningless. I thought it would never stop. After so many years of being desperately poor, I had no idea how to handle a business, nor had I ever dealt with money of any kind. In fact, I felt guilty about it. I felt I was overpaid. I would shop with my girlfriend and feel badly that I could afford more than she, so I'd buy her things—a $300 silk shirt, clothes for her daughter, objects for her house. . . . She took it, too, which created a huge imbalance in our friendship and eventually destroyed it. I didn't understand that I was paid well because I was earning profits for the companies that hired me. No one does you any favors in this business. Money was also another problem between Alan and me. He understands the value of it. He appreciates every dollar. We would argue over my excessive spending on clothes. I loved clothes and couldn't believe I could buy anything I desired. I would say, "It's my money," like a spoiled child. I hadn't learned the concept of "ours" or of saving. Someday I would learn, but it was going to take some work.

NINE

During my next hiatus, in 1979, I was scheduled to star in three independent feature films. None of them was exactly the perfect vehicle for me, but Jay said to keep throwing projects against the wall until something stuck. He told me, "I want to spread you into so many areas of show business that it will take five years before you can possibly fail." This was what it was like working with Jay. He always interjected the negative to keep me insecure, to keep me needing him. Nonetheless, I was excited.

At the conclusion of the *Three's Company* season, Alan and I, Bruce, and Stephen packed our bags and took off for London, England. Leslie wasn't talking to us. Earlier she had deliberately gotten herself thrown out of Ojai Valley School for smoking marijuana. There was a strict "no drugs" policy, so she was immediately expelled, with no tuition refund. Leslie was a free spirit. We had forced her to go back to Ojai for a second year and she was not going to do anything she did not want to do. Now she was back at Beverly Hills High, which was where she wanted to be.

We arrived in London and were met at Heathrow by producer Elliott Kastner's 1957 chauffeur-driven, maroon-colored Rolls-

Royce Silver Wraith. There were only two like it in the world, and I was told the other one belonged to the Queen of England.

When Alan had first read the script for this movie, he'd said, "It's a piece of shit."

The movie was *Yesterday's Hero*, and I played a successful rock and roll singer opposite Ian McShane, an English actor, who played an alcoholic soccer hero. I hardly needed to act in this one. I knew the dance with the alcoholic all too well. The promises, apologies, pledges to clean up his act. Then the broken promises, because I understood the only real love affair the alcoholic has is with the bottle. Everything else is a distant second. This was the first and only Jackie Collins novel to be made into a feature film; the rest have been television movies.

Alan was right. It wasn't a very good script. But between the director and Jay, they convinced me I could make something of it. The director, Neil Leifer, was a famous American sports photographer and recorder of athletes and political legends. His photographs appeared regularly inside and on the cover of *Life* magazine. One of his most famous pictures was of him lighting Fidel Castro's cigar while Castro lit Neil's.

"It's a lousy script," I told Neil long-distance to London one night. I had never heard of Jackie Collins at the time.

"I know," Neil said. "But we'll rewrite it as we go along. We'll essentially throw this script away and work from the outline. We can make it great, and I promise I'll take fantastic pictures of you."

I was intrigued.

Jay went on to convince me. "It's an important career move," he said. "Nobody knows you in Europe, but everyone there loves soccer. So this is a way to get them to notice you."

Alan still protested until Jay lost it and screamed, "We need a European movie! It opens up another whole arena for her." Jay and Alan were at each other's throats more and more often those days. Whenever Jay had the chance, he'd take me aside and tell me, "We need to talk alone, without him. Alan's always there, and he doesn't understand you like I do. He's not a people person. He doesn't understand your heart. I can make the public know what a good person you are. That's what they will respond to. You need to be loved because of your background. It's different with Farrah. She doesn't give a shit 'cause everyone has always loved her. I understand you, Suzanne, because I started in this business wanting everyone to love me."

Whenever Jay would get me alone, my thinking would become confused. He'd make me feel that without him, I'd be nothing.

But Alan felt that we should not be so anxious to jump into just any feature film. He thought we should wait until the perfect vehicle came along for me. "I'll support you in whatever you choose, Suzanne," he said. "I just wish it was a better project."

Once in London, we met with Elliott Kastner. He was a nice guy with an agenda. Charming as can be; you couldn't help but like him. He was a transplanted New Yorker, from Brooklyn, and had produced hundreds of movies. A few were moderate hits, including *Missouri Breaks* with Marlon Brando. But mostly he did movies that were released in Europe. Elliott had a friendly face and impish sparkling eyes, white straight teeth (his own), and a captivating smile. He was of average height and wore beautiful, hip, expensive clothes, like cashmere overcoats and designer suits, with the casualness of a rock star. Instead of a shirt and tie, he'd pair a T-shirt with a $2,000 suit.

The making of *Yesterday's Hero* was a glorious job for me. Every morning James, the chauffeur, would pick me up in Elliott's Rolls-Royce in front of the elegant and famed Dorchester Hotel. I felt like a princess. In the backseat would be crumpets and tea, jams and jellies, and I would nibble away as I was driven to the English countryside. While I was filming, Bruce and Stephen had a great time discovering London, which kept them busy, since they had only a brief two weeks during their spring break. It was one of the few periods where their sibling rivalry dropped. They needed each other for companionship. London could be a big, scary city if you were alone. But together, they took English cabs, rode the double-decker red buses, saw Big Ben, Windsor Castle, Trafalgar Square, Harrods, and much, much more. It was fun to come home at the end of each day and listen to them both excitedly replay their day's adventure. It was a glimpse into the possibilities of familial harmony.

I enjoyed working with Ian McShane. He had a rough-and-tumble cockney demeanor and he was a good actor.

One day, out of the corner of my eye while shooting a scene on location in the countryside, I noticed a striking woman standing next to Neil. She was tall and had beautiful smoky eyes and long brown hair pulled straight back into a gorgeous high ponytail that reached her bum. She was wrapped luxuriously in a full-length white fox fur with brown suede knee-high boots.

"Hi," she said, "I'm Jackie Collins."

She was as beautiful as her sister, Joan. We became instant friends, and throughout the filming, Alan and I spent a lot of time hanging out at the London hot spots with Jackie and her husband, Oscar. They owned the hottest disco/nightclub in London at the time, called Tramps. It was reminiscent of Studio 54 on the inside without the "scene" outside. The beautiful and famous hung out at Tramps. Most nights Jackie would put together fabulous parties with Michael Caine and his beautiful wife, Shakira, Jackie's sister, Joan, and dukes, duchesses, and counts with various (and sometimes dubious) pedigrees. The visiting Hollywood glitterati all made it a point to stop by Tramps—including David Soul and Paul Michael Glaser (who were in London filming *Starsky and Hutch*), Michael Douglas, and Alan Alda.

We were three weeks into shooting and, contrary to my deal, I still didn't have a paycheck. My contract specified that

I would be paid at the end of each week of filming. Jay was home in America at this time, taking care of Farrah, so Alan took charge.

"Don't worry," Elliott told Alan. "The new production office is not geared up yet. You'll get it next week."

Alan had to be the bad guy. "Elliott," he said, "you've gotta pay Suzanne or I'm taking her back to America."

"Don't worry, Alan," he answered reassuringly. "I'll have it tomorrow. Hey, why don't you guys come to my house for dinner tonight. I live at Runnymede. It's the site of the signing of the Magna Carta. Tessa and I would love to have you."

That was Elliott's way. He'd charm the pants off of you. Tessa Kennedy was Elliott's mistress of fifteen years. She was in her late thirties, blond, and great looking. She looked like she could have been a former model. She had big beautiful round doe's eyes and was pencil thin. They had two children together. When I asked Elliott why he didn't divorce his wife, he said he didn't want to hurt her feelings. That was Elliott. Always padding his space; always keeping the balls in the air, never quite letting them fall, so no one could ever get really mad at him. So Elliott, Tessa, and their two children lived happily together at Runnymede, while his wife lived in a posh Mayfair flat.

"Elliott," Alan said on the telephone that night, "can you give me directions to Runnymede?"

"Sure," he said, and proceeded to do so.

"Okay," Alan said. "We'll see you in thirty minutes." Alan and I enjoyed Elliott, so we were looking forward to the evening.

Runnymede was like something out of a medieval fairy tale. A glorious twelfth-century manor with a long driveway that had originally been used for carriages delivering noblemen. Inside was perfection. Tessa had incredibly good taste and was an interior designer, her biggest client being King Hussein of Jordan. The king regularly sent his private Boeing 747 jumbo

jet to fly her to the palace to continue redecorating one sumptuous room after another. Tessa was elegant, sophisticated,
and aristocratic—a complete contrast to Elliott and his "deez"
and "doze" Brooklynese. Tessa graciously showed us around
the mansion, each room lovelier than the one before. Price-
less antiques, windows spewing brocades and silken tassels,
Aubusson rugs everywhere, unbelievable art covering every
inch of wall space.

Two perfect little English children appeared. The little girl
was five years old and dressed in a simple white voile dress with
stitching and smocking that only the most expensive stores
would sell. The little boy was seven years old and wearing gray
pants, a navy blue blazer, and a tie.

"Good evening," they said as they curtsied.

"Well," Tessa said as she stood up and gestured toward the
dining room. "Shall we have dinner?"

"Where's Elliott?" I asked, bewildered.

"Oh," said Tessa nonchalantly, "he just got a phone call and
had to go to a funeral."

Alan and I looked at each other, confused. We had just talked
to him thirty minutes earlier. Someone had died and was already
having a funeral service within thirty minutes, at night? Well,
that was Elliott.

"He'll be back later," Tessa said calmly.

I felt like I was in the middle of a John Cleese English comedy. It was absurd.

The table was set with antique Limoges, heavy lead crystal,
and sterling silver. The table itself was a long mahogany Queen
Anne that could easily seat thirty or forty people. The five of us
huddled at one end. The butlers brought us our dinner, each
plate covered with a silver dome. Yum, I thought. I'm hungry. I
wonder what we're having? The domes would be removed all
at once. My salivary glands were working overtime. Duck à

l'orange? I wondered. Rack of lamb with mint sauce? Filet mignon with béarnaise sauce?

None of the above. The butler uncovered my plate, and I was staring at . . . macaroni and cheese!

"Well," I said, trying to hide my surprise, "it sure makes me feel like home. Isn't this a nice change." I mean, it tasted good, but the presentation was a little grand for such a humble meal.

As we were having our "gourmet" dessert of vanilla ice cream, Elliott arrived. "Hey, you two," he said with his charming grin. "Look at that *punum*," he added, holding my *punum* (Yiddish for "face") in his hands. Then he sat at the other end of the table—forty chairs down—and started absentmindedly polishing the mahogany surface with his napkin. Alan and I stared at him blankly while pressing our knees against each other's under the table in astonishment.

After he showed us the spot outside where the Magna Carta had been signed, which was marked with a stone that said "Magna Carta," we went home. Elliott never explained his absence, and we never asked.

Of course, the money wasn't there the next day, so Alan decided to pull the plug, which meant I would not be going back to work until Elliott fulfilled my financial contract. The phone rang in our suite.

"Alan, sweetheart, whatcha up to?" Elliott asked innocently.

"We're going home," Alan said firmly. "A deal's a deal. I can't let Suzanne work for free."

"Don't worry about a thing. I'll have the money tomorrow morning," Elliott answered sweetly.

"Okay," Alan said. "When we have the money, Suzanne will go back to work."

"No problem," Elliott answered. "Meet me in front of the Mayfair branch of the Bank of England tomorrow morning at eleven sharp."

"I'll see you then," Alan said matter-of-factly, and hung up the phone.

The following morning Elliott met Alan in front of the bank. He had payment in full for the entire movie in cash. Elliott handed Alan a large paper bag filled with money.

You cannot open a bank account in England unless you live there, so Alan was stuck carrying the money himself. He had cash stuffed inside his underpants, T-shirt, even his socks. We couldn't mail it home; we couldn't leave it in the hotel room; we couldn't wire it into our bank account. We didn't feel comfortable keeping it in the hotel safe, so we were stuck with the cash.

In the middle of shooting *Yesterday's Hero*, we had to fly back to Los Angeles for me to shoot an Ace Hardware commercial that was to look like a fabulous Las Vegas show—stairs, feathers, legs, dancers. It was like a marathon, all that flying back and forth. But at least Alan was finally able to deposit the money in our bank.

At the wrap party for *Yesterday's Hero*, Elliott was all smiles. "I had a good day," he said. "I sold this movie for more money than I got for *Missouri Breaks*—all because you are the hottest property in America right now," he said, pinching my cheeks.

"Good," Alan said, smiling. "Then maybe you'll sell us your Rolls-Royce. Suzanne loves it, and I'd like to buy it for her."

"I'll do better than that," Elliott said. "I'll give it to her."

Wow! I couldn't believe it. Four days later we were on our way back to America and the Rolls-Royce was already steaming across the Atlantic Ocean, "Deliver to Los Angeles" stamped on the side of its crate.

Five months later we were back in London for the premiere of the movie. The critics liked it; it looked like we might have a hit. At the premiere party after the movie, a woman tapped me on the shoulder. She was well dressed, but her face looked ravaged. She was holding a drink and appeared to be drunk, but I couldn't be sure. Her voice was trembling. "You've taken away the only thing that means anything to me in the whole world. You took my car!" Suddenly Elliott appeared and his wife disappeared.

Just like that!

"Hey, youze guys. Havin' a good time?" Elliott asked with his usual charm. That's when I found out the car belonged to his estranged wife.

"I'll send it back," I said in shock.

"Naw, I've been wantin' to get her a Jaguar. This just kinda speeded things up," he said smiling. Vintage Elliott.

———

There was a joke around town. A famous French actress is at the Cannes Film Festival being interviewed by a reporter. "If you could make love with any three men in the world, who would they be?" he asks.

"Well," she says, her English dripping with a French accent, "Robert Redford and Tom Cruise and Elliott Kastner."

The reporter says, "I understand Robert Redford and Tom Cruise, but why Elliott Kastner?"

"Because," the actress answers, "everywhere I go in Cannes, everyone is saying 'Fuck Elliott Kastner!' "

TEN

 Two weeks after finishing Elliott's movie, we packed up once again and headed to Toronto for the second movie I was to do that hiatus. The boys would be joining us as soon as school let out in two weeks. I was starring in a feature film with Donald Sutherland called *Nothing Personal.*

In spite of my incredible success, I still had no grasp of the power I held in my business. I wanted to return to Los Angeles to attend Bruce's graduation from Ojai. He was an Honor Student and he wanted me to be there to watch him receive his award. "Absolutely impossible," I was told by my producers. "We can't stop shooting for three days until you come back. It will cost the company a fortune and the insurance company won't stand for it."

I was intimidated and afraid to upset everyone, so I reluctantly called Bruce and told him I could not come. "I'm sorry, sweetheart," I told him. "But Grammy and Gramps are coming. So is your Aunt Maureen and Uncle Bill. Also, Alan has offered to come and videotape the whole ceremony; and then you, Alan, and Stephen can fly back to Toronto together."

"Alan's coming?" Bruce asked nervously.

"Yes. I think it will be a good thing for the two of you."

I regretted not attending. Alan as an emissary was the last person Bruce wanted to see on that day. Being alone with Alan was an unsettling experience for Bruce.

"How was the graduation?" I asked when Bruce arrived in Toronto.

"Well, I wish you could have been there, Ma. I didn't know what to say to Alan."

That night we watched the video that Alan had made of the ceremony. I sat next to Bruce on the sofa and squeezed his hand when his name was called.

"I'm proud of you," I whispered to Bruce as we watched. It wasn't the same as being there, but it was something and I was happy Alan had gone and had made the effort.

Nothing Personal was being produced by American International Pictures, which was headed by Sam Arkoff, the larger-than-life Hollywood producer best known for always having a cigar stuck in the side of his mouth. I played a lawyer fresh out of law school who, along with a college law professor (Donald Sutherland), tries to save the seals in Newfoundland from being slaughtered for the fur industry. Because of our protests, someone was trying to kill our characters.

I was looking forward to working with Donald and was also nervous about it. After all, Donald was very famous, not only as the star of numerous huge movies, like *M.A.S.H*, but also as Jane Fonda's former lover. In the '60s, Jane and Donald were prominent political activists calling for the end of the Vietnam War. I used to see both of them regularly on the evening news while I was giving Bruce his nightly bottle.

Donald was a megastar to me, and I hoped my acting skills were honed enough to keep up with him. The first time we met was accidentally at Vidal Sassoon in Beverly Hills, where I had gone to have my hair touched up for the movie. When I arrived, the receptionist whisked me into one of the private VIP rooms, away from the watchful stares of the other patrons. As the door to the VIP room opened, a man with hundreds of pieces of tin- foil stuck to his head to make fresh blond streaks looked up. If I didn't know better, I would have thought he had stuck his fin- ger in an electric light socket.

"Hello, I'm Donald Sutherland," he said perfectly comfortably.

"Oh, my God! I'm sorry," I stammered. "They put me in the wrong room."

"It's okay," Donald said good-naturedly. "Now you know! I'm not a natural."

"Me neither," I said, laughing; and I closed the door.

Donald was famous for changing hair color and style for each new role. He had decided to have blond wavy locks for this pic- ture.

We met again two days later in Toronto. The way Donald smiled at me, I knew we were going to get along.

"I like your hair," I told him, and winked.

———

Alan and I rented a large Tudor house on Oriole Parkway in a lovely neighborhood. Bruce and Stephen would have their own rooms and there was a swimming pool. Leslie would be joining us periodically throughout the shoot. We enjoyed being in Toronto. Alan had been born there and had been the biggest star on Canadian television until he decided he could no longer take the cold Canadian winters and moved to Los Angeles. Lucky for me, or I might not have met him. Also, Alan's parents, sister, and niece and nephews lived in the city. So this was to be a good time for all of us. Alan liked getting away from the western United States at this time, because he had had incredible success with a little side job he had taken doing commercials for a grocery store chain called Alpha Beta. The campaign was so successful that soon Johnny Carson had taken to doing Alan Hamel–Alpha Beta jokes in his monologue on a regular basis. The slogan of the commercial was "Tell a friend"; so everywhere we went, people would stick their heads out of their cars and yell "Tell a friend" at Alan.

It wore thin. He was truly accomplished, having started with *Razzle Dazzle*, which ran from 1960 through 1965, the most popular kids' show in Canada. It was a tongue-in-cheek show meant to entertain adults as well as children. Alan's mischief was always apparent. There was a peanut gallery of screaming kids, and Alan would come out and yell at the kids to "Shut up!" They thought that was really funny, so they'd scream even more. He was no Buffalo Bob. He talked to the kids the way parents wish they could.

Alan went on to be the most sought-after host for every type of program. He hosted *Midnight Zone*, a weekly variety show for two years, then starred in *Nightcap*, a one-hour weekly show that ran for five years, which was the predecessor to *Saturday Night Live*. Alan was the Chevy Chase of Canada long before Chevy began his career. The show was meant to shock, and it did. Alan interviewed a topless woman live, which had never been done before on Canadian network television. After that the Canadian Parliament set up a special committee to investigate how this had happened. They confiscated the tape and didn't return it for six months. The show was out of control. The viewers had never experienced anything like this. Canadians, by nature, are very conservative, so this represented a breaking of the mold. It was the most watched TV program in the nation, after hockey. People arranged their week around this show to find out what crazy Al Hamel and his cohorts would do next.

After *Nightcap*, he hosted a one-hour weekly show called *The Observer*, which was much like our *60 Minutes*. In 1964 Alan hosted Canadian coverage of the Tokyo Olympics. He also hosted *Sightline*, a weekly live actuality show from different parts of Canada; *Lively Arts*, a weekly half hour of interviews with the current stars of the day; and *Saturday Sports Date*, which he took as a way for him to get to warm places in the winter. Alan hates to be cold. To this day, when we are in cold weather, his teeth chatter until he can get under the covers or into a warm bath.

In fact, in 1967 Alan woke up on a freezing Toronto morning to what sounded like gunshots. He started out of bed on the ready, only to find it was the sound of frozen tree boughs heavy with ice breaking off and falling to the ground. At that moment he made his decision. He had gone as far as he could on Canadian television. He was cold. He jumped on a plane that afternoon and headed for California. When he got off the plane in Los Angeles, he was greeted by the warm Pacific air and declared L.A. home.

Alan continued to commute to Canada for a while. Then he finally moved his family to California.

He landed the job on *The Anniversary Game* for ABC almost immediately, which is where we met. After that and around the time of his divorce, he and Dick Clark produced several shows together: *Mantrap*, out of Vancouver; *The Sensuous Man*, out of Montreal; and finally, three years before we were married, *The Alan Hamel Show*, Canada's answer to *The Tonight Show*, in which Alan starred for five years. His last few installments of *The Alan Hamel Show* included a five-part in-depth interview with Groucho Marx, which turned out to be Groucho's last interview.

You can imagine how after all his previous success, being best known in the United States as the "Alpha Beta man" rubbed him the wrong way, and why more and more he welcomed opportunities to work outside of Los Angeles.

ELEVEN

 The shooting of *Nothing Personal* was going well. We were all enjoying being in Toronto. It was a great time for me to connect with Alan's family. The boys were now settled into our rental house. Stephen got a job working in his uncle's clothing store and Bruce got a job as a delivery boy.

I loved working with Donald Sutherland. He was a consummate professional and a lot of fun to be with. On the first day, the director asked after a scene, "Did you guys get that?"

"Us?" Donald asked incredulously. "Don't you know if we got it?"

At that moment, Donald realized he had to take over. From then on, Donald called the shots. He pushed me creatively.

"Don't wear any underpants in this scene," he told me.

"Why?" I asked incredulously.

"Because if you've just finished making love upstairs, and you've come down to make coffee, and you're planning on getting back into bed to make love again, the most you would do is grab my shirt to keep away the chill."

He had a point. Features were rooted in reality, whereas television, particularly sitcoms, was not. But I decided to keep on my underpants anyway.

Jay eventually came to Toronto. He was still making sure he peed on his territory. I couldn't believe it when he showed up on the set. I was making a film about saving the seals in Canada, and he arrived with a nine-piece set of real sealskin luggage.

I liked Jay, though. He is the most eccentric man I've ever known. I asked him how he could dare bring *seal*skin luggage to the set considering the topic of the movie. Jay replied, "Suzanne, I've cultivated being eccentric because then 'they' don't know what the fuck I'm gonna do next. It's my shield. And 'they' hate it because they can't fire me!" That was Jay!

He arrived in town with his usual flamboyance, pounds of gold jewelry dripping from his neck, wrists, and fingers, including a Christmas present from me—a gold medallion inscribed "I love you, Mr. Mean." That was my nickname for him because he changed moods at the drop of a hat. His mood could shift from rosy to black in an instant. It would happen unconsciously or he could make it happen at will. Another unpredictable man in my life. Only this time, I wasn't walking on eggshells like I did with my father and to some degree still did with Alan. My dad and Alan had control over me because I had so much to lose. Jay knew if he acted badly or tried to push me around, I'd tell him to take a hike; so I was never the object of his ruthless behavior. He was too clever to let that happen. He worked on my emotions. He knew where I was vulnerable.

Jay and I had a lot of fun when he wasn't messing with my head. He was doing less and less of that as he realized Alan was hovering and ready to take over. I was taking my time before I turned over full control to Alan. I wasn't worried about Alan's abilities, but I was worried about our arguments, which continued to happen—albeit less. He was still starring on and producing *The Alan Hamel Show*, in Vancouver, and had to be away every other weekend.

It was an unsettled time for me. It seemed that I was being pulled in every direction at every moment. I was hot. Everyone wanted a piece. I hardly had a piece left for me.

I hired my first assistant, Marsha Yanchuck, at Jay's recommendation. She had worked for him for ten years, then left because she could no longer handle his tyrannical outbursts. Marsha was calm, efficient, and unflappable. Finally I was getting some order in my life—I had someone to remind me to write thank-you notes, someone to return the many business calls that came in daily. "Did you read the script from so-and-so?" she'd ask. The stairs to my bedroom were piled high with scripts yet to be read. There was no time. To this day I wonder how many incredible projects I passed on because I couldn't find the time to read. If a producer bugged me too much, I would tell Marsha to pass, just to get them off my back.

As soon as *Nothing Personal* finished filming, I was set to costar in a movie with Michael and Kirk Douglas called *Final Countdown,* but the Douglases kept moving the schedule until I ran out of time as *Three's Company*'s fourth season was starting. At Jay's urging, our lawyers threatened to sue for the money we would have made because the time had been set aside and I was unable to use that period of time for other projects. From a business standpoint, it was legitimate; but when you are the product, it is an uncomfortable experience. In retrospect, I would rather have had the opportunity to work with Michael in the future than get the money. Instead, the legal hassles left a bad taste in their mouths where I was concerned. But once again, at the time I was still not making my own decisions.

Months later, Alan and I were invited to Cliff Pearlman's house in Palm Springs for dinner. Cliff was the owner of Caesars Palace in Las Vegas, and I was hoping one day to try my luck in the nightclub business. I had always loved singing, and in my head, I saw myself as a successful nightclub entertainer. When I was a child, my daydreams were always about singing and enter-taining. It was my escape. I would fantasize I was on a big and important stage with a packed audience of beloved fans; and always, always, my mother was in the front row. She would be proud and happy and without worry. I had no idea that visual-ization is a key to success. In visualizing, you see yourself where you want to be, focus, then do the work to get there.

Cliff was known for throwing interesting dinner parties. "Come over tonight," he said. "I'm inviting a few people." His tone clearly stated not to ask who they were.

As we arrived at his front door that night, a Rolls-Royce pulled up. After ringing the bell, I saw Kirk Douglas and his wife, Anne, in the front seat. I could only imagine what they were thinking. Luckily, Kirk is a pro and the subject of litigation never came up. Business is business. He seemed to understand that better than I. Thank God, because if he had mentioned it, I probably would have said, "Oh, let's just forget the whole thing." Uncomfortable situations made me nervous.

Cliff and his wife, Cindy, Kirk and Anne Douglas, and Alan and I talked comfortably for about half an hour. Kirk was charming and in incredible shape. He was wearing beautiful white linen pants, and it looked like he had no underpants on. It was hard not to stare, probably much the same as when a woman shows cleavage; and I must say he looked good.

It was also obvious we were waiting for someone. The table was set for eight. The bell rang. A familiar voice. Who is that? I was thinking when Frank Sinatra and his wife, Barbara, walked in. What a life I was living. Frank sat next to me and told me he loved my show and thought I was a "doll." Frank thinks I'm a "doll," I was thinking incredulously. I didn't know what to talk about with him, so I asked him about his mother. I had always heard how much he loved her. For the next hour he told me one enchanting story after another. We were sipping wine, and the conversation became easier, looser. Soon he was talking about the plane, her death, and his pain. (His mother had been killed tragically while flying in Frank's private jet in bad weather to see him perform in Las Vegas.) He became teary and stopped talking for a moment. I was touched by his humanity and vulnerability. I stopped thinking of him as Frank Sinatra and instead saw him as a human being who had experienced the many textures of life—the highs and the lows, the ecstasy and the agony. I asked him if he ever felt her presence now, and that got him back to feeling good. "All the time," he said. "Onstage, at home, in the kitchen, a lot."

———

"Dinner will be served," we were told. I was seated with Frank on one side, Alan on the other. To Alan's right was Barbara. Cliff was at our end of the table, Cindy at the other with Kirk and Anne. It was a wonderful evening until Alan asked Cliff if he had read the new unauthorized Meyer Lansky biography.

Meyer Lansky was a Mafia gangster whom Alan had unwittingly befriended in Cuba when he was in his early twenties. Alan loved Cuba and had even tried to get a job there at the TV network. (Again, lucky for me he couldn't, or I might never have met him.) Alan went to Havana the first time with a friend he had been working with in Miami while Alan was doing commercials for Chrysler. They stayed at the Riviera Hotel in Havana, and Alan's friend introduced him to a little guy named Meyer Lansky. Next thing Alan knew, he was in Lansky's vast suite, which Alan remembers had a lot of crystal chandeliers. Over the next few days, Meyer took a real liking to Alan. He moved Alan into the adjacent suite and picked up the tab. He recognized his street smarts. Luckily, Alan had to go back to Canada, or Meyer might have gotten his claws into him. It wasn't until Alan returned home that he found out who Meyer Lansky was. Two years later

Alan ran into him one more time in the lobby of the Diplomat
Hotel in Miami after Castro kicked Meyer out of Cuba.

"Why would I want to read a book about Meyer Lansky?" Cliff
asked Alan gruffly. Rumor had it that all Vegas executives were
connected guys. Maybe Cliff felt Alan's question was provocative. This question hung in the air like a big black cloud. The
silence was deafening.

Coming from an alcoholic environment has its advantages. I
knew how to take over uncomfortable situations and act like an
elephant really hadn't just walked into the room. The adaptive
dysfunctional codependent in me saved the evening. I became
my most charming, funniest self and soon the table returned to
normal.

"Are you crazy?" I asked Alan when we returned home later
that evening. We laughed at the whole situation. It was an incredible experience to spend the evening with such interesting people. Another perk of celebrity. Doors open. Big private doors.

TWELVE

When Jay had persuaded Farrah Fawcett to leave *Charlie's Angels* after only one season, the ABC network pronounced him persona non grata. He would never work with them again. Fred Silverman was beyond angry. Farrah had been the primary reason for the unbelievable success of *Charlie's Angels*. In one year she had become a phenomenon. Jay was told by an executive who had been present in a meeting at ABC regarding Farrah that Fred Silverman said he didn't want to do business with Jay ever again regardless of his client list. "Let's smoke him out" were his reported words.

I was feeling the effects. *Three's Company* was the number one show on television; yet I was not asked to participate in the Emmys, which ABC hosted that year, or specials or movies of the week. Anything that came up on ABC seemed to be closed to me. No one at ABC would return Jay's phone calls. He called me and said, "I've got an idea. I've decided to sell your hiatus. ABC is not sending you any extra work, so I called Bud Grant, president of CBS Entertainment, and asked if he would like to have a contract with you for the next three years. You would continue to star on ABC for the run of the show, but on hiatus

113

you work for CBS on projects that interest you. You can do specials and movies of the week."

The situation made me nervous. "I don't want to upset Fred Silverman," I told him.

"He doesn't care about you," Jay said. "He wants to get back at me for pulling Farrah, and he's using you to do it."

CBS offered me a deal to have my own show, called *Suzanne*, at the end of my series. Before I signed with CBS and without telling Jay or Alan, I called Fred Silverman's office to tell him about the situation, but he was out of town; so I was put on the phone with the senior vice president. I explained my situation—that I felt loyalty to ABC, they had been so good to me, and I needed to know what they wanted to do about this contract offer from CBS. Handling this myself was very naive. I should have left it to my lawyers, manager, and adviser, but I was still rather green to big-time show business. Jay, however, practically had my foot in the CBS door.

"You'll be the only star with a series on ABC but with an exclusive contract with CBS," he would say, "plus a guaranteed series deal." Still, I did feel a loyalty. I waited and waited, but ABC never responded; so finally we signed with CBS. Not a good move. It was big news. "Fred Silverman Furious Over Suzanne Somers' Desertion To CBS" was the story in the trades. I felt awful, so I called Fred.

"I talked to your vice president ten weeks ago, and he never called back," I explained.

"You could have tried a little harder to get me," he said angrily. "How could you do this? I gave you your big break. Don't you think you owe us any loyalty?" he asked.

"But I tried," I stammered, feeling upset.

"Yeah, well good luck," Fred answered, and hung up.

I was devastated. I had not wanted to create ill will. Two weeks later it was announced that Fred was leaving ABC and defecting to NBC, which had offered him a better deal. So much for loyalty.

I felt angry with myself. But Jay also had another agenda. By signing with CBS, he would be getting his fifteen percent of my future. If I stayed at ABC, he knew he'd be gone before it was necessary for me to make any long-term deals. I'd walked right into this one.

Now ABC had no need to nurture and coddle my career. "Just get as much out of her while we've got her" was the attitude. What I couldn't know was if this choice would eventually affect my future negatively or positively.

THIRTEEN

Outside of the industry, the public responded to all three of us on the show with unbelievable enthusiasm. It was as though the country was our playground. Everywhere I went in America, people responded to that "lovable Chrissy." In Miami, the famous Joe's Stone Crab House opened the restaurant on a Monday just for me and my family. Piles of delicious, succulent crab were placed on the table, with key lime pie for dessert.

"No charge," Joe said when we were finished. "We're just happy you chose our restaurant. If you wouldn't mind, maybe you could send an autographed photo for the wall."

In New York, *Good Morning America* was on the "stop by" list. I walked onto the set while David Hartman was doing an interview with someone else. Ha! Ha! Ha! went David. It seemed like the old days of Bob Hope doing walk-ons on *The Tonight Show*.

While in New York, Alan, Jay, and I stopped by unannounced at the office of Tony Thomopoulos, the new president of ABC. Tony didn't have any leftover animosity toward me from Fred.

Tony was on the phone and held up one finger, meaning he'd be with us in a moment, while gesturing to us to come into his

116

office and have a seat. "I'm just on the phone with Bob Daly" (who was president of CBS and Bud Grant's boss), he whispered with his hand cupped over the speaker. "Do you want to talk with him?"

"Sure," I said, exhilarated, and he handed me the phone. This was heady stuff.

"Look out Tony's window," Bob said to me. "I'll wave a white napkin in the window so you can see me."

Sure enough, in the high-rise building opposite ABC, I saw a white napkin waving in a large window on the thirty-second floor. "I see you," I said excitedly.

"Hurry and get out of Tony's office," Bob said. "We can't wait to have you on our network." Everybody laughed.

Fifteen minutes later we were visiting Bob Daly at CBS and he called Tony. "Look who I've got over here," he said mischievously. "She's waving a white napkin."

"Hi, Tony," I said on the phone as I waved the napkin furiously. We all laughed uproariously. What a life!

———

But at the same time, back on the homefront, Alan and I were continuing to have major problems with Leslie. It was her total "screw you" attitude. She was living with her mother, but her heavy presence was felt in our lives every day. It seemed to be more like minute by minute. Every time the phone rang, it was either Leslie or her mother or someone with bad news about Leslie. "I saw your daughter hitchhiking on the Pacific Coast Highway this afternoon. It seems kind of dangerous," one friend said.

I found I couldn't trust her.

I would ask, "Leslie, did you take my new Armani shirt?"

"No," she'd say defiantly.

"I know she took it," I'd say to Alan in bed at night.

"Why do you always want to blame Leslie?" he'd ask angrily.

"Because every time something is missing, it ends up in her closet until her mother gives it back to me."

Night after night, Alan and I would argue about Leslie. Alan was in total denial that there was a problem. He always turned it around so that it appeared I was the one with the problem. My insides were always upset. I felt misunderstood and alone. The more upset Alan would be with Leslie, the more he would pull back from Bruce and me. Stephen would get up in the morning and ask, "What kind of mood is Daddy in today?" We walked on eggshells around Alan, trying to sense his mood. If anything, all three kids bonded as a result of Alan's moodiness. He was scary to them and they were intimidated. It wasn't like Alan to be like this, but he was upset over Leslie's problems and his lack of control over his own life. He didn't know how to talk about it. Once again, I was in familiar surroundings—back in my father's house—controlled by the moods of others. My life felt schizophrenic, from incredible highs to the lowest lows. Alan was unable to express his sadness and exasperation over Leslie. For the first time in his life, he couldn't control the situation, so he reacted with anger and silence and looked for reasons outside of his real pain to blame and get angry.

We all knew Leslie was a walking time bomb, but none of us knew when it would detonate. Somewhere in my gut, I knew the explosion was coming. I just hoped we would all survive it.

FOURTEEN

"I had a great idea last night," Alan said excitedly over breakfast.

"What?" I asked.

"You and six thousand sailors."

"What do you mean?" I asked.

"I see you singing and dancing on an aircraft carrier with six thousand sailors as your audience," he said enthusiastically.

"That's a great idea," I said, understanding. I could immediately visualize the whole program. Even though America was not officially at war with any other country at the moment, we needed to rebuild the "dream" again, which the Vietnam War had shattered. We had not been victorious for the first time in our country's history.

The idea of rebuilding the image of our armed forces while at the same time entertaining America with my own television special was thrilling. Uniformed men not only look great, they are also an enthusiastic audience. I had grown up watching those famous USO Bob Hope specials from the living room of my family home in San Bruno and had always loved them.

119

"We'll hire the most beautiful dancers in Hollywood, and we'll work up a great act for you and your 'girls.' Then we'll fly everyone to the nearest aircraft carrier to do the show, and the sailors will go nuts."

I had been wanting to sing and dance all my life, and it was customary in the 1970s to give hot stars their own television specials. It was a chance for the audience to get to know them better in different formats. Cher had had several specials, as had Bette Midler, Barry Manilow, Carol Burnett, Julie Andrews, Cheryl Ladd, and Lynda Carter. And now, hopefully, me. I was ecstatic.

The following week Alan and I walked into Bernie Sofronsky's office (he was the vice president of specials) at CBS, which was now my new contractual home, to sell the idea. Bernie was Alan's age, with prematurely white curly hair. He was smart and likable.

"Suzanne and six thousand sailors on the *U.S.S. Ranger*," Alan said.

"Let's do it," Bernie replied immediately.

It was visual. You could see the show and its appeal in that one sentence. "We'll shoot it next spring," Bernie said.

"Okay, sounds good to us," Alan answered.

Alan always says, "When the deal is done, talk about the weather." We agreed on the idea and Bernie told Alan to get together with Business Affairs to prepare a budget. Done!

"Nice weather we're having," Alan said; and I knew it was time to go.

———

Now that Farrah Fawcett was separated from Lee Majors, she required more and more of Jay's time to handle her events. Jay was her escort at premieres and parties. He traveled with her to Mexico, London, and Cannes. I relied upon Alan to take over when Jay wasn't available. My deals for the next three years were in place and the bulk of my time was spent fulfilling those obligations.

In reality, Alan was now ready to take over. He felt that "three was a crowd." He really didn't want Jay in the equation anymore. I was torn in both directions. I could see the sense of Alan taking over, but I worried that without Jay we might falter.

"Jay is not really managing you anymore," Alan said one afternoon. "All the calls are coming through my office. I've learned a lot from him, but I now have a clearer vision than he does of where you can go with your career."

• "Maybe you're right," I said, concerned. "But let's wait until after Christmas."

———

And what a Christmas it was. Alan's parents came from Toronto and I wanted to share our success with the whole family. I wanted to make this the Christmas that no one would ever forget. Never mind that Alan's parents were Jewish and didn't celebrate Christmas. Just to be with their son and grandchildren was enough for them. My mother-in-law, Margaret, loved me and had accepted her "blond shiksa" daughter-in-law and all that came with me. Even though I wasn't Jewish, she could see that I loved her son dearly and made a nice home for him. She didn't care that I was on television. It was amusing but meaningless to her. She saw only the good parts of us, never the bad. She had no concept of the ordeal of blending families. Her disapproval over Alan's divorce was long gone. Originally, when Alan had separated from his wife, his mother had said, "Nice boys don't leave their wives and families." I think this cut through Alan's heart. He had never done anything to offend or displease his mother. He was utterly devoted to her. I can't remember a day, regardless of where we were in the world, that he did not call her. But ten years had passed. Alan and I were now joined at the hip. It was clear to all that we were "soul mates," even though we were still working out the "soul" part. She called us the "love birds."

I had tried so hard to make this a great Christmas. I meant well. Truly, the excess came from love and a wanting to share; but inadvertently, it was overkill, overindulgence to the point of boredom and embarrassment. We gave Margaret a diamond and gold bracelet, among many other things; my father-in-law, Izzy, got leather Bottega Veneta slippers that were as soft as velvet and a cashmere robe. My father received a solid gold Rolex watch; my mother, three beautiful designer suits from Giorgio, Beverly Hills.

The kids had so many gifts that they got tired of opening them. I wished I hadn't wrapped everything individually. It took three hours to open all the presents. Bruce seemed thrilled with his new bike. He also loved getting a television set for his bedroom. Stephen was happy with his stereo plus a new television set of his own. Leslie got skates and a small diamond on a gold chain. She actually put on a big smile and said "Thank you" in a meaningful way. She looked at me pleased, and for a moment we shared something nice. It was a thrill to see her happy in my presence, even if I felt I was "buying" her happiness. I was starving to make any kind of emotional connection with her. Alan gave me a beautiful pair of antique diamond and emerald earrings, tasteful as always.

When I looked at Margaret, I could see she disapproved. I realized immediately that I had done the wrong thing. Margaret had survived the Depression. She did not believe in overindulging. For example, Alan had had only one toy during his entire childhood. It was a block of wood with two leather ears nailed on the sides and he called it his toy elephant. Margaret said nothing to me, but I knew what she was thinking: What about saving? Why are you spoiling the children? This is too much. Nobody needs all this! Like my husband, Margaret appreciated the value of a dollar and the hard work it took to earn each one.

On the other hand, I still did not feel worthy of my enormous salaries. It was almost as though I was trying to get rid of it, so I could feel normal again. I didn't see my talents as anything special. I saw Chrissy Snow as special, but I couldn't connect "her" with me. That same day, trying to be so perfect, I cooked dinner for thirty people by myself: a delicate light wild rice soup, crab salads, roast turkey, cornbread/pine nut stuffing, baked yams dripping with butter, creamy mashed potatoes, giblet gravy, brussels sprouts, homemade cranberry sauce, and pumpkin pie with fresh whipped cream.

Before dinner, but after the Christmas morning gift bonanza, I had flown my entire family from San Francisco and had them picked up by a parade of limousines and brought to the house. As they entered, a mariachi band of seven men greeted them. We danced, drank, sang, and nibbled on homemade (by me, of course) appetizers in front of the eighteen-foot Christmas tree (which, naturally, I had decorated).

Everyone laughed and had a great time except Leslie, who was now in one of her black moods because Alan had caught her with her girlfriend in his closet smoking pot during the Christmas festivities. It was as though she couldn't handle having a good time in our presence. She had to screw it up. We never had any lasting satisfaction with her. After Alan's reprimand about drugs and sneaking behind our backs, she came to the Christmas dinner table with a scowl on her face. She toyed with her food and would not join in any conversation. To me, the black cloud of Leslie's mood darkened the dinner table. Everyone seemed nervous that something out of control might happen . . . and it did. I lost control. The words just popped out of my mouth.

"If you don't want to be here, Leslie, just go home," I said tightly, trying not to yell but not doing a very good job.

I had had it. I was overtired from trying to make a perfect day, a perfect meal, a perfect house, a perfect Christmas. I had overdone it and now I allowed Leslie's mood to ruin everything. Giving her such power was an indicator of my emotional state. I was still feeling responsible for everyone else's good time. I guess I didn't feel important enough to take care that I had a good time.

"I hate Suzanne!" Leslie yelled at anyone listening, and threw down her napkin. "I'm going home!"

Everyone at the table became quiet and uncomfortable. I wanted to cry, but I put on a happy face so as not to show my true feelings.

I couldn't see what was really going on with Leslie, which I can only chalk up to my lack of development and understanding. I saw the situation only from my own point of view. I guess anyone who feels that she has to be superwoman would have trouble gaining insight into a little girl ravaged with pain over the losses in her short life. In retrospect, a day like we were experiencing could only bring sadness. She might have felt badly that her own mother was not included; or she might have felt badly that she no longer had her mother and father under the same roof. When she was a child her grandparents had stayed with her; now they were with us, in particular with me, and nothing was the same anymore. At that time, people thought of divorce as something that happened to the parents, not the children. Yet the children of divorce are the biggest losers. The adults find new lives and the children are expected to fit in. They all react; some burst with anger and some stuff it down like Stephen and Bruce, but the anger smolders and will eventually erupt like a volcano.

FIFTEEN

That night after my family was safely tucked back into their limousines for their return trip to San Francisco, I washed all the dishes and then fell exhausted into bed. I lay there for a while reliving the day. It had been a lot of things—wonderful, glorious, and upsetting. Almost everyone had had a grand time. I was grateful, but I didn't feel happy.

Alan put his arms around me and whispered that it had been a great day. We didn't talk about Leslie. It was too painful. Then we fell asleep. To this day, my favorite moment always is sliding into bed next to my husband—his skin, his smell, his warmth make me feel safe and content.

December 26 brought a blow that threatened everything I had accomplished. Jay called and said, "You'd better sit down."

"Why?" I asked shakily. "What's wrong?"

"Your mug shot is the cover of this week's *National Enquirer.*"

Alan ran down to the newsstand, and there it was. Big as day, my police mug shot complete with my ID number: SUZANNE

SOMERS ARRESTED FOR FRAUD. Never mind that the arrest had happened a decade ago. The cover made it appear as though it was now. Back then, at twenty-three years old, living in Sausalito with my child, I had been arrested for writing bad checks. In retrospect, it was inevitable. I had no work, no husband, no child support, no skills, and no family who could help. I kept us fed and clothed by my ability—indeed my need—to live on the edge. I would play games with my bank. A check was due me from my modeling agency, so I would write a personal check for groceries, hoping my paycheck would arrive in time to cover it. It was constant juggling, but it fed into my need for living on the edge. I needed to teeter on the brink of crisis at all times to "feel" anything. It was how I had been raised. My childhood was so painful that I numbed my feelings to protect myself from the pain of my father's drunken violence. The only time my heart would pound, that I would "feel" anything, was when there were real crises—when we had to hide in the closet, or Dad had to go to the hospital because my brother Dan had hurt him in one of our physical family brawls. I didn't realize I had become addicted to crises. If I hyperventilated, I "felt" something.

This syndrome followed me into my new young adult life. So "kiting" checks was a way to continue the patterns I had created. In practical terms, it kept Bruce and me alive, fed, and clothed. In emotional terms, it kept me sick. But I didn't know this. No one wants to be "sick." I was surviving, just like when I was a little girl. I lost touch with reality. I pretended life wasn't what it was. If I needed groceries, I wrote a check. If my rent was due, I wrote a check. I knew it would be a matter of days before it cleared or bounced, but that was okay. It bought me time. When you've lost touch with reality, borrowed time allows the unreality to continue.

But now, all these years later, and after having made restitution, it had come back to haunt me. Only this time, it was national. All of America would now know the awful truth about me. There in front of America was the picture of my scared little face, eyes vulnerable and pathetic.

Every phone call that day brought worse news. "Now what!" I said to Jay, frightened. "What am I going to do?"

"I think you should go to Vernon Scott at United Press and tell him your story. Tell him the truth." Which I did.

I told Vernon, a longtime Hollywood reporter, of my teenage marriage, divorce, and destitution. I told him I never meant not to make good on the checks, but that payment from my modeling agency was slow and bouncing checks became part of my routine as a means of survival. I was sincere. I truly felt badly that *Three's Company* and ABC were embarrassed by my past. Vernon was touched by my sincerity. He put his arm around me and told me not to worry.

"Everyone will understand that you did what you had to do to survive. Frankly," he continued empathetically, "in a country as wealthy as ours, young girls shouldn't have to resort to such desperate measures to take care of their children." I left Vernon feeling slightly relieved.

Then more bad news came the next day. The weekly tabloids announced in their headlines: THREE'S COMPANY CONSIDERS DROPPING SUZANNE SOMERS AS ADVERTISERS THREATEN TO PULL THEIR SPOTS OFF THE SHOW. Now it was out. The country knew what I knew. I was a worthless piece of shit. But to my surprise, instead of turning on me, the people rallied around me. Letters to the editor came in from everywhere. Everyone felt sorry for poor little Chrissy. Everyone felt protective.

By telling my story honestly, I was forgiven. I was given the gift of compassion. The truth had set me free. *Three's Company* said to the advertisers, "No, we are not going to drop Suzanne from the program"; I was back in the news big time and once again took my spot as the tabloids' darling. I felt like Mary

Magdalene, the biblical figure to whom I most related. She was a sinner who was so bad she washed Christ's feet with her tears and dried them with her hair to show her repentance and be forgiven. Figuratively, I wanted to wash my feet with my tears to show my gratitude.

A part of my secret had been released; but instead of the truth destroying me, I was repaired. I no longer had to worry about being found out. I was an absolved sinner this time.

SIXTEEN

To celebrate New Year's Eve that same week, Alan and I packed up the boys for New York City and a week at the Regency Hotel with Jay. I was cohosting *Dick Clark's Rockin' New Year's Eve*. Bruce and Stephen were quite excited about the adventure. Leslie was mad at us over the Christmas fiasco, so she did not want to come. She was going to act out until we understood her; but we were still too ignorant to see the problem.

Bruce and Stephen loved New York, especially hanging out with "Uncle Jay." Jay had never had children of his own and had no concept of spoiling. After the "mother of all Christmases" the previous week, I was trying to make sure I put a cap on things. I was even worried this trip would be too much overload, that they would become indifferent to these extravagances. I'd seen that bored look on the faces of so many Hollywood children. "Members of the lucky sperm club," Alan called them. I did not want to be responsible for taking the excitement of life away by overindulging.

"Why can't we fly first class, too?" Stephen asked.

"When you're both grown-up and working and making your own money, then you can fly any way you choose," I would tell them. "You're only one row and one curtain away from us, so you can visit us, and I'll save my dessert for you."

Stephen liked traveling with us. He was integrated into our lives now. His own room, chores, allowance, and house rules were all a part of being involved in this family. Now that he was living with his own father, he felt less threatened by Bruce. But he wouldn't permit me to touch him, and I had never been able to kiss him. In this way, he stayed loyal to his mother. At times I would allow my feelings to be hurt. In my adult reasoning I would get angry that Stephen wanted to participate in our lives on his terms. But perhaps he was too young to be thinking in such a sophisticated way. Probably, he was confused and sensitive. I assume he felt guilty about leaving his mother alone while he dipped into the excitement of this family. He would get quiet, brooding. As with his father, his mood could pervade the house, while Bruce and I acted like dancing circus dogs, twirling, twirling, trained, and obedient, always pretending that what was going on really wasn't happening. Human evolution is a slow process. Three steps forward, two steps back. It is the dance of life. I wanted to keep moving on in my emotional growth, but at times I would feel overwhelmed.

Scott Peck writes in *The Road Less Traveled*, "Life is difficult; but it is the wise man who welcomes problems and mistakes, because through them we grow spiritually and emotionally." With each step, I was moving toward my goal of gaining inner peace and serenity, and with each backward move, I was learning my lessons. The whole process was as it was meant to be. I had chosen my teachers long before I understood the concept that negatives are opportunities to learn our lessons of life. My father, my husband, my son, Stephen, Leslie, even Jay were all my teachers. We were all together for a reason. Together we had an opportunity to learn some of the greatest lessons of our lives, or we could remain stuck in our thinking and never grow to our full potential. Subliminally, we must have all known this to be true, because for reasons unknown, we "stuck it out."

———

Bruce, Stephen, Alan, Jay, and I arrived at the Regency Hotel in Manhattan. Ours was a beautiful two-bedroom suite and Jay occupied a suite one floor above us. The boys enjoyed Jay. He had no rules and filled them with stories of his conquests with the beautiful women of Hollywood. Jay didn't like to date girls who were under eighteen or over twenty-four years old. He said that at twenty-four, girls start asking too many questions. When that happened he would have to get rid of the present one and move on to the next beautiful starlet.

"We're going to Jay's room to watch the football games," Bruce and Stephen told me. Unbeknownst to me, Jay was teaching them how to gamble. He gave them each $300 and they could bet on whatever games they wanted, at $100 a game. Points, players, scores were all part of the pot. Winner take all. Both boys came back to our suite loaded with cash.

"Take it back. Right now!" I said when I saw their bulging pockets. They thought I was mean.

On New Year's Eve, I pretaped my part on Dick Clark's show. Even though Alan and Dick were no longer business partners, Dick and his wife, Kari, and Alan and I remained dearest friends and still are to this day. I enjoyed working with Dick. In the early days of their business, I was always Alan's girlfriend, hanging around the set. It was fun now that I was "hot" enough to be working alongside him.

After the show, we all went to the River Cafe under the Brooklyn Bridge to have New Year's Eve dinner. I had an armed bodyguard with me, which had become standard procedure in big cities. Suddenly my safety was my new worry. There had been threats and strange people hanging around outside our house. Paparazzi and threatening-looking fellows were waiting at all times outside our hotel, so we were cautious.

While we were eating dinner, what sounded like a gunshot went off in the restaurant. The bodyguard grabbed me and threw me to the floor. Alan grabbed Bruce and Stephen and threw himself on top of all of us. Jay had already dive-bombed under the table. I looked up. The restaurant was silent, but all around the room were personal bodyguards with guns drawn, like in an old shoot-'em-up. The "gunshot" turned out to be a cherry bomb (a kind of big firecracker) going off, which someone thought would make a good joke. We were shaken but strangely excited. It seemed like we were in a movie, only the movie was real life. The shocking part was realizing how many people moved about with armed guards. My world was changing. No one had armed guards where I grew up.

Safety brought relief. Jay ordered a bottle of Dom Pérignon and the rest of the evening was truly fun. Bruce was so excited about New York and Uncle Jay, the Brooklyn Bridge, limousines, the suite at the Regency, gunshots, armed guards, and my fame that he started shaking his head back and forth in a comedic frenzy. Not in a bad way; he just did not know any other way to release all the overwhelming energy. For the first time he was realizing the change that had come over our lives. We were living a fairy tale. I hugged him and laughed, too. I loved seeing him so happy. I hoped it all wasn't too much.

It was hard to imagine two young teens having more fun than Stephen and Bruce that weekend. The Regency was their playground. They scoured every inch of that hotel inside, outside, from the bowels to the roof. It was Stephen and Bruce's incredible adventure, and this night put the crowning cap on it.

At midnight we took the boys back to the hotel, and Alan, Jay, and I went to Studio 54. It was the hippest, most happening disco in the land, owned by Steve Rubell and Ian Schrager. They and they alone handpicked those who could enter. You either had to *be* somebody or look like you *were* a somebody. It was all attitude, looks, costume. Paparazzi were everywhere. Flash! Flash! "Suzanne, over here! . . . Suzanne, Suzanne," I heard as I got out of the limo. Transparent, pearlized balloons as big as the tires on a 747 kept falling from the ceiling. Beautiful naked dancers were hanging by harnesses from what looked like the sky above. They would dip down throwing sparkling confetti on all the people dancing. Diana Ross was hanging over one of the balconies looking very "out of her mind," like she had smoked a lot of pot, but I couldn't know for sure. In the corner Halston was holding his usual court with Bianca Jagger and Liza Minnelli.

Alan, Jay, and I walked in and started dancing. The music washed away all reality. The strange smell of popping amyl nitrate capsules was all around us. Barry Manilow's "Copacabana" was the music of the moment. Flash! Flash! Pop! The paparazzi were on the dance floor with us taking those crazy pictures you see in the tabloids. Turning and turning, Alan and I were spinning around and around, giving in to the madness, the excitement, the excess of it all. It was like great sex. I didn't want it to end. Not just this night, but also my life as it had become. It was so far away from my old life. Far away from the constant worry of simple existence. I had had to count every dollar back then. I was able to fill the gas tank in my Volkswagen for five dollars a week, and I had become expert at dinners for Bruce and me for under two dollars—pan-fried Petrale sole in butter with shallots and garlic and parsley, boiled new potatoes, and a green leafy salad. Bruce still says, "I never knew we were poor." I got us through it somehow, but the stress of it was unhealthy. I would grind my teeth at night and wake up with the inside of my cheeks bloody from the nervous nightmares. Headaches, backaches, neck aches were my norm. All the tension would come to a head in my restless sleep.

By contrast, my new life was like a dream—a beautiful husband, an adorable son, a great job, a new home that was paid for,
travel, fun, and excitement. I was sure the problems of the
stepchildren would work themselves out one day. I truly wanted
harmony.

SEVENTEEN

We returned home to Los Angeles and life resumed as "normal." That Friday night we taped one of my favorite episodes of *Three's Company*. It was the show where John Ritter and I accidentally got handcuffed together and Chrissy had to go out on his date with him in a way that his new girlfriend wouldn't realize we were cuffed together. I think it is the funniest episode of all our seasons together. John and I laughed from our bellies all week. The whole idea of it was so absurd. It was pure farce, my favorite form of comedy.

The ponytail on the side of Chrissy's head had started as an accident because one year into the show I had had a little problem. Every Friday morning, I would go to Vidal Sassoon in Beverly Hills and have Virginia bleach the roots of my hair white. It had been established at this point that Chrissy Snow had snow-white hair, so even the smallest showing of darker root growth was unacceptable. Virginia was colorist to the stars, her biggest client being Rod Stewart. (She had created his bleached white, jagged-edged spiked hair look.) While the bleach was

135

"cooking" on my scalp, Virginia was gabbing away on the telephone. Suddenly she ran toward me with panic on her face. "Oops," I heard her say as she toweled off the bleach. She had left it on too long and the hair on the top left side of my head broke off at the roots, leaving a huge bald spot. This is the stuff of lawsuits today, but I wasn't interested in anything but a solution. We solved the problem by bringing the hair from the other side of my head over the top of my head and catching it in a ponytail. Luckily for me, I'd inherited my mother's thick hair. Thus the one-sided ponytail was born.

On the night we taped the handcuffed show, my studio hairdresser was having trouble getting the ponytail "look" just right. We were running late. Mickey Ross came storming into my dressing room screaming, "What's going on? Cast intros were supposed to be five minutes ago!"

His anger level was totally inappropriate for the situation, but he still was able to control me. He yelled so loudly, I started to cry.

"I'm sorry, Mickey, but we're having trouble with my hairstyle tonight," I stammered.

"This is not a show about hair!" he screamed, and stormed off.

Five minutes later I was ready and standing backstage waiting to be introduced. John was trying to comfort me. Like a bad child, I felt terrible that I had upset "Daddy" once again.

I walked onstage as my name was announced to thunderous applause and screaming. "We love you, Chrissy," they yelled. I looked out at the audience, and as my eyes adjusted to the light, there, to my delight, was the entire center section of the audience filled with teenage girls, each one of them wearing the Chrissy ponytail. Like a line of dancing donkeys, the ponytails bobbed with the girls' laughter and excitement. Well, Mickey, I thought, maybe this *is* a show about hair.

As I look back, I now realize that the idea of a producer ever screaming at anyone is preposterous. No one in any workplace has the right to yell or scream. Part of the old Hollywood cliché was the ranting and raving director. That I allowed Mickey to do this was clearly evidence of my continuing lack of self-worth. I let him treat me like a child, so he kept doing it. It was control. The producers of *Three's Company* were intent on keeping us the "kids." If we were good "kids," we'd get a little pat on the head. If we displeased "Daddy," we were in trouble. Joyce was so into it that she took to talking baby talk. She would arrive at work and immediately change the sound of her voice and her body movements. She would snort and gurgle and call me "Zannie" in her teeniest little baby voice. We all still bounced around the set like kids on a jungle gym. John, Joyce, and I were all pretty naïve about accepted procedures, and the producers took advantage of our naïveté. None of us had designated dressing rooms, as is standard in the industry. Individual dressing rooms are for "stars"; bull pens are for "kids." They did not want us to have any concept of our value outside of the rehearsal room. They did not want to lose control. We had no privacy. On Monday, Tuesday, and Wednesday we were all in one large rehearsal room. All our phone calls were overheard. At lunch I usually had one or more interviews to conduct on the telephone. So much was going on in my life that I had lost touch with the fact that not everyone on the show was being offered big-money deals on a regular basis. This was my new reality, and everyone who interviewed me asked me about it.

One day Norman Fell, who played Mr. Roper, our landlord, flipped out. "I'm sick of having to listen to her talk about how damn successful she is."

"I'm sorry, Norman," I said, "but I don't have any place to conduct my interviews."

Looking back, I don't blame him. I should have kept all business deals to myself. I would never, ever talk about money or deals today. But back then, I was still pretty much a yokel. Everything was "gosh," "gee whiz," or "holy cow." I walked around in a constant state of amazement that my life had taken this incredible turn. I was anxious to tell everyone, thinking they would be happy for me. In actuality, it was insensitive of me. Success can make others feel inferior or resentful.

On Thursdays and Fridays we were given CBS staff dressing rooms because we were busy with camera blocking. Friday was the actual taping, and I couldn't allow my concentration to be unfocused by giving interviews.

John was "hot," doing features every hiatus. I was "hot" and doing the same. Joyce was doing TV movies but not features, and that created tension. Norman Fell and Audra Lindley (who played Mrs. Roper, our landlord's wife) were old troupers and most of the time were just happy doing their work. The fact that we were all on the number one show in America had escaped everyone. There was an underlying competition among the cast. We were each looking over our shoulders to see if the others were gaining. Because we weren't a real family, the generosity that exists in a real blood family was not present. The stakes were too high. All work outside this show preserved us a place with the public long after *Three's Company* was over. The goal was to rise above our show, to become so ingrained in the public's awareness that the show became secondary. This was happening to John and me and, to some degree, Joyce. All the magazine covers, interviews, television specials, and movies were building our story. All of us wanted to be sure that when *Three's Company* ended, we wouldn't end.

Somehow I had understood this from the beginning. That is why I had given Jay every penny of my first six weeks' salary to make me so visible that future work would land in my lap. And for all his eccentricities, head messing, conniving, plotting, and scheming, he kept his part of the bargain. He made me a star. He took care of me. He made America love me. That is why I liked him and still do. He was a survivor, and I could relate to that.

Around this time, Barbara Walters called Jay to ask if I would let her interview me for one of her famous specials. Jay was enthusiastic. Alan was not. "She'll eat you alive," he said. He was worried that parts of my past would come up and I would not be able to handle it.

"Give me more credit," I told Alan forcefully. "I can handle myself. I'll just tell her the truth. It worked the last time."

Alan was reluctantly convinced but felt protective.

The Barbara Walters interview was my most important public appearance up until that time and remains important to this day. Now, almost twenty years later, people still come up to me and recall that interview.

———

Barbara is good. She interviews for hours and then edits down to the vital twenty minutes. She gets you relaxed and trusting. It is an important foreplay. Then, just as you start to sway back and forth, moving gently with the rhythm, BAM! She hits you with a big fist. In my case it went like this:

Barbara: "I hate doing this, Suzanne, but, well, I really have to."

At that point she pulled out a topless picture of me—an ad that I had posed for years earlier which I hoped would never surface again. I looked at the picture with horror, totally forgetting the camera was on me in close-up. In that instant the memories flooded back. The humiliation, the desperation.

"Why did you do it?" I heard Barbara ask.

I took my time to answer. Then slowly, quietly, sadly I explained. "Have you ever been so poor, so destitute, that you had to sacrifice all dignity to get through your life?" I continued, "I was in my twenties and divorced. I was alone in the world with no means of support and a child recuperating from being run over by a car, which happened when Bruce was five and nearly killed him. I had to do what I had to do to put food on the table. Taking my clothes off was a humiliating experience, but I had run out of options. The rent was due. I remember arriving at the job and deciding that I must be professional about the whole thing. I went into the dressing room, took off my top, and walked into the studio like it was the most natural thing in the world. Inside I was dying, but I was expert at pretending; so I smiled the biggest smile I could muster, hoping that by doing so, we could take the picture of the happy nude girl and get it over with. I guess I've always hoped it would never surface, that it would be some kind of secret-service job; but that is pretty naive thinking." I told her I was ashamed. I was afraid the public would turn on me for posing for such a low-class picture.

Barbara was quiet for a moment. I was overcome emotionally. I couldn't look up. I stared at my lap, wishing I could walk away and never come back. "Well, that explains a lot," Barbara said. "I thought you had done it recently."

"No," I said. "It was years ago."

"Did you write the poem about your son around that time?" Barbara asked softly.

"Yes," I said.

"Will you read it to us?"

Good, I thought. This will change the mood. But instead, as I started to read the poem, it intensified my emotions. Tears were streaming down my face.

> *Sometimes I see my son*
> *and remember when I thought I'd failed*
> *Because . . .*

There was a long pause and then I had to stop because the words would not come. I was overwhelmed with feelings. I felt I would choke from the ball of tears I was holding in my throat.

Three times I tried to read the poem and each time my emotions overcame me.

Finally Barbara said, "I can't make you do this. It doesn't feel right to me."

"No," I said. "I want to read it. It's important to me." Finally I got through it:

Sometimes I see my son
And remember when I thought I'd failed
Because so many told me
A mother who bore a boy
Should not send away his father.
Sometimes I see my son
And remember the pain of unloved pregnancy
And the resentment I sometimes felt
At raising him alone
When I could not have the freedom I deserved.
There were days I was as much a child as he
When I wanted someone to give me
The love I gave so grudgingly to him.
Days that we learned together about life
And had as many questions.
Sometimes I see my son
And wish his mother had it all together
To give him strength and courage I only sometimes have
To listen when my own hurts need hearing
To hold him even though I am alone.
But sometimes I see my son
With trust in his eyes no one else could give
With a smiling, shining face that says there was no
*   failure*
No monstrous mistakes
Only good things and memories of love and caring.

Sometimes I see my son
  And he touches me in secret corners
  And I know that everything is fine
    And will always be
Sometimes I see my son and I love him.

The day after the show aired, Barbara was inundated with requests for copies of the poem. Once again, truth showed me its unbelievable power.

People were different toward me after the airing of that show. Suddenly I had texture; I wasn't just that "ditzy blond." I was a survivor with a heart and a soul.

EIGHTEEN

﹏ "I guess it's time," Alan said. It was 1980, four seasons into *Three's Company*. "Let's ask Jay to dinner tomorrow night and we can discuss the whole thing in a civilized way."

My heart started to pound just thinking about it.

We had already made plans to have dinner at Michael's in Santa Monica with Tony Thomopoulos, the ABC president, and his wife, but, naively, neither Alan nor I figured the dismissal of Jay would come as a major blow. He had to have been expecting this.

We invited Jay to our house for a drink before dinner, deciding to use that time to tell him of our change in plans. We were really out of touch not to realize that Jay would go ballistic.

Alan started the conversation while I sat on the couch of our office, my eyes transfixed by the sofa fabric as if it were the single most *fascinating* chocolate brown corduroy I'd ever seen. "There's no easy way to do this," Alan explained, "so I'm just going to tell you. I know you assumed this was coming," Alan continued. Then he took a breath and began. "We've decided that Suzanne and I can handle her career."

Jay's face turned ashen.

"You've been great," I interjected nervously. "I wouldn't be where I am today without you, Jay. It's just that it feels right to let Alan take over now."

As I babbled on, I could see Jay's eyes becoming smaller and smaller slits in his face. The color in his cheeks flushed a strange combination of red and purple; the veins in his neck popped out.

I had forgotten that the canes Jay always carried concealed a razor-sharp sword within. Jay stood up slowly, like a warrior preparing to attack. His voice was trembling and deep. "You can't do this to me," he roared. And with that, he pulled the sword out of his cane and slashed it back and forth between Alan and me. His eyes were crazed, like a mad dog's. I tried to reason with him while dodging.

"Think of the good times," I said, ducking from his sword. My voice was high-pitched, nervous. "Think of all the fun we've had together."

I wasn't really frightened. He was playing out a part. Errol Flynn was one of his heroes. But it was nerve-racking.

"I knew you'd do this to me. In the end everyone leaves me," he yelled.

Swoosh! Whish! I jumped onto the sofa, bending, weaving, avoiding his brandished sword. I never really thought he'd kill us, but Jay could be crazy, and you never knew. On and on the yelling and screaming continued. Our office was located on the back side of our home directly above Stephen's room, so he could hear everything going on. Poor Stephen was terrified, looking at his ceiling, the source of the noise, and not knowing what to do. He later told us that he called his mother and said, "Come and get me. It's crazy here."

It took two hours to calm Jay down and get him to put his cane away. We were now over an hour late for dinner with the Thomopouloses. We kept calling the restaurant and apologizing, assuring them we were on our way; and then Jay would start in again. Jay adored drama, but he also was truly upset. So was I. It had been a great ride with him, and I would miss his outrageousness, but not the head messing.

I hoped this change would allow me to calm down and not feel so crazy. What did it matter who was on more covers each month? There was room for all the '70s girls—Farrah, Cheryl, Jaclyn, me! Jay had created the race. I wanted out. I also wanted out of the tug-of-war between Alan and Jay. I couldn't take it anymore. I needed to find some peace and balance.

Why we didn't cancel dinner this night still puzzles me. It was a disaster waiting to happen. Did I really think Jay was going to put on a happy face and act as if everything was okay?

Finally, somewhat calmer, we all left for the restaurant. Now Jay was in a mean, foul mood.

We arrived to find, not surprisingly, that Tony and his wife were irritated. Jay's date, Linda, whom they did not know, had arrived on time; so Tony and his wife, Penny, and Linda had been sitting together uncomfortably making chatter for close to two hours. Linda was wearing a fishnet T-shirt with no bra, and her nipples were sticking out through the holes in her shirt. She had beautiful breasts, but I'm not sure this helped to make conversation any easier, although Alan did mention later that evening how much he enjoyed sitting across from Linda.

Jay was obnoxious throughout dinner and would not talk to anyone. He also wouldn't eat. He sat through the whole dinner with a mean stare fixed on me, and I, the dutiful daughter of the alcoholic, felt obliged to keep inane chatter going. "Isn't this food great? What a beautiful night. I love your T-shirt, Linda. . . ." All the blathering I could think of. "What are you having, Tony, the veal or the fish?" I asked without caring about the answer. It was perfect for me. I could pretend nothing was wrong. I had been trained from childhood not to see reality.

When I look back, I wonder who was sicker, Jay or me.

Finally, dessert arrived. "Um-m-m, crème brûlée," I babbled on. "I've always loved it. I make it myself and I think mine is quite good." Blah, blah, blah, I carried on.

Jay continued to stare at me with beady little eyes. He never said one word. He never looked at anyone but me. Intent, mean, and messing with my head. I felt like I would explode from the tension. When will this night be over? I kept thinking.

When we left the restaurant, Jay did not say good-bye to any of us. He looked at me one last time, grabbed his cane, and walked out the door. I knew he would eventually calm down and we would be friends again. He was that way. He could put feelings aside and resume in a new way. But he would never forget. I knew that for years to come, maybe for the rest of my life, anytime I saw Jay he would remind me how I hurt him by firing him. As I watched him go out the door of the restaurant, I remembered what he'd once said to me: "I'll get you up there where the air is rarefied, you'll become deified, then I'll become nullified." He had been there before; he would be there again. He knew the game. It was show business.

NINETEEN

Now Alan had the job. He was in complete control of my career. I was pushing the envelope by turning myself over to him. Either the power struggle would find its balance in equality or we would self-destruct. And a delicate balance it was. Alan understood my career better than I, so I needed his guidance; but at the same time, he was my husband, and I would not, could not, allow myself to be swallowed up by him.

I had control issues. I had allowed my father to bully and badger me, physically and emotionally, all my life. Through success I was able to put my father in perspective. Why had I given him so much power? I thought. He's a guy who didn't achieve his dream of becoming a star player in big-league baseball. He never saw his good qualities—his humor or the talent it took to have made it as far as he did in the minor leagues. He did not see the qualities that attracted people to him like a magnet. He was a great dancer, and his friends loved to watch him cut up. He had a beautiful, trim, toned physique from all his years of athletics. Instead of appreciating all this, he focused on his negatives and the demons that lived within him. To deflect his pain, he took out his anger on his family. As a grown and successful woman, I stopped letting him push me around. I yelled back. I stopped accepting unacceptable behavior.

And then I married Alan. I had lived with two people who were not going to give up control so I could learn what I needed to learn. Once again, I find myself amazed at the inherent intelligence we all possess. Deep inside we have an inner voice, and the messages are there. We are always hearing them but rarely listening.

Somewhere along the road of life, in order to find the softness in yourself, it is essential to let down your guard and begin to trust. Alan was such a controlling person that I had never, in all our years together, seen him cry. It would have been too revealing for him. I was so concerned with telling Alan over and over that he didn't own me that I was afraid to tell him that I needed him; that I respected his vision and wanted his advice; that we could do this thing together and be more powerful as a unit than either of us would ever be individually. I was afraid he would see me as weak. But this is why we found each other. To find our softness and to learn for the first time in our lives that we could trust; that we could need another person without giving up our personal power. In this lesson, we were learning together that we would get the greatest of all gifts—a deep, enduring, respectful love. A love we both had longed for all our lives but had never allowed ourselves to have. It required surrender. It required a give-and-take and an understanding of each other's strengths and weaknesses, and it was important to take care that we never belittled or sabotaged the parts of each other that were most vulnerable.

Most marriages never find this balance of mutual trust. Most couples are too busy defending their personal control. They hang on to it with a ferocity, never really understanding what they are holding on to. All they know is that they will never let the other partner win. In the end, what has been won? A lifetime of anger and put-downs and hardness. You can see it in the eyes.

My darling
dancers and me.

Leslie designed
the costumes
for the acts.

A *Harper's Bazaar* layout photographed by Bill King.

Being featured on
magazine covers
has always been
a big event.

WALKING

★ 10th ★
Anniversary
Special Issue

The Walking Dr.'s Anti-Aging Prescription

7 EASY STEPS TO FITNESS

Special Section: How to Be Active, Eat Well, Beat Stress

25-Minute Anti-Stress Walk

Spice Up Your Lowfat Food

Test Your Weight-Loss IQ

Warning: The Surgeon General has determined that inactivity is detrimental to your health

Suzanne Somers, 49, celebrates America's

JUNE 1996
U.S. $2.95 CAN. $3.95
DISPLAY UNTIL JULY 1

Atlantic City

FEBRUARY 1993 $2.95

OFF-OFF-BOARDWALK THEATER ■ BONUS: GUIDE TO GREAT SHOPPING

MEET OUR VALENTINES:
THE 60 MOST ELIGIBLE WOMEN IN TOWN

SEX & VIOLINS: HOW TO FIND ROMANCE IN CASINO CITY

PLAY, GYPSY! DINNERS WITH STRINGS ATTACHED

CARAMEL KNOWLEDGE

M-BOOM VICINI'S

Who will love Suzanne Somers?

Journal

$1.95
May 1992
Ladies' Home

LOW-FAT DIETS THAT PREVENT DISEASE

100 WAYS TO LOOK GREAT THIS SUMMER

How to feel up when life gets you down

Clair Huxtable says good-bye

SECRETS OF GREAT SEX

How to help your kids take tests

Life without Michael by Cindy

SUZANNE SOMERS
She had an alcoholic father, was an unwed pregnant teen, then became TV's best-known bimbo. Now, at 45, she's found the self-respect she always wanted

---

People
weekly

JANUARY 22, 1996

How the stars FIGHT FAT

Celeb tips on eating smart, feeling great and losing 5 pounds fast

SUZANNE SOMERS, 49

Insets: Baywatch's David Chokachi, Wynonna Judd, Cindy Crawford

---

McCall's

MARCH 1978   95 CENTS

EXCLUSIVE: "MY FATHER, CHARLIE CHAPLIN"

Quick shape-up for spring
THE LAZY WOMAN'S DIET AND EXERCISE PLAN

MAKING LOVE
The subtle art of matching moods

Special Sunday dinners your family will love

A HILARIOUS PREVIEW OF ERMA BOMBECK'S NEW BEST SELLER

The truth about homosexual teachers

THE HIDDEN MONEY IN YOUR HOME

What to do about sexual pressures on the job

Special 8-page section "WHERE IN YOUR TWENTIES, THIRTIES, AND FIND YOUR PLACE"

SUZANNE SOMERS OF "THREE'S COMPANY"
A very intimate interview with TV's biggest new star

APRIL 18, 1988 $1.85

People weekly

- Tiffany vs. her mom
- War of the gossips
- Why women fight women at work

CHILDREN of ALCOHOLICS

Going public with a very private problem, these four famous people—and some courageous kids— tell what it takes to live through a nightmare

---

HEALTH • FITNESS • BEAUTY • EXERCISE • FASHION • NUTRITION

SLIMMER

FEBRUARY 1985 1.95

SHAPE-UP

With TV's Solid Gold Dancers' Five Day Workout

Goodbye Chrissy: Meet Sizzling Suzanne Somers

HOLIDAY DEPRESSION: EXERCISE YOUR BLUES AWAY

Dieting With Low-Cal Frozen Entrees: Can It Work?

Fitness Follies of '84: A Look Back At The Year In Fitness

Oct. 22–28   89¢

TV GUIDE

A SPOOKY GUIDE TO HALLOWEEN TV

Special episodes of 'Roseanne,' 'The Simpsons'—and more

Where the ghosts are: TV's new supernatural craze

An interview with the 'Vampire' author, Anne Rice

JAY LENO: 'We'll be number one again'

Suzanne Somers of ABC's Step by Step, and host of a new syndicated talk show

---

TV GUIDE

Local Programs May 20-26
30¢

Canada's Parliament on TV: A Lesson for America?
Page 12

AMSEL

Suzanne Somers, Joyce DeWitt and John Ritter of 'Three's Company'

Revolutionary Cancer Treatment ■ Homeopathy for Pets

Alternative Medicine Digest

Issue 20

HEART DISEASE
You Can Clean Your Arteries

ANXIOUS OR DEPRESSED?
Balance Your Hormones Naturally

HYPERACTIVE KIDS
Natural Alternatives to Ritalin

SUZANNE SOMERS
Immersed in Alternative Medicine

November 1997
$3.95 U.S. / $4.95 Can.

PLUS Seizures, Arthritis, Muscle Pain, Diabetes, Headaches, Fibroids ■ Brain Power Boosters ■ Organic Olive Oil ■ Flower Essences for Cats ■ Prostate Protection ■ Anti-Aging Tips

With Glenn Zottola,
my band leader.

My "pal" Tanya
the elephant
poses with me.

Sammy Davis, Jr.,
and me in Las Vegas.

Starring in
"The Moulin Rouge"
at the Las Vegas Hilton.

George Wyner,
Alan, and me in
She's the Sheriff.
Alan made a
guest appearance.

She's the Sheriff.

My brothers, Michael and Dan; me; my sister, Maureen; Dad; Mom; and Phil Donahue, appearing on his show for the publication of *Keeping Secrets*.

Hosting *The Late Show*.
The baby monkey tries to nurse.

Performing in London at "The Talk of the Town."

They hold no sweetness, no softness for each other. And what happens to the children of these marriages? You can see the truth in their eyes also. The nervousness; the darting, quick looks from parent to parent; analyzing, adapting, never siding too closely with either parent for fear of losing the other. In the end, to retain control, everyone loses. And nothing is won.

———

"I really want to sing," I told Alan.

"You're going to," Alan answered, laughing. "As soon as the season ends, we're shooting the TV special. You'll be able to sing your heart out in front of six thousand sailors," he said.

"I know, but I'd like to put together an act before that."

Alan went to work. I loved that about him. I called him the "wishmaster."

When the time came to put together a Vegas deal for me, Alan made good use of all the relationships he had forged while hosting his own show. He called everyone he could think of and asked them how the Las Vegas business worked. One after another, they each pointed out that no one had ever successfully crossed over from television to nightclubs. These were two different mediums; the latter had no safety net. Many TV performers had tried, but not one person had lasted longer than two weeks—Carroll O'Connor, two weeks; Sally Struthers, two weeks; Ted Knight, one night.

My hiatus periods from *Three's Company* would give me time to pursue this new career. Before Jay had left, he and Alan were offered a two-week deal for me at the Riviera for big money. They said no. Then they were offered two weeks and more money at the Sahara, but it, too, was declined. After Jay was gone, Alan went to Bernie Rothkopf at the MGM Grand, and before Bernie had a chance to say anything, Alan said, "I want a two-year deal for her and I don't care what the money is."

"Why?" asked Bernie.

"Because if she falls on her face the first time, I want her to be able to come back again and again until she figures it out. And she will."

I now had a two-year deal at the MGM Grand Hotel, eight weeks a year, plus a big million-dollar music special for CBS; and Alan had never heard me sing a single note. He was the manager. I was the performer. If I said I could sing, he believed me.

I knew I could do it. I wanted to live out my childhood fantasies. I wanted to be an entertainer and have the audience love me.

Now I had the opportunity. I also realized something about Alan. He had taken the reins from Jay and he was continuing to build my career without my feeling crazy. My initial fears were not justified. He wasn't telling me what to do or trying to control me. He kept talking about diversification. "Have more than one thing going for you," he would say. He would capitalize on my areas of interest and expertise. It was the beginning of our incredible partnership. I had always admired Ann-Margret and her husband, Roger Smith, and the way they had built a business out of her career. She was multidimensional—Vegas, movies, television, recording. I wanted a career like hers. Alan said, "You'll have it and more."

We slid easily into working together. It wasn't cliché. It wasn't the manager hovering and criticizing. He provided the business expertise. He was a deal maker; he was a salesman. I was the product. His job was to sell his product for the best price and to place the product in the right arena. I kept charge of quality control. I made sure I kept myself rehearsed, rested, and fit, and I ate properly for maximum energy.

With no illusions we entered into our partnership knowing it would be hard work. As Frank Sinatra told me one night in his dressing room, "It's those who hang in there who make it. Never despair." I was not going to give up. As a team, we were committed to creating a business that was ours. We each knew our jobs, and we had the energy.

We hired Carl Jablonski as my first choreographer, Saul Ilson as writer/producer, Earl Brown to write special musical material, and Ret Turner to make the costumes. These were the behind-the-scenes "stars" of television variety. Carl choreographed for Carol Burnett and Julie Andrews. Saul and Earl wrote special material for the Osmonds, Elvis, Cher, Bette Midler, all the greats. Ret designed with Bob Mackie for every major entertainer in the business. Among them there was a mantelful of Emmys. Quality was what we were after. I needed a great act, and the only way we knew how to get it was by hiring the best and the most creative minds.

Every day after I finished *Three's Company*, my group would come in and we'd work until one or two o'clock in the morning for weeks. I had rented the same hall in which we rehearsed *Three's Company*. It was easier for me that way. I didn't have to move my stuff, and my people only had to roll in a piano.

It made me feel vulnerable to begin rehearsals of any kind. Everyone stood around watching while I tried to learn a new form. The writers were looking for keys to my personality, the choreographer was searching for natural movement skills, and the musical director was listening for vocal strength. Night after night we'd work. My feet ached and burned with blisters; back pain was constant. I lost weight and slept jerkily from nervousness. The enormity of what I was taking on loomed over my head. What if I failed? What if I made a complete fool of myself? I was losing my confidence as other people were molding and shaping my abilities into something that didn't gel with the vision I had of myself. I had seen myself as smooth, seamless, easy, sexy, and self-deprecating. I had seen my movements as gawky and goofy, the way I danced for Alan when we were alone. Suddenly I was expected to move like Liza Minnelli and sing like Barbra Streisand. The only time I felt comfortable was when I put on the chicken suit and walked across the stage singing the Colonel Sanders theme song as a non sequitur. It was silly, but it fit my onstage personality better than the Ann-Margret moves being thrust upon me.

I had to start somewhere, and the only way to learn what didn't work was to try it in front of an audience. If it failed, we'd throw that part out and start again until we honed in on the little "jewels" of performance where I could emerge.

For some reason, I couldn't bring myself to sing in front of Alan. I felt the ground would slip away from under me if he heard me sing and hated my voice after all the work he'd done to make this deal happen.

One night Alan walked into the rehearsal hall while I was singing, and I immediately stopped. "Suzanne," he said, "you're opening in two weeks in front of two thousand people. If you can't sing in front of me, how are you going to sing in front of them?"

He was right. It was ridiculous to be afraid of Alan's reaction.

"Okay," I said. "Here goes." I took a deep breath. "Just feed me chord changes, Dick," I said to my piano player.

Slowly and with my eyes closed, I started singing, deep, slow, sexy. "It had to be you . . ."

I was feeling confident. I opened my eyes and Alan was smiling that special way that he does when I undress for him. And I knew it was going to be okay.

Two weeks to go. I still couldn't eat or sleep. The thought of opening night was overwhelming. There was no safety net. If I failed, I failed—in front of everyone. *Three's Company* was so far ahead of anything else on television that one week it aired twice and tied with itself—number one and number one. We were still on an incredible roll. The ABC television show *20/20* was now following me everywhere to produce a documentary piece called "The Making of a Las Vegas Star." At any given time,

I had a crew of at least twelve people around me. They were in my kitchen filming breakfast before work, and then they'd film the *Three's Company* rehearsal and into the night with the Vegas rehearsal.

We were trying out the act the week before we opened at the MGM Grand, at The Turn of the Century, in Denver, Colorado. The club was a dump that entertainers such as Bill Cosby and Paul Anka used to break in new material.

It was freezing in Denver and very high, a mile high. I ran out of breath just crossing the street. I woke up Saturday morning, the day of the big opening, with a major sore throat and every flu symptom imaginable. In the episode the week before, Chrissy had experienced her first kiss, and the actor whom I was kissing had a terrible cold. Naturally, with all the stress, my immune system was weakened and I caught his germs.

"How am I going to sing tonight?" I wailed to Alan. I wanted to curl up in a little ball and stay in bed all day.

"Just imagine yourself well," Alan said. "You've worked too hard to sabotage the whole thing now."

I knew he was right. All day, over and over, we practiced the dances and the material. "Point your toe! Remember your hands! Attitude!" Carl was yelling. It was like my memory had gone. I couldn't remember anything, not even the words to the songs, let alone the dance steps.

Dancing has never been easy for me. I'm mildly dyslexic, and right and left create big problems for me. We got past that one by painting my right shoe red. "Red, red, black, black, red, black, red!" Carl would call out.

I couldn't count; I couldn't remember colors; my throat hurt; I had a fever and wanted to throw up.

Slappy White was my opening act. He was a really funny comedian who was a regular on the circuit. He played the Catskills, small clubs, and Vegas lounges and occasionally opened for name entertainers. Bruce and Stephen got a big kick out of watching him rehearse. Bruce was a quick study.

"Mom," he said to me while I was getting ready backstage, "listen to this one that I heard Slappy say. 'We were poor, really poor. We didn't have no smoke detector at our house, so at night we used to pour kerosene on the dog.'"

It made me laugh and I loosened up a bit. Bruce always had that way about him. He laughed from his toes and made me feel good. "Thanks, Bruce," I said.

"You're going to be real good tonight," he said sweetly. "I love the way you sing."

"Thanks, Bruce. I love you."

"Ten minutes, Miss Somers," I heard the stage manager say on the other side of my dressing room door. Now I really had an upset stomach.

I was in a black bugle-beaded gown with a breakaway skirt. The first number was "I Want to Be Happy If I Make You Happy, Too"; a little desperate, but that's how I felt. Then the skirt would rip off. I would put on a black top hat and go into "When My Baby Smiles at Me," an old Ted Williams song. At that point, two male dancers in top hats and tails would join me in a really clever dance routine. Carl had done a great job. I had good material. My only enemy was me. I was terrified and my fear had stripped away what little self-confidence I had left.

"Five minutes, Miss Somers," the stage manager said through the door. Now it was just Alan and me alone in my dressing room. We were both nervous. Alan's eyes were misty, liquid. He held me tight.

"You'll be great," he whispered. I hoped so.

Together we walked to the stage. The band was in place, the overture began, and then I heard my name being announced.

At that moment, I would rather have been sitting in the dunking chair at a county fair having people throw balls at me. I wished I didn't have to walk out in front of this audience. I was sick, frightened, and unconfident and felt as though I'd developed a severe case of amnesia. What's the first song I'm supposed to sing? I thought, panicked.

But it was too late. I couldn't back out now. I had gone past the point of no return. All my prior work had led to this moment . . . now.

I took a deep breath and walked into the light. My legs felt like those of a newborn colt trying to stand for the first time. The audience applauded enthusiastically. After all, I was their adorable Chrissy. They came to see me in the flesh. They came out of curiosity.

"I want to be happy," I heard my thin little nervous voice singing. The rest of the hour was a blur. Saul Ilson and Earl Brown sat directly in front of me in the front row mouthing each word nervously. At one point, I blanked and Saul held up a flash card. The guys were my lifeline. With their help, the material started coming back to me. My memory returned. I began to relax, even enjoyed it somewhat. The last number was "Razzle Dazzle 'Em" and the final lift in the air by my two dancers, Randy and Barry. The ceiling was low and my head bumped a pipe that was in the way. Clunk! Ow! The audience thought I was being dumb old lovable Chrissy; but really, I had forgotten to watch out for the low-hanging obstacles that Carl had reminded me about over and over again during the rehearsals in Denver.

"Razzle dazzle 'em and you'll be a sta-a-r!" The end! The curtain closed with the audience still applauding. That's a good sign, I thought.

It was all over in an hour. I had gotten through it. It was good . . . wasn't it? I didn't know—couldn't know. Backstage was filled with newspaper reporters, well-wishers, bigwigs, and photographers.

"How was I?" I asked Alan while I lay in his arms later that night.

"Good," he said, "and you'll get better." Alan never lies, but I knew "good" meant mediocre or worse. I felt vulnerable.

The next day the reviews came out in the local Denver newspapers. I remember only this one: "And then she sang, 'I Don't Know Why,' and I still don't know why."

It was a disaster. The papers creamed my performance. "She should stick to TV," said one reporter.

"How do you feel?" Dave Marash, the producer and host of my *20/20* segment, asked.

"I'm not giving up," I said.

Six days to go to my big opening at the MGM Grand in Las Vegas. I'm so used to the *20/20* crew, I forget they are there. I cry, wig out, lose it, all on camera. Too bad, I think. I can't help it. The pressure is enormous. (It was all included when the segment aired.)

We threw out half of the new material from the Denver show. Rehearsals became intense. No big laughs. No more joking around. My whole family and most of my hometown were coming to the MGM opening. This made me more nervous than knowing that half of America was going to see the same thing on *20/20*. I can grasp the reality of two thousand people in a theater; I have no real way of visualizing a viewing audience of twenty to forty million people.

I allow *20/20* to interview Bruce. I won't let them show his face because I worry about security. Celebrities' children have been kidnapped; besides, it is not for me to give up Bruce's anonymity. The shot of Bruce is from behind, walking and talking with Dave Marash. Bruce feels none of the pressure I was feeling to excel. "Mom's been singing all my life," he says. "She always used to sing me to sleep. I love her voice." He is pure, unaffected. Just a son who loves his mom. "Mom is not Chrissy. Mom is Mom. She's always there, and I like her cooking. She always makes me Grasshopper Pie when I ask. It's my favorite," he says. Just a sweet fourteen-year-old boy.

The MGM was overwhelmingly big. I couldn't see the back of the room from the stage. The room was laid out in tiers. In front of the stage there were long tables parallel to the stage with chairs on both sides, followed by the first row of red leather half-moon-shaped booths. These are "Kings Row" and saved for celebrities, high rollers, and big tippers. Behind Kings Row is another row of similar booths for those who can't be fit into Kings Row. Following that, on the fourth tier, are the less expensive tables. Tickets are priced according to the audience's ability to see the stage.

Always, there is the Frank Sinatra table in every Vegas showroom, the maître d' had told me. It's a booth reserved in Kings Row just in case Frank Sinatra should show up without a reservation. After the show has started and it's obvious Frank isn't coming, this booth is given to a late arrival with deep pockets. It takes a big tip to sit in that booth.

The room was carpeted in red and had silver walls and large crystal chandeliers.

I had already lost ten pounds that week. Ret Turner was backstage feverishly altering my gowns. They had to fit skintight.

"Your mom is here," Alan said to me backstage. It was opening night.

"I can't see her till later, Alan. I can't see anyone right now. I'm too stressed-out! Please explain."

Why did I do this? I keep asking myself. Why did I put myself through this? *20/20* is there in the dressing room. I don't even see them now. I'm sitting on my stool in front of the mirror with my head in my hands. I'm afraid to go out. *20/20* keeps filming. I'm over my sickness; now I am just sick to death.

The changes feel right. But I won't know until I try them out. Will the audience be kind and understanding? Will they like me, or will they want to see me fail? This is big business. Each couple will have paid close to $200 to have two lousy drinks and see me. Am I worth it? I must deliver. I must deliver. Please! Please, God, be with me tonight!

"Time to go," Alan says.

I feel like I'm walking to the electric chair. Everything is shaking—my hands, my feet, my legs. We're backstage now. I can see my Uncle George sitting in the row right in front of the stage. I see my mother, my father; my sister, Maureen, and her husband, Bill; Bruce, Stephen, and Leslie. Friends I grew up with, Auntie Helen, Uncle Dave, Uncle Ralph, Auntie Ann, cousins Judy, Dan, Tom, David, Joan, Jan. Everyone I've known all my life has come to support me. I want to cry. I don't want to let them down.

There's nowhere to hide, nowhere to run. The overture begins. We've spent big money. Spared no expense. There will be no profits because of that, but it doesn't matter. Just succeed. DO NOT FAIL! I hear my name: "Ladies and Gentlemen . . . Suzanne Somers." I want to die. I freeze.

"I can't do it," I say to Alan.

"Yes, you can," he says firmly.

"No!" I say. I want to run.

"Now go out there!" Alan says. "They'll love you!"

Then he put his foot on my butt and actually pushed me onto the stage. I'm there! It's the big time. Everyone is clapping. They are excited. This is their Chrissy come to life! This is the hometown girl making good. Can I meet their expectations? My legs shake like Jell-O for the first two numbers. Then I do Saul Ilson's brilliant piece of material. I turn myself into Chrissy before their eyes while explaining with memorized words about her posture, her walk, her purity. While I talk, I put two ponytails in my hair, one on each side. Randy and Barry, my dancers, hold my breakaway, bugle-beaded skirt in front of me while I slip on a one-piece Chrissy outfit that looks like a tight, hot pink satin T-shirt and black short shorts with suspenders. They pull the skirt away.

My shoulders go up, like hers, the feet turn in; and in front of all of them, I become Chrissy. They scream with delight. They love her. I'm finally comfortable.

I start to sing à la Chrissy, with all her wide-eyed innocence. It conveys her purity of spirit and her lack of complication. Maybe that was the attraction. She was nonjudgmental and simple. Her approach to life was with the same wonder and focus as that of a two-year-old. She threatened no one.

At the end of the song, both boys kiss me on the cheek.

The audience loves it.

Alan insisted that at the end of the show I sing "God Bless America."

"Why?" I asked. "It will sound stupid."

"No, it won't," he says. "That way you'll get a standing ovation."

Sure enough. I told the audience at the end of my show how grateful I am that I was born in America. Only in this country can you become "somebody" no matter where you are from or who you are. I believe it, too! Then I sing,

America, America, God shed his grace on thee.
And crown thy good with brotherhood
From sea to shining sea!

The audience leaps to their feet. Alan has the pyrotechnic guys blow off mortars, aerial displays, and enough fireworks to light up Manhattan. The audience is clapping, screaming, yelling. "We love you!"

It's a success!

TWENTY

As a husband and manager, Alan was warm, devoted, supportive, caring, and nurturing to me, yet his treatment of Bruce was still very cool. We had made only some progress. He now accepted that Bruce had to be in his life, but Alan wouldn't allow himself to show any enjoyment while in Bruce's presence. He was merely civil to him. The average stranger got a warmer reception. Because of this I was always a step away from feeling angry. Yet with Stephen, Alan hugged and kissed and instigated loving little wrestling matches. Strangely, Stephen reacted to this attention by stiffening his body and pulling away. Stephen had an anger he didn't understand. He always looked disinterested when I was around. In return, I reacted by being sickeningly sweet while trying to lift his spirits. I'm not surprised that Stephen wanted nothing to do with me.

Because Alan's moods were not consistent, all three children were nervous around him. I tried to make up for it by being overly nice and overly understanding to all of them. There were days when Stephen was Alan's favorite; other days, it was Leslie. Bruce was never at the top of his list.

Bruce's overriding feeling relative to Alan was fear. Most of the time, it was fear of making Alan angry; Bruce was afraid to speak up.

"What did I do to make him not like me?" Bruce asked me one day out of the blue. I couldn't explain what I didn't understand, and I felt ashamed.

Stephen's mood lifted when he was around his mother. He adored her and felt protective. On the rare occasions that I would hear both boys laughing together, my heart would feel joy. Sometimes Leslie, too, would come over and I would hear the three of them laughing. But that was usually when they were hidden in one of their rooms, as though they didn't want us to see them having a good time. Perhaps, subliminally, they wanted to continue punishing us for being happy together.

Bruce would look to Alan like a shunned little orphaned puppy. Just a little pat on the back would salve his confused soul. He was really needing an important male presence at this time. His own father was five hundred miles away during these years, so the only adult he could count on day to day was me. But how does a mother fill the needs for her son in a way that only a father can? I was doing my best, but I knew that sometimes my best just wasn't good enough.

That I let this go on for so long is something I live with to this day. What was missing in me that I allowed Bruce to be exposed to Alan's indifference? I am still shocked by my behavior. My denial permitted Alan to continue to inflict emotional damage on Bruce, whom I loved more than anyone in the world. I know I would throw myself in front of a moving train if it would save his life; yet under my own roof, I allowed his soul to be wounded over and over, which is surely as difficult to endure as any physical pain. This was my greatest prevailing dysfunction. I was still afraid of my imagined wrath from Alan, a wrath I had never seen.

This feeling was rooted in a place deep inside from years of watching the original family of my childhood. The first relationship I had ever observed was that between my mother and father. My mother was afraid of my father, and because of this, we always tiptoed around him, adapting to his behavior; never saying anything provocative; never doing anything to change the present mood if we could help it, because the consequences were dire. He would explode into violent rages, drunk or sober, if one of his many buttons was pushed.

Without knowing it, I had unwittingly carried this learned behavior into my present marriage and now Bruce was having the same experience with Alan. We are affected by our past until we take the steps to change. I didn't know I could insist upon it. I didn't know when Alan was "cool" and unloving to Bruce that I had the right to say, "When you treat Bruce with indifference, I feel hurt and protective. I feel I must take Bruce's side because he is powerless, which makes you the enemy."

This could have started a dialogue of reasoning. I know Alan didn't want to hurt me. If we had been communicating properly, we could have worked on breaking down the emotional barriers he had constructed. At this point, he was acting from a place of habit. But I was still afraid to bully back and take my full power with him in our personal relationship. It was easy to take my power in our business partnership. We were scrimmaging on a level playing field. But in our home I felt emotionally handicapped. I should have demanded he treat me and my son the way we deserved to be treated. The other underlying fear I had was rejection. What if I demanded fair treatment and Alan rejected the notion? Then I would have to decide to leave and mean it. Empty ultimatums render one powerless. Resolve behind an ultimatum is the only way and I wasn't emotionally ready to leave. So his behavior continued. With it came confusion. How could I love someone so much, so passionately, and still feel so much anger at the same time? You can't force someone to love you or anyone else. I hoped that time would help.

At night, in the dark, I would ask the God of my understanding for help. How can I reach Stephen? What can I do to bring Bruce and Alan together? Help me to love Leslie. Parts of my life were under control and the other parts were beyond my reach. When I was happy and enjoying myself, I could always feel a little tug, like a puppy nipping at my skirt and making me walk slowly for fear I might trip. I could never relax completely. I knew something needed to be done, but I didn't know what that was. This was the stuff of my prayers.

———

Stephen still wouldn't allow me to get inside where he lived with his closed-off feelings. But every once in a while, I would get a clue. One sunny day Stephen and I were in the kitchen together. I was making a mango tart for that night's dessert, so I was busy and not looking at him; but I was enjoying his presence. Out of the blue, he said, "One day I hope I make a lot of money and then I'm going to buy Mummy a really nice house and send her traveling wherever she wants to go." That was all he said. It was an insight. Obviously, he was pained by his perception of his mother's existence. Perhaps he perceived her to be lonely and living a lifestyle that did not seem fulfilling to him. In reality, she lived in a really nice house with a swimming pool in a safe neighborhood. She had her longtime housekeeper, Margo, living with her as well as Leslie. In addition, she had created a successful career for herself as an artist. Maybe Stephen felt guilty about his decision to live at our house with his father instead of with his mother at this time and for choosing to live among the luxuries of our new good fortune. Perhaps it was guilt that made him so glum. Perhaps it was simply adolescence and the accompanying confusion. He liked living our way, but maybe showing his enjoyment didn't feel right.

Whatever it was, I heard the sweetness within his statement—just a kid who wanted the best for his mother. I felt his fierce loyalty, and I admired it. I had no desire to be his mother or take anything away from his mother. I was only looking to be another asset in his life, someone with whom he was comfortable. It was selfish in origin. I knew that if I connected with Alan's children, he would love me even more and in turn, by example, would want to love Bruce. I wanted Stephen to be able to let down his guard and relax in our home. If he could relax, I believed, Alan would be able to relax also. Then, little by little, the tension would ease. I wouldn't have to be nervous in my own house, nor would Bruce. Home should be safe and free. For now, ours was not. But we continued to take small steps.

Sometimes the tension in the house, coupled with the pressure of my work, would make me feel crazy inside. Then, once again, I would have one of my inappropriate explosions. It wouldn't work its way out unless I threw something that made a loud crash and bang. Or sometimes I would try to hit Alan. He would grab my wrists hard before I connected and look angrily into my eyes. "Don't hit me!" He meant it. I would struggle and writhe while he held my wrists until I would crumble in a heap of tears and confusion on the floor. Then I would feel ashamed and apologetic. I wouldn't know why I had gotten so out of control. I was so sorry, I would sob uncontrollably. We'd been through the same scenario so many times before.

When would I be able to figure out the source of this pain, confusion, and anger? I had never considered the importance of seeing a lifetime pattern laid out over my past and present life like a blueprint of my behaviors. I never saw the triggers. Every time my life whirled around me out of reach and out of my control, I stuffed my feelings down, down, down; and then, like Mount Saint Helens, I would erupt.

Each time it took a piece away from us, a little piece of our hearts and souls. How many pieces do we have before we run out? How many times could we tolerate the craziness and the violence before we would simply self-destruct? What I really failed to see during this period was that we all were unable to be truthful. That was the problem. Five people, angry, hurt, threatened, jealous, resentful, and afraid; mostly afraid. Each of us was acting as though the other was the one with the problem. Once again, the elephant was sitting in the living room and we all pretended we didn't see it.

I don't mean we were lying. As a result of my initial therapy, I had explored the lying phenomenon, which I wrote about extensively in *Keeping Secrets*. I had lied as a child and as a young girl about my reality. I had lied to make myself appear better than I thought I was. But at this time of my life, lying was abhorrent to me—it still is today. Even an exaggeration is a red flag. I now realize that during this period of my life, I hadn't explored truth and honesty deeply enough. Pretending is dishonest. Not sharing feelings is dishonest.

My dear late friend psychiatrist and author David Viscott said, "If you lived your life honestly, your life would heal itself." How true. As a family, we were unable to be truthful about our feelings. As a family, we desperately needed truth in our communication. We needed to reveal how we really felt about each other. Our success or failure as a family depended on how much truth we could tell and hear. Only when we were able to express our true feelings with each other, no matter how unpleasant, could our relationships begin to right themselves. But we weren't ready yet. As work continued to surge at us like a swollen river, Alan and I would immerse ourselves in its current. It was a wonderful, creative distraction. The joy and pleasure that came from doing what we loved overshadowed personal problems and gave us needed relief. Soon negative feelings were pushed away and the pain was replaced by this new anesthesia called work.

TWENTY-ONE

We were now on the nightclub circuit. Hiatus weeks were spent playing clubs all over America. My stage show was declared a hit. Every place we went, it was received with glowing reviews. We sold out at almost every venue. It was a very exciting time. I had a lot to learn, but what I lacked in polish, I made up with charm. If I made a mistake, I would fall into goofy Chrissy behavior and all would be forgiven. Chrissy was everybody's child.

I was also getting much-needed experience under my belt before we taped the CBS special *Suzanne Somers and 6,000 Sailors* at the end of the *Three's Company* fourth season. I wanted to shoot the show live, start to finish, complete with ad-libs and mistakes. I missed the old days of television, when great entertainers like Frank and Sammy seemed to simply walk onstage and give a show. It never seemed rehearsed or staged, simply polished. I wanted to bring that type of entertainment back and remove the safety net of videotape. Live. By the seat of my pants. A one-hour show should take one hour to tape.

We rehearsed for the special for weeks. Again I was working with the same team. Carl Jablonski choreographed in a way that

166

protected my untrained feet. I had rhythm, I knew how to move; but between the dyslexia and not quite understanding about counting, I needed dancers who were so good and so tight that I could simply move in my special and personal way right in the middle while the dancers did all the fancy stuff around me.

Alan loved girl dancers. And I liked having beautiful women onstage with me also, especially with an audience of six thousand American sailors. But I needed a couple of good strong male dancers to do the lifts and the catches. We hired fourteen girls and four guys.

These rehearsals were more fun than those for the original act. The "Can she do it?" pressure was off. I was now on the road constantly and with each performance was gaining a little more confidence. I liked entertaining and felt comfortable in front of a large crowd. It felt natural, like I belonged there.

Maybe childhood dreams are more potent than we realize. All those nights hiding in the closet, shaking with fear from the violence downstairs, were spent dreaming of being on a stage. It was my distraction, my salvation. My dreams lifted me out of the desperation of our miserable existence. In my dreams, I was a fairy princess, the fairest of them all, loved, adored, wanted. It was always a beautiful stage as I had imagined Broadway stages to be and I was always in the middle, covered with crystal and shimmering light.

"I want my opening costume to look like crystal," I said to Ret Turner. Dreams can come true. He designed a magnificent gown of chiffon that made me look nude, with crystal beads creating an intricate but smooth pattern all up and down my body. When I walked, it caught the light and outlined my curves.

He also made me a plain baby pink jersey slip dress, simple and beautiful, that fell softly against my legs to the floor. Hanging off my shoulders was a cloud of wispy pink tulle to blow softly in the wind while I was singing a powerful Bruce

Webber song, "I'm Coming Home Again." We staged it so that I stood on the wing of one of the fighter-bomber jets with the sailors at my feet.

Doing a TV special is exhilarating. The network gave me an enormous sum of money to produce one hour of programming. I took no personal fee. I wanted every penny to show up on-screen. I was living my dream and building a career.

We booked the guest stars—my pal Marie Osmond, whom I knew from appearing on *The Donnie and Marie Show* so many times, Gladys Knight and the Pips, and Flip Wilson.

I wanted to do the strip number from *Guys and Dolls* called "Take Back Your Mink," but word was that Jo Loesser, the widow of Frank Loesser, who had written *Guys and Dolls*, owned the rights to the material and had never let anyone do "Take Back Your Mink" on television.

"Maybe if you called Jo personally, she'll soften," my director, Art Fisher, said.

I still found nearly every influential or famous person intimidating, but I knew I could really score doing this adorable musical number in front of the sailors. If I could excite my audience on the ship, it would translate through the TV screen to those watching at home, and I wanted to succeed.

Jo Loesser couldn't have been nicer. "You are Adelaide," she said sweetly, and gave me permission. I'm told that gay bars all around the country still rerun this number over and over on their television screens, which is a big thrill for me.

The day to shoot the special finally came. We were ready. We had all arrived at San Diego, where the ship was docked. I was nervous but not in a fearful way. It was nervous excitement. I knew we had a great show.

The *U.S.S. Ranger*, under the command of Captain Dan Pederson, was ready too. The aircraft carrier was shined, scrubbed, and picture perfect on the shimmering Pacific Ocean. We had the complete cooperation of the U.S. Navy. A stage was built in the middle of the ship's airstrip, flanked by eight fighter-bombers, four on each side. We'd designed the stage in the shape of a cross so I could work the entire area side to side. No one had a bad seat. Months of fine-tuning performances in theaters-in-the-round had been good training.

Art Fisher brought sixteen cameras, one for every imaginable angle. There was even a camera in a helicopter for that perfect aerial shot from time to time. The sailors were asked to wear their dress blues, and the captain wore his formal dress whites.

Bernie Sofronsky, head of television specials for CBS, looked around approvingly. Excitement was in the air. Beautiful girls, half made up and in curlers and leotards, were everywhere. An army of crew from Hollywood was laying cable, hanging lights, and making last-minute adjustments with the stage and sound equipment.

I was standing on the stage marking the space and getting a feel for its size when I looked up and saw Gladys Knight and the Pips on the sidelines, ready to rehearse. I walked over and introduced myself. I had been such a fan of Gladys for so many years that I felt nervous meeting her. Her eyes were soft and liquid, like windows that allowed outsiders to look inside and see her heart and soul. It was obviously a kind place; it was also warm, sweet, and loving. I was thrilled she had agreed to guest star.

"Thank you so much for coming," I said genuinely. The Pips were already doing their "Pip moves" in place. They couldn't help themselves. Soon a crowd gathered, watching them slide, spin, and snap their fingers, as only they could. "I'll see you later," I said to all of them.

"Good luck," Gladys said as she nodded approvingly at me.

Gladys Knight and the Pips are the most professional people with whom I have ever worked. They were there on time, complete with their own costumes. Rehearsal took ten minutes to get their sound correct, and then they quietly, patiently waited in their dressing rooms for the show to begin.

Marie Osmond and I rehearsed a brilliant piece of special material written by Earl Brown, called "You're Not Like That at All." It had to do with our perceived images—she being Donny's little sister and a good little Mormon girl with no experience in "romance" matters, and me being the bad girl that everyone thought was dumb. It was tongue-in-cheek, naughty and nice.

But where was Flip Wilson? One hour until show time and no one had seen or heard from him. His agent said he had left his house the night before and should have been there. Flip had been known to use a lot of cocaine, as were so many entertainers of that time. "Users" carried around little mirrors, a razor blade, and a teeny little spoon called a "coke spoon." It didn't shock me when I would see people "using," because it was so commonplace. Luckily, it held no interest for me, or I might have been one of the many who took their pain away by getting high. I didn't like the way people behaved on coke. The effect made them act like extremely hyper children—they literally bounced off walls. I was already in a constant hyper state. The last thing I wanted was to add to my anxiety. I wanted to feel peaceful and serene; and although I didn't realize it at the time, I had begun my journey to truthfulness.

No one back then realized the destruction that cocaine wreaked on their lives. No one understood the eventual paranoia that cocaine brings with it. It destroys marriages and families; and for those who don't get help, it will kill. In the '60s and '70s it was everywhere—at fancy parties, backstage, in back alleys. Even the *Three's Company* group had its "cokeheads." I'd joke about it. "Choppin' and snortin' again, huh?" I was ignorant. I didn't know about its evil consequences.

"We're gonna have to do the show without Flip," the director said to me. "It's ten minutes to show time. Even if he shows, there's no time to rehearse. The only thing we can do is post-tape him after we lose the audience and slug it in in editing. In the meantime, I want you to do a longer interview with the sailor you'll pick from the audience."

Damn, I thought. I wanted this to be live. No stops. Damn Flip Wilson! I had been warned he was unreliable. Still, he was one of the funniest, quickest guys on television, and I needed his wit to balance all the music.

"Okay, let's go," Alan said. "Time to start."

My heart was pounding excitedly. The fighter-bombers were covered with sailors sitting and standing. Each bridge was dripping with uniformed guys, and the airstrip around the stage was a sea of white hats. It was beautiful, just as I had hoped.

The music started and fourteen fabulous-looking girls danced onstage in white sailor suits with hot pants. They started singing "Why Do Fools Fall in Love?" Then I came out in the middle, just like in my dream. The screams of the sailors drowned out the music. Everywhere I looked I saw an ocean of dancing white hats. Before the number was over, I ran offstage and quick-changed into the nude-and-crystal "killer" gown. My hair was long, straight, and white, like the crystal beads. For the moment, I was the fairy princess in the middle of a beautiful fairy tale just like in my childhood fantasy.

After the guys had quieted down, I told them to close their eyes and imagine their arms around their favorite girl as I sang Neil Sedaka's "Breaking Up Is Hard to Do." They were left swooning as the Pips entered stage left, doing that incredible "Pips" thing while Gladys entered center stage singing "Midnight Train to Georgia." The sailors screamed with excitement.

Backstage I thought Bernie Sofronsky would pee in his pants. "This is great," he said, laughing.

"Take Back Your Mink" brought down the house (or was it the ship?). Fourteen girls and me doing a strip was more than the guys could handle. One of my dancers, Marine, a French girl who later became the double for the incredible dancing in the movie

Flashdance, finished the number as we all did, with a falsetto "Well, wouldn't you?" with our arms in the air. What none of us knew was that both Marine's nipples came out of her corset. So maybe that was why the sailors went so crazy. (Days later, when I asked her why she didn't tell us, she said in a heavy accent, "We don't care about such things in France.")

. . . Still no Flip Wilson . . .

Marie and I finished our number, and while I changed, she sang alone. In the meantime, Alan was on the phone with Flip's agent, who was no help, so Alan was placing calls to the Highway Patrol. Several numbers later there was still no Flip Wilson.

Now we were at the end of the show. I was singing my tried-and-true closing number, "God Bless America," in a long, skintight, red bugle-beaded gown with a high neck and long sleeves.

Sure enough, the captain had a tear in his eye, and the sailors held their hats over their hearts. The show finished with a standing ovation and thousands of white hats thrown into the air.

I whispered, "I love you," and I meant it. Then I blew them a kiss and walked offstage. I could hear the hoops and screams behind me. Alan was waiting and took my arm to steady me down the stairs. I was a combination of so many feelings. The dream had come true. I had lived out my childhood fantasy. I felt good; the audience felt good. I finally felt I was doing what I was meant to do. I was high with excitement and full of satisfaction. Very few moments in my life have equaled that feeling.

———

"Flip's here," Alan said flatly as he hung up the phone in my dressing room. He was thirty-six hours late.

"I thought it was tomorrow," Flip said through a drugged fog when we met him. It was obvious he would not be able to perform that day. We called his agent to fly down immediately to try to keep Flip sober until he finished taping his piece the following day.

TWENTY-TWO

I would have liked to have John and Joyce on my special, but seeing as how they hadn't come to my opening at the MGM Grand in Las Vegas or sent the customary flowers or telegrams, I realized they either didn't know about opening-night rituals or they weren't terribly supportive of my outside career. Flowers are sent for support. When you're backstage, they remind you that others in your life wish you well, even if they're not able to be there for the performance. They also create a festive and uplifting mood in the dressing room. In fact, no one from the entire *Three's Company* cast, crew, or production team had come to my opening night. No one had wished me well, and no one had asked how it went.

My feelings were terribly hurt. What had I done to alienate everyone? We had been together for four seasons. Rather than us connecting as a group, my popularity with the public had disconnected me from everyone on the show. I felt misunderstood. I was too young and too new in the business to have downplayed my excitement and enthusiasm for all that was happening in my career. When I was around everyone, as I look back, it must have appeared that all I cared about was me, me, me! But the reality was disbelief that someone like me, who had spent a lifetime thinking I was worthless, had been dropped into a life that was so unbelievable. Because of that, I could not stop talking about it. To speak of it made it tangible and reinforced its existence.

The producers probably saw my success as further erosion of their control. I also believe Joyce had a problem with me. I liked her, and at times we had incredible laughs together. She was sweet, kind, and wonderfully talented. But as each day passed, it seemed the more fame I garnered, the wider the gap grew between us. Each magazine cover with my picture put up another barrier. But at the onset, Joyce had chosen not to do publicity. I always understood that television is a commercial business. In TV, I sell my talent. As TV actors, we must understand this; and if we cannot handle the commercialism, we need to restrict our talents to the theater or some other venue that's not overtly commercial.

Here's where we can get into that "What is art?" conversation; and for each person, the answer is as different as one's explanation of "What is God?" To me, art makes the viewer and the participant feel something, anything—good or bad, beautiful or ugly. After a play, a movie, a symphony, or a rock concert, you'll often hear the remark "I was moved." That means that person felt something. Feeling makes us think; we feel our truths.

So, perhaps my enthusiasm for and my understanding of this medium made Joyce angry.

Maybe it was because from the beginning, I enthusiastically and gratefully embraced this opportunity. Maybe it started the moment I gave all my money to Jay Bernstein. It had been the break of a lifetime, and I had decided to grab it. Maybe the lack of support from the *Three's Company* group was resentment that I was spreading my wings, that I didn't appear to need them quite so much; maybe because Alan and I were stronger as a unit than they were individually. Maybe we threatened them. Or, more simply, maybe none of them understood that what we were really doing together was business. Whatever it was, I take responsibility for not being sensitive enough to the group. Obviously, my behavior put everyone off.

But business is a big part of the "show." Because the product is people (actors), egos get out of balance. My ego was certainly operating at full speed.

Over the last twenty-five years that I've been a part of show business, I've come to realize that the one thing that keeps getting in the way of great business ventures is the "out-of-whack" egos. It's about control. It's about loss of power.

I couldn't know at that time that the seeds of destruction were being sown within the show. The mood of resentment and fear was trickling from the producers' offices down onto the set.

On most television shows, the dream of the producers is a "breakout" character. The *Three's Company* people had achieved this breakout dream, but the producers resented it. The more attention I got as either the character or myself, the more popular it made the show, which in turn produced revenues. Even so, the producers were the ones sharing the profits. I wasn't entitled to an extra dime. I was making them rich, and I was happy to do it, at least in the beginning. But they were so worried about losing their control over me that they allowed an atmosphere of veiled contempt to permeate the show.

Everyone's real character was starting to emerge. I could feel it—like a chill. I would walk into the rehearsal hall to an icy reception and wonder what I had done. It didn't feel good. I liked all of them and wished they liked me. But the way I'd dealt with my fame had created an imbalance and there was nothing I knew of that could change the situation. The party was essentially and unofficially over. To my amazement, I had become the problem in the room that no one wanted to talk about. The producers did not want to acknowledge the value of my character. In their eyes, that would have given me power. I already had the power, but I wasn't using it and didn't intend to use it frivolously. I wasn't making any demands. I wasn't a prima donna. I was merely trying to build a great career for myself. I had realized the incredible opportunity from the get-go.

None of them seemed concerned with building anything. They weren't thinking beyond this show; not the producers, not Joyce. Only John seemed to understand better than any of them.

It was becoming harder and harder for the producers to include me as one of the "kids." And they didn't like it. The three of us were like siblings on the show, and siblings don't like it when one of them rises beyond the family. Maybe the group was left feeling "Why not me?"

It's the producers who set the tone. Instead of embracing me as a valuable business asset, they were trying to keep me down on the farm after I'd seen Paree. Still, you can't stop an individual's progress. It's impossible.

Mickey Ross wasn't a businessman; his background was in theater. He was a former vaudevillian and writer for Norman Lear's company. This was his first and only sensation. From a business standpoint, I believe he saw this project only relative to his profits. This was his "baby," and no one was going to tell him how to raise it. He never saw the big picture. He never understood the steamroller effect of all the magazine covers, specials, feature movie projects, Barbara Walters interview, *20/20*, *Newsweek* cover, *Harper's Bazaar* layouts, *Vogue* editorials. Not even being featured on *60 Minutes* meant anything to him. I remember asking if I could come in late for rehearsal one morning because I was shooting the cover of *People*. Mickey bellowed, "We are doing a show! The only thing that is important is what goes on in this rehearsal room!" He would not allow me to be late. The same thing happened when Dustin Hoffman requested my availability for the next movie he was doing. It would have meant shuffling the *Three's Company* schedule around a bit. "Absolutely not!" Mickey yelled. And I cowered. I didn't want Mickey mad at me. We never even got to the negotiations. My producers were intractable. It was NOT going to happen. Yet every TV appearance to promote the movie would have been an appearance to promote *Three's Company*. Never once did I sit down in that glorious chair alongside Johnny Carson when he didn't say, "How're things back at the apartment?" There wasn't a person in America who didn't know what apartment he was talking about.

I think Mickey believed that the success of the show was about him. It was as though in his mind, the world had finally recognized him for the creative genius that he knew himself to be. So everything I did that did not involve his show was an unnecessary distraction. He was unable to see all the parts of the puzzle. He was king of his little fiefdom, with no one questioning his judgment.

The most intelligent member of the producing trio, Don Nicholl, had died of lung cancer during the first year; the third producer, Bernie West, Mickey's old vaudevillian comrade, was just along for the ride. He was the silent sweetheart partner, Mickey's faithful and dedicated yes-man. Thus Bernie was always able to carry the swing vote, because he always went the way Mickey voted.

The other two team members, Don Taffner and Ted Bergman, were the "business" guys but creatively uninvolved. "Just send me the check" was their MO; and what checks they were. Don Taffner bought the two former Vanderbilt mansions in downtown Manhattan. He knocked down the center wall, added a grand staircase, and began living the life of a potentate. Ted Bergman bought two new Rolls-Royces and a big house overlooking the Pacific Ocean and he got a new girlfriend.

And I honestly believed they all deserved the money, the success, the perks, everything! They had had the business acumen to buy the rights to an English comedy series called *Man About the House*, adapt the script to meet American tastes, hire Mickey Ross along with Don Nicholl and Bernie West, and put them to work. Don Taffner and Ted Bergman had done their jobs, and now they were raking in the rewards; except for one blunder. As they were off enjoying the good life, they left Mickey in charge, which was a dangerous decision. As my success began to grow outside of the show itself, he became intent on destroying it. He wanted to keep control no matter the cost.

I credit so much of what I learned to Mickey. Together we had created something way beyond what we had initially perceived. But rather than enjoying the creation, he became angry that I had learned to fly from the nest alone. Back and forth I would fly. Each day my wings became stronger. Instead of professional and even parental pride, he felt rejected. I didn't need him to teach me anymore. I now heard the beats and the rhythm of comedy on my own. The music had always been there, but he had taught me to "hear."

Just like the father in the movie *Shine*, instead of letting go with joy and pride, he became angry that I was no longer doing it his way. We were Rex Harrison and Audrey Hepburn. I believe we were involved in a Pygmalionesque dance with incestuous underpinnings. He loved me, hated me, wanted me, and hated himself for feeling this way.

The "ego" was about to land!

———

Meanwhile, back in the rehearsal hall, Joyce was still talking baby talk. She had a character she'd invented called "The Little Princess." This character was a bossy little princess who scolded everyone in her "itty-bitty little voice." We would laugh hysterically when she went into this character because the character could say all the things Joyce never could. The character could tell people off and zero in on all our little personal quirks.

The Little Princess especially liked to pick on me. But I loved the character. Relating to each other this way was the only time Joyce and I had any honest communication. We could clear the air without either of us feeling attacked.

I used to beg her to do it. And in time, to make the others in the group laugh, I started mimicking Joyce by doing my own imitation of her doing The Little Princess. One day while I was doing this, Joyce stormed out of the room. I ran after her. "What's wrong?" I asked.

Joyce stopped on her heels and did an about-face. Then she said, "You are the cruelest, most manipulative person I have ever known in my whole life!"

"Why?" I asked, "Because I copied The Little Princess?"

"Because you copy everything," she yelled. "I am never doing The Little Princess in front of you ever again!" Then she stalked off.

Wow! I thought. I didn't think mimicking The Little Princess was a big deal. It was just funny, a joke, a way to get laughs. I wasn't trying to "steal" or "copy" anything. But The Little Princess blowup was a metaphor for everything that I felt was bothering Joyce about me. She was the one with the training, and because of that maybe she thought she would emerge triumphant as the star performer. I don't think Joyce ever anticipated I would learn as I did. I believe she resented my abilities to observe and imitate. I think that she felt I was trying to steal her talent from her. In fact, I did learn from her. She is incredibly skilled and knowledgeable. But once I had watched and learned by observing, I absorbed the skills and incorporated them into the simplicity that became my character. I was Chrissy. Chrissy had subtext and a back story, just as we all do. We all are who we are as a result of how we were raised and the life experiences we have along the way. Because of the back story I had given Chrissy, my character on the show ceased to be work for me. I could fall into Chrissy in an instant. I knew who she was and how she thought about things. It was as easy as being me. (Maybe easier.)

In any event, Joyce and I did not know how to communicate. If we had, all these petty problems could have been avoided. My ignorance contributed greatly to the prevailing mood.

The problem with noncommunication is that we can never know what someone else is thinking or feeling if that thought or feeling is stuffed inside. Only a wizard can figure that out. The rest of us have to assume or presume.

I am constantly telling Alan in our lives today, "State your feelings! Don't make me guess at what is going on with you, because I'm probably going to get it wrong." If I am not told, "I'm angry" or "jealous" or "hurt" or "threatened" or "in pain," I will most likely assume that the silence has something to do with me. It throws me off base. "What did I do?" I ask. And then the stupid dance begins.

"Nothing" is usually the response.

"Well, you seem quiet or upset," and on and on and on.

How simple it all becomes when the statement "I feel" is made as soon as an encounter begins. Now the other person knows where they stand. There is no guessing.

But true, honest, forthright communication is one of the most difficult human skills to master. Why? Because of fear! Everything that has ever held me back in my life has been due to fear. Fear of consequence. Yet what we fear is what we draw to us so that we may learn.

But I didn't have this insight back then. I just felt confused. I was the bad girl again, just as when I was a child and had thought that if I could figure out how to be a better daughter, my dad would love me enough to stop drinking. At this point, not much had changed. Here I was, an adult in my thirties, and the same old demons still rode on my back.

I assumed Joyce didn't like me because of something I had done. I never questioned what was missing in her that she allowed me such power in her life. I believe my presence made her miserable, but that should not have been my problem. Because of my own dysfunction, I took it on. We were both doing the dance of misunderstanding, but neither of us understood the real problem. Although, looking back, I can see that even in this scenario, we had made some progress. For the first time, Joyce had verbally confronted me; and most important, she had done it while using her own voice. Truth was desperately trying to break through, even if it was uncomfortable to let it do so.

TWENTY-THREE

Tony Thomopoulos and Elton Rule, CEO of ABC, were now my drinking buddies, so to speak. They dined at our house; we met in New York, partied at Studio 54, hung out in Los Angeles restaurants and went to A-list parties together. I was on the "inside," privy to all corporate and network gossip—which stars were trouble and which ones were not. Heady stuff! I had always been on the outside of the popular crowd while growing up, so I placed undue importance on my new relationships with the top guys. I naively thought we were forming real relationships. I could pick up the phone and get either of them immediately anytime I wanted. It never entered my mind that down the road I was going to have to negotiate with these guys, nor did it enter my mind that perhaps I was being set up. How can you play hardball when you're sitting across the table from your "good pal"? It takes it out of the realm of business. "How could you do this to me?" would be the obvious way to burden me with guilt and weaken my position.

When I look back at this scenario of my own making, my naïveté is glaringly obvious. I was so impressed with myself at being "connected," so smug about having firsthand knowledge, that I found it hard to keep it to myself. It's fun to be the one who knows what's happening next, before everyone else does. Afflicted with a bad case of the "stupids," I let little bits of insider information slip out to others in the business. Remember, this is big business and programming is akin to war. What was told to me over wine at a dinner party was privileged information. I guess it made me feel like a big shot, which was more evidence of my insecurity. A secure person doesn't need to seek attention to feel powerful. Anyway, this move on my part was a huge mistake. As high as the stakes are for network actors, they are equally high for the network executives. Slipped information travels like wildfire. A pickup on a show means that show has been given a time slot on the air, and this is coveted information. Making it common knowledge gives the rival network a chance to counter. Savvy network strategy parlays into entrenched positioning for an executive. It also translates into dollars personally for the executive and big revenues for the network.

My big mouth left egg on my friends' faces. I received a phone call in the rehearsal hall at *Three's Company* one afternoon and heard the dreaded words vomit angrily out of Tony's mouth. "How could you do this to me?" I had passed on information about a private conversation Tony and I had had, and it made Tony look bad in front of his bosses.

Apologies, embarrassment, and self-flagellation couldn't really change anything. I would pay for my error. Big time.

As with honeymoons, unless you do the work after the initial seduction, the glow fades easily. I wasn't working hard enough on the most crucial element of my life. Growth was not my professional priority. I had been caught up in the dance of success and now I felt confused and bewildered that the party seemed to be ending. I no longer fit in with the "kids" at work, and there was intense friction with Mickey Ross. Now I also had an extremely high-powered enemy at the network.

My hiatus of 1980 began in the spring, so we planned a three-month tour with my act. There was Las Vegas, Atlantic City, and all the outdoor eastern venues, including Connecticut, Rhode Island, and Massachusetts. We had state and county fairs booked everywhere. We played venues with Bob Hope and others with Buddy Rich, the world's greatest drummer.

I truly loved being with my group. None of the petty rivalries existed that were so prevalent back at *Three's Company*. Alan and I were in charge. I liked that. Bruce, now fourteen, and Stephen, fifteen, came along for the whole tour and asked if they could work as stage crew. We piled the group in a caravan of buses and lived within our joyous circus atmosphere. The pace of our schedule smoothed out the problems of our family. Life on the road was a fun distraction, and we were all finally getting along, at least for the time being.

We'd take over entire floors of hotels in big cities and wings of motels in small towns. I would see the wardrobe assistant running around barefoot, delivering cleaned costumes to dancers' rooms. The bar in the lobbies would be filled with guys from the lighting and sound crews. The road manager was always at the front desk going over phone bills and reservations.

We'd arrive at the venue with our many road cases loaded with sound equipment, speakers, sound boards, lighting grids, stage risers, special curtains, onstage changing booths, and cases and cases of costumes. It was quite a production. All production decisions were made by Alan, which allowed me to be free of any responsibilities except the actual show itself. Our tour ran like a well-oiled machine.

We'd take our group out for lobster feasts after the show if we were on the East Coast and champagne and chicken drummettes in my dressing rooms in Vegas. It was a very happy experience for all of us. I was with my family, and Bruce and Stephen were learning to relate as brothers. It was our family business. The boys loved the backstage excitement. They helped hang the lights and set up the sound equipment, and they liked hanging out with the group. They felt included and needed. It was too bad that Leslie was not able to be a part of our adventure. She was now in teenage overdrive. Understandably, friends and activities at home were more interesting to her. Because of her rebellious nature, we worried that taking her with us would have put us in a constant state of watchdogging. We were afraid it would have made it difficult to focus on the show, which was usually in a different city every other day. We felt we couldn't trust her, so Leslie's mother carried the burden of her rebellion during this time.

My personal-appearance agents would put together co-headline packages for different theaters. Sometimes I was with Don Rickles, sometimes with Bob Hope or George Burns or the Smothers Brothers or Tim Allen. This particular summer, we were doing a lot of venues with Buddy Rich. I had never met him before but I used to love watching him banter with Johnny Carson on *The Tonight Show*.

One afternoon we were rehearsing at a Rhode Island theater-in-the-round. It was a large tent and Buddy had already rehearsed with his band, and, as was our deal, I used his band for my show. They were great musicians, young guys, eager to learn from the master. Buddy watched my rehearsal from the fourth row, and as I tapped my way through "Sweet Georgia Brown," he flashed that great smile/smirk of his, shaking his head in mock disgust. "What?" I asked, smiling, after we finished.

"You can't tap worth shit," he said good-naturedly.

He was right. I was queen of the fakers. I made sure people were watching my face instead of my feet. I'd mug and laugh because I knew dancing was not my forte. But Buddy tapped in his head all the time. The beats never stopped. It translated to his hands until it built to an incredible orgasmic frenzy night after night. I always made sure I was dressed and ready long before my show started each night, so I could stand in the wings and watch his creative energy as he lost himself completely in the beats of his genius. Very few have ever had or will have the abilities of a Buddy Rich. He was a "cool cat," one of the last of his kind.

Our final show that summer was at the Kennedy Center in Washington, D.C. I was co-headlining with Bob Hope, and President Carter and his wife, Rosalynn, were to be in the audience.

What a nice way to end the tour, I thought. The theater was a masterpiece—red carpets and crystal chandeliers and tiers of gilded balconies. After months together, there was a closeness among all in the group.

That night was our best show, and our excitement was not even tempered by the fact that the Carters didn't arrive. After the show, Alan and I took the whole group to the lounge at the Four Seasons Hotel for a midnight supper. We nibbled on french-fried zucchini, chicken wings, and quesadillas while sipping Dom Pérignon. All of us took turns singing around the piano. My road manager sang "You Are So Beautiful," à la Joe Cocker. I sang "Adelaide's Lament" and Alan sang "Mouth to Mouth Resuscitation."

Around four o'clock in the morning, Alan and I, and a very exhausted Stephen and Bruce, went upstairs to our hotel suite for a short night's sleep before we caught our plane to Los Angeles that morning. School was starting soon and so was the *Three's Company* new season.

TWENTY-FOUR

The fifth season of *Three's Company* was in full swing. It was late August 1980. "My contract is up in a couple of months," I told John and Joyce while backstage one night. "I'm going to ask for profit participation and I hope you guys will support me, because whatever I get, you also get. You don't have to do anything, because you both already re-signed your contracts last year. If the two of you stand by me, we will all have more power."

They both sat and stared at me.

Finally John said, "Go for it, babe."

"Sounds great," added Joyce, without conviction.

It was naive of me to count on them or even to ask them. They had not been supportive of me or my projects up to this point. Why would they start now? But I figured money would be a good incentive. I was the one renegotiating. I would be the "patsy." All they had to do was say they agreed with my requests for a salary increase. Then John, Joyce, and I would be entitled to reap the rewards. We had a parity situation. If I was paid more, then all of us would have to be paid the same.

Looking back, I realize I should not have involved them at all. I was in this alone and it was perfect fodder for them, along with the others on the show, to point the finger and label me a greedy businesswoman and not an "artist."

I felt that after five years of holding the top TV spot, John, Joyce, and I were entitled to an increase. The original investors involved with the show were already receiving huge financial compensation. Alan and I saw that other actors like Alan Alda and Carroll O'Connor were being paid a percentage of the profits, plus $250,000 a week, on their shows. At that time, and still today, that is an incredible amount of money. But they were worth it. Why? Because their names brought in profits. People loved Alan Alda and Carroll O'Connor. The public adulation translated into viewers, and viewers translated into revenue for the network through advertising dollars.

But no woman had ever been paid that much except Lucille Ball, who owned her own studio, Desilu. It was risky to go for the big pot of gold, but these were new times. Gloria Steinem had paved the way for women in business. Women were worth as much as men. I wanted to try for the big money in my business. If John and Joyce supported me, we could win. They couldn't fire all three of us. Individually, we might be replaceable, but replacing the whole trio would be the demise of the show. The producers would not be that stupid. The network wouldn't allow it.

Being an actor is like no other career choice. If you go to law school and pass the bar exam, there is no guarantee you will be rich, but there is a guarantee that you will become a lawyer. If you go to medical school, you will become a doctor if you finish your schooling.

An actor has no guarantees. You can study, perform in local and amateur theaters all your life, and never get one paying job. It is a career based on spec; the actor puts in the time and effort, studies and reads, works his or her craft—all on the "speculation" that maybe one day he or she will get a job. There are hundreds of thousands of actors who never get a single paying job.

At the time of my decision to renegotiate, I had several things going in my favor. First, my contract was up and required renegotiation. Second, the show was a runaway hit. And third, my demographics and TV Q ratings were the highest on television with women ages eighteen to forty-nine. That was the demographic most coveted by advertisers at that time.

I felt my positioning was solid. My entertainment lawyer, Gunther Schiff, who had handled most of my contracts thus far, said this would be a slam dunk. He had just finished negotiating for Penny Marshall and Cindy Williams, the stars of *Laverne and Shirley*, and had gotten them each a whopping weekly increase and a piece of the back end. I felt assured, but nonetheless nervous. I was finally taking the huge step that would most certainly upset "Big Daddy." Mickey would be furious at my audacity. It was everything he had been afraid of since the very beginning. He had never wanted to allow me to get "too big for my britches"—and now I was about to demand a level playing field.

I had recognized my power and would ask for my deserved piece of the pie. From this moment on, I could not, would not, remain "one of the kids." This was the greatest opportunity I'd ever had, and I didn't want to blow it. Besides, there was plenty for everyone.

Three's Company had already been sold into syndication for the highest price per episode in the history of television. Syndicated reruns had become a new phenomenon in the '70s. *Three's Company* was sold for hundreds of millions of dollars. It would run several times a day, every day, for the next couple of decades. This did not even include foreign rights. The pie would be divided among Don Taffner, Ted Bergman, Mickey Ross, Don Nicholl's estate, Bernie West, and a few other minority holders. I felt that I, along with John and Joyce, deserved to share in the wealth; and for that, in turn, I would agree to stay with the show until the public said, "No more."

Three's Company was an anchor show for the network, the same way *Roseanne* was an anchor show for ABC in the late '80s and early '90s. That's why Roseanne was paid $700,000 an episode plus given ownership of her show, because the network could use her popularity to bring viewers to ABC. The same goes for *Seinfeld*. Why do you think Jerry Seinfeld was given a pay increase to $1 million a show plus ownership even though it turned out to be his final season. Because Jerry anchored the network. Any new show placed before or after *Seinfeld* succeeded because of its proximity to Jerry's show. Viewers planned their weeks around his show. *Seinfeld* gave NBC cachet. It lent an air of success and winning. Imagine the profits involved if the network can afford to pay not only $1 million an episode to Jerry but $600,000 per episode to each of the other cast members as well! They are worth it because they bring in profits, and as long as they are bringing in profits, the network wants to keep them happy.

Networks and producers pray for chemistry, that undefinable "something" that hits a nerve with the public; that "thing" that Jerry Seinfeld had with Julia Louis-Dreyfus, Jason Alexander, and Michael Richards. Viewers enjoyed seeing these people together. What would have happened to the show if they replaced any one of them? The chemistry would have been off.

Today's producers would fight to the death to protect their chemistry. That is why Roseanne was able to get away with such outrageous behavior. She had power and she used it. At times she abused it, but as Ted Harbert, the former president of ABC Television, told me at that time, "If all she wants is money, no problem. We'll put up with her demands because hers is our most important show. She is our anchor. When you mess with an anchor show, you are messing with the entire network."

There was plenty of money to go around. But I was forgetting one thing, which was identified so eloquently by Michael Douglas in the movie *Wall Street:* "GREED!"

Greed and ego were to be my opponents. I knew this going in, but I didn't think that in the end my opponents would be stupid. Surely, giving up a small bit of their huge profits would be better for everyone than cutting short the life of the series by a few years. Egos aside, in the end everyone would realize that keeping the public happy would ensure extra years of life for the show, which equaled more profits for everyone. Everyone would end up winning—the producers, the network, the advertisers, the creators, the actors, and the public. It was simple math. At least it seemed that way to me.

But a series of strange events started to happen. (Only in retrospect years later did I understand.) Friends of ours received a phone call from an executive very high up in Corporate Affairs at ABC in New York who was a friend of theirs. He said, "Tell Suzanne I just came from a strategy meeting, and they are going to 'hang a nun' in the marketplace and it's going to be Suzanne." The phrase "hang a nun" refers to a practice in olden times. When leaders wanted control, they'd stop at nothing—even hanging a nun.

"What's going on?" I asked my friends. "Is this some kind of Deep Throat thing? What was that message supposed to mean?"

I later heard from a retired network executive who had been there that, unbeknownst to me, the network had decided to make an example of the next big star who asked for a salary increase in order to discourage other series players from asking for the same. Word must have gotten out that I was about to ask for an increase. They wanted to put an end to skyrocketing salaries.

Word around the network was that my lawyer got them last time but he wasn't going to get them again. If this was true and if we had all known it, I'm sure Gunther would have suggested we use another attorney, but because we didn't have that information, we entered the negotiations with a huge handicap.

———

That same week I was booked for another appearance on *The Tonight Show*. I always loved doing *The Tonight Show*. I was a regular, one of Johnny Carson's favorites, and lately Fred De Cordova (his producer) had asked me to perform whenever I appeared. I decided to do a number from my act called "The TV Medley." It was special material, a medley of the country's favorite TV theme songs—from *The Jeffersons*, *All In The Family*, *The Mary Tyler Moore Show*, to name a few. It was choreographed to include two male dancers, a high-energy number with lifts and intricate footwork. Even though I had done this medley hundreds of times, I was feeling a lot of stress as a result of all the strategy meetings with my lawyer. I was beginning to wish that I hadn't started the ball rolling. I felt scared. What was I risking? What if I lost everything? The closer I got to "the big meeting," the more frightened I felt. I didn't want to create friction and bad feelings. I didn't want Mickey to be mad at me. Deep down, I cared about him. It would certainly be easier to stick with the status quo. Fear was permeating my being. Fear distorts perception. I was losing sight of my value. I was doubting my worth.

In the middle of my dance number on live television, before the millions of viewers who faithfully watched *The Tonight Show*, my thoughts veered to that fear, and I lost focus. A simple dance turn and I felt a shooting pain through my ribs. Adrenaline kept me going through the number and my interview with Johnny. But every laugh brought excruciating pain, a sharp shooting fire, like a hot poker. It felt like my ribs were broken, but how could that be? I hadn't slipped or fallen or done any intricate movements. I got through "paneling" with Johnny, but to me our spot together was a blur. I was desperately trying to manage the pain without Johnny or the audience knowing.

After the show I needed help getting out of my costume. Bending over to remove my shoes became an unendurable chore.

I called in sick the following day to *Three's Company*. It was the first day I had ever missed. The doctor X-rayed my ribs, and sure enough, they had been fractured by muscles so tight, they had snapped the fragile bones. I told the producers and gave them my doctor's name. They didn't bother to call him.

Getting out of bed was a task. So were the simple daily routines of bathing and dressing.

I missed a second day.

Gunther called. "The producers think it's a renegotiation ploy, and I don't think that's a bad thing. Get them scared. I'll set up the meeting for tomorrow."

"Tell them to call Dr. Uhley," I said, whining with pain.

I didn't like the idea that my injury was being used to set the tone. I felt the two things should be kept separate. But I was still allowing others to make my decisions, and I did need another day to recuperate.

The meeting was set for Wednesday. It would still give me Thursday and Friday to learn that week's show, and I was a quick study. I woke up feeling nauseated. There was so much at stake.

"Don't be a hard-ass," I told Alan over breakfast. "I don't want to lose the show, so make sure you don't push them too far."

"Well," Alan said, "it's pretty hard to negotiate without taking a position. I can't say to them, 'Suzanne would like a small piece of the profits, but if you won't give it to her, it's okay.' I have to tell them this is what we need. You deserve it, Suzanne. You've worked your ass off. You've brought more publicity to this show than anyone else."

I stood at the kitchen counter, looking worried.

"Don't worry," Alan assured me. "These guys don't want to lose you; they're just negotiating. We'll ask for what we want;

they'll counter; we'll come back; and so on until we reach an agreement. But you have to know, there's always a chance, I even believe it's a possibility, that Mickey's ego could screw the whole deal," Alan continued. "He comes from that Eastern European background. I've seen it with my mother. They take a stand and won't budge." Alan looked into my eyes earnestly. "If he won't move at all, do you want me to back down completely?"

I didn't answer.

"Will you be happy to continue working in that atmosphere? Can you live with the fact that they won't give you an inch, not only in salary but also in your ability to do outside projects?"

Alan wanted me to think hard on this. It was my decision.

"This is your career," Alan said seriously. "You have to tell me how you really feel."

I turned away, frightened, and walked slowly and painfully into the living room. I lowered myself uncomfortably into my white linen club chair and stared at the ocean for a long, long time. My heart was a mélange of feelings. I had never considered that this could be the end of the most glorious job of my life. Yet if the *Three's Company* producers and ABC weren't willing to compromise in any way, maybe it would be better if I moved on. CBS was waiting to put me on their network. I could bring back this beloved character in another form.

"Okay, Alan," I finally said. "Go ahead. I want a small percentage of the profits; and if they won't agree to that, then a substantial pay increase." Alan looked at me with searching eyes. "Go," I said. The decision had been made. Before Alan left the house, he said reassuringly, "Don't worry. If it all blows out of the water, we can move on. You've got a series deal and two more specials at CBS. You've turned down feature after feature because of their intractability; you've got nightclub bookings into next year. You're gonna be okay."

I hoped he was right.

Then Alan left to meet with Gunther at George Sunderland's office at ABC.

Gunther was one of the most respected and powerful entertainment lawyers in the business. He was about the same size as Danny DeVito, and there was something about his demeanor and presence that reminded me of Danny in an expensive suit. I liked Gunther, and he had always handled my legal affairs nicely, but always with Alan looking over his shoulder overseeing each deal.

Gunther greeted Alan in the lobby of ABC Television in Century City.

"Well," Gunther said, "I talked with both John's and Joyce's lawyers today, who said their clients are happy with their contracts just the way they are. In other words, Suzanne is on her own."

This was not good news. They would have been powerful allies going into the meeting. Somehow Mickey must have gotten to them. Maybe he gave them the "Hey, kids, the only important thing is the show" speech; or perhaps he alienated them from me by telling the cast after I had missed two days of work, "She's trying to ruin our show." Mob fury is always effective. Who can go up against that?

Now, I was alone in everything.

"I could tell as I walked into the office that they were prepared to play hardball," Alan said later. Mickey sat in his chair looking dour, mad, and determined. He puffed angrily on his cigarette butt. He wore the same nondescript clothes he always wore. His skin was flushed underneath his almond-colored tan and his white curly hair was wet, as though he had just come from swimming.

Mickey didn't say hello to Alan. Not a good sign. According to Alan, the two lawyers spoke their usual lawyer bullshit, trying to lighten the atmosphere; but what did they care? They got paid no matter what happened. Only their egos made them want to win. Other than that, there would be other clients, other meetings.

Mickey and Alan were like two prizefighters circling the ring, sizing up their opponent. This meeting was about more than my wanting a piece of the profits. It was ego all around. All these egos in control of my destiny. Only Alan had my best interests at heart.

Back home, I was painfully pacing back and forth in my living room. My stomach was in knots. I kept looking at my watch. It had been about an hour. They're just sitting down in George's office, I surmised.

"As you know," Alan said confidently to the assembled group, "Suzanne loves doing the show, and she will be happy to stay put throughout the entire run; but her contract is up and her present deal is no longer commensurate with her value to the show." Alan sat forward in his seat. "Both Suzanne and I feel that the public has spoken. They have embraced Suzanne and her character in a way that rarely happens. Even Ted Bergman told Suzanne at the wrap party that he thinks she's in a category with Lucy. Now," Alan continued, "regardless of Ted's opinion, it's obvious that what Suzanne is doing on the screen has struck a chord. So we feel it only fair that Suzanne now participate in the profits because she has contributed so much to the success of the show, and will continue to do so in the future."

Alan later reported that the whole time he was talking, Mickey's chest was heaving from his heavy breathing. Sweat formed on his upper lip and the veins in his neck bloated with blood. His eyes turned to steel. When Alan finished talking, Mickey threw down the butt of his lit cigarette and slowly rose to his feet. A sound came from deep within, almost hoarse, like something from *The Exorcist;* and then he bellowed with seething rage:

"YOU WANT ME TO SHARE MY BLOOD WITH HER?"

He stood over Alan, his posture in bully position until Alan stood up, nose to nose, and said, "YES!"

"NEVER!" Mickey shouted, and then went into a tirade. "Who does she think she is? I taught her, I molded her, I made her, I owe her NOTHING!"

Alan and I had been right. Mickey truly believed *he* was the show, and he was obsessed with being right. He wasn't going to allow a couple of upstarts like Alan and me tell him what to do. He was not listening to his instincts anymore. His reaction wasn't information-based, it wasn't experience-based, and it certainly wasn't business-based. His ego had taken over. He felt he had created all of this, and he didn't need anyone.

On and on Mickey ranted. The lawyers on both sides sat smugly. It was a good show. Finally there was a pause in Mickey's bellowing, and George calmly said, "This is what we are prepared to do. On behalf of the network and the *Three's Company* producers, we are willing to offer a small increase payable at the end of the season *only* if she behaves. No points and no further negotiations."

Alan sat stunned. This would have moved me to earning one seventh of what the top men in television were earning. It was a demeaning slap in the face—If she behaves? he thought. In five years I had missed only the past three days of work because of fractured ribs, and I had X rays to prove it.

"Why are we at this meeting?" Alan asked Gunther, seething. "This offer is insulting," Alan said to the group. "You don't deserve Suzanne, and the only way you can have her is $150,000 a week or ten percent of the profits!"

"This meeting is over," George pronounced. Mickey stood alongside George in solidarity.

It was over!

Car phones had not yet come onto the scene in 1980, so I waited in my living room an agonizing three and a half hours before I heard Alan open the garage door. I had been all alone during this time. The boys were away at school. Alan was fighting with the lock. My heart began pounding like a tom-tom.

It was too painful for me to get out of my chair and walk downstairs to greet him, so I waited impatiently.

"Alan," I yelled out.

"Be right with you," he answered.

Boom! Boom! went my heart. If it were good news, he'd be running up here to tell me, I thought. Alan's footsteps sounded labored, deliberate, coming up the stairs. I strained from my chair to see his face.

He was not smiling. His face looked ashen. "Not good," he said flatly.

"What do you mean?" I asked, panicked.

"This was not a negotiation," he began. "They had already decided what they were going to do. It was take it or leave it; a small, little pittance of a raise at the end of the season, and only if you 'behave.'"

I was stunned. I couldn't believe my ears. I meant so little to them.

"I'm really sorry," Alan said sincerely. "I feel responsible, and I know that had I said okay to their offer, you'd still be on TV. But I couldn't let them do that to you. Either they were going to humiliate you into returning to be 'one of the kids' again, or they were going to get rid of you. I know you're feeling vulnerable right now," Alan said as he put his arms around me, "but you're going to be okay. I've been around a long time, and I know if we continue to press forward, you will eventually get what you want."

Suddenly it seemed like the electricity had gone from the house. It felt dark. Cold. I stared at the Pacific Ocean from my living room window, even though the picture had long since gone black. I was looking, yet could see nothing. I couldn't believe it had all gotten so out of hand. In the background, coming from the kitchen, I heard about my departure on the television news. "Suzanne Somers quits over contract dispute. Army Archerd reports that Suzanne Somers walked off the *Three's Company* set after making outrageous salary demands. Suzanne Somers and her husband demanded $150,000 per episode and ten percent of the profits."

I felt like my vocal cords had been removed. I no longer had a voice from which to be heard and understood. I was not angry with Alan. I had given him the power to run the meeting, and I know he did his best for me. There really had been no option except accepting what was essentially the status quo. Nonetheless, I felt lost. Suddenly I no longer belonged to Chrissy or the show. My TV family had shunted me out the door. "Get out!" they had said to Alan; and in doing so, they had said "Get out!" to me.

I was decimated. Too stunned to cry. I was distraught that I had let the most incredible job of my life slip through my fingers. There had hardly been a fight. It was a knockout in the first round. Clang! went the bell. And then it was all over.

The winner was declared. Mickey stood victorious. His attitude was smug. He was sure he could replace me with no problem. He could get another blond for no money and have complete control.

All the television reports made me sound petulant and greedy. Added to everything else, *Three's Company* demanded I complete the remainder of the season in humiliation.

I presume Mickey had devised this sinister plan. I was instructed to report to work on Fridays for the rest of the season only to tape a one-minute tag at the end of the show. They changed the story line to accommodate my banishment from the set (Chrissy had gone away to care for her sick aunt, who was never to recover).

A special set was built behind the main set. It was out of view of the audience and any unnecessary crew. Most important, it was out of sight of the cast. Every week I was met at the back door of the studio and escorted to the set by a uniformed guard, where I taped a one-minute phone call to Jack or Janet into a dead telephone. As soon as I finished doing my one minute, I was escorted out the back door by the guard.

In all the weeks of this degrading treatment, neither John nor Joyce nor anyone else on the show ever came out of their dressing rooms to say hello or to show any compassion for my predicament. Knowing Mickey, either you were on his side or you were the enemy. No one had a choice. To continue working in his fiefdom, you had to choose to be on his team.

I guess it was easier for them to pretend they didn't know I was on the set. They couldn't give up being the "kids." "Daddy Mickey" was too powerful a force to deal with. I had been controlled by his power myself. The longer their silence continued, the harder it would be for them to confront me.

Several times I broke down in tears while taping these one-minute tags. The lone cameraman would have to wait until I regained my composure. All the producers' offices had monitors directly linked to the stage. So did the dressing rooms. I knew everyone was watching. It would be too compelling not to. But no one responded for fear of incurring Mickey's wrath. He was the one who signed their checks.

Mickey had won. While he was at it, he managed to turn every single person, including the director, the script assistant, even the wardrobe department head, against me.

People from my former job would cross the street if they saw me coming. I saw the wardrobe assistant one day on Beverly Drive. He pretended he didn't see me and dashed across the street. It happened often with others from the show as well.

———

Mickey's satisfaction was short-lived. He had convinced the network that blonds were easy to come by. He had trained me, he told them. And he could train another one—like a seal. What Mickey never realized was the power the three of us—not two or one, but three—wielded.

American TV viewers did not like having their favorite threesome dismantled. They were used to the original cast. Mickey had messed with the most important element of any series. Without the original chemistry, the show lost something crucial. It was like a death in the family. The family was never the same. The public mourned the loss of Chrissy. Even to this day, nearly twenty years later, people say to me, "That show was never the same without you." And it wasn't. It had lost its setup. Strange as it seems, I can only guess that the writers, headed by Mickey, had never understood what my character was really about. They had never understood the public's relationship with Chrissy's pure and simple soul.

They replaced me with one blond actress and then another. The chemistry never reignited, and the show began to fade quickly. It was no longer the same show. I never went out of my way to watch it after that. Sometimes I would come across it as I channel-surfed; but I never lingered very long. I didn't like this apartment or its inhabitants anymore. I didn't think they were nice people.

In the end, Mickey failed everyone—the network, the partners, the cast, and especially the show itself. *Three's Company* continued for another three years, but it had lost its command with the public. The ratings had been averaging a 40 share; but after Chrissy's departure, the show eventually slipped to a 29 share. With this tremendous dip in ratings, the network had lost hundreds of millions in advertising dollars.

Having power for the first time in one's life is like having money for the first time. When you've never been used to having money, as I experienced, the tendency is to spend it. It has no value; there is no understanding of the meaning behind it. The same is true with power.

I like to think that maybe I paved the way for change. Years later, I am still being used as an example. In talking with Cindy Williams one day, she told me that a year later both she and Penny Marshall had wanted to try again for another raise, but Penny said, "Remember what they did to Suzanne." Maybe because of the *Three's Company* fiasco, the networks changed their strategy. There had always been disdain toward actors in the industry because of the power they derive from their popularity.

But today's television executives understand show business. Nothing personal. Everyone gets to win. Years after the *Three's Company* debacle, Alan ran into Elton Rule, and all Elton could say was that he couldn't understand how it had gotten so out of hand. Neither could we.

My nature is to go deeper, beyond the surface, but I have no control over the ways of others. It seems to me, as I look back over this whole scenario, I was in the right place at the right time with the wrong people at the wrong time. To date, the "tag" of humiliation has been edited out of all the reruns. I don't know who made that decision. I'm sure it was a money thing. I don't get paid if I'm not in the show. Anyway, I'm glad. It would be painful for all to relive that slow death.

Despite everything, I do not see this entire blip in my life as anything other than something that was meant to be. At the time it was painful and depressing. But these were my lessons. And through all of this were to come my greatest opportunities.

Part Two

THE OPPORTUNITIES

TWENTY-FIVE

It would have been easy to sit back and give up. It would have been easy to become the poor little victim. But then who would be the loser? This is my life! Nobody cares if I get what I want out of it but me. I'm the only one who knows what will make me happy; therefore I am the only one who cares if I move forward and find my way to peace and satisfaction.

There is little to learn when all is going smoothly. It's nice, it's peaceful, and it's even necessary to have some periods in life that let up from the pain. We all need respites, time to breathe. But it's the pain of life's experiences that confuses us, depresses us, and tortures us so that we define ourselves and are forced to decide what to do about it. It is this frame of mind that helps us grow and evolve. How can we know what we want if we don't have an opposite experience to define what we do not want? I had to lose everything to learn what was truly important to me.

That first year was devastating. I felt embarrassed to be seen in public. I felt I was nothing. Without Chrissy to define me, I didn't know where I fit in. I hadn't saved my money because I'd thought it was a faucet that would never stop pouring forth. Money had been meaningless. I hadn't realized the lifestyle we had set up. Bruce was still going to Thacher, Stephen was now at Menlo College, and Leslie had enrolled at Parsons School of Design in Paris and Los Angeles. Tuition for private schools is very expensive. When money was flowing like water into our household, I never noticed. But now signing checks made my hand quiver. I watched our savings diminish. To Alan's credit, he never said, "I told you so." I was learning this lesson the hard way. I didn't need him making me feel worse.

Also, I hadn't realized how expensive my personal upkeep had become. Bjorn, my favorite makeup and hair stylist, charged $1,500 a day! Sometimes the network had paid and other times, for my own personal appearances, it was out of my pocket. Again, when I had the show, his fees meant nothing to me. Now he was a luxury I could not often afford. Without Bjorn, I was unable to re-create my "look." My look needed changing. I was no longer Chrissy Snow with the snow-white hair.

Who was I?

Restaurants, travel, new clothes, decorating the house, cars, flowers—all were extravagances I had taken for granted. It had to stop.

I couldn't buy a new dress to take the pain away. There was no money coming in. I was still giving interviews about what happened, but they were dwindling. My interviews were boring. I was trying to make sense to the American public of why I wanted to be paid $150,000 a week, and the public got turned off. "She has some nerve," a woman said in a letter to the *Chicago Tribune*. It was time for me to shut up and stay home. I felt like a failure.

TV Guide put me on their cover as the "Fallen Sitcom Star." It was a dreary picture with me wearing a dreary gray sweater with a dreary gray background. The inside article made fun of my new dreary existence. The writer described me as sad and cold and lonely, sitting in my dark living room staring at the fog.

I shut the doors of my house and stopped taking phone calls. I no longer wanted to see or talk to anyone.

In looking back, throughout the whole experience, I realize I had become my accomplishments! I had conned myself into believing that people loved me because of what I could do for them. Like a marionette—when the strings were pulled, I danced. Like the circus dog—bow wow, throw me a treat. Tell me you love me. It took losing everything to understand how needy I was. I was trying to please everyone—my husband, my son, my stepchildren, my family, and my fans. I felt like I was trying to take care of the whole country. No wonder I was spinning out of control. The scenario of my childhood repeated itself all over again, this time with new players. I thought I was "well"; but once again, I had chosen to place myself in a position in which to learn about control. My relationship with Mickey, the domineering "daddy," echoed my childhood experiences with my father. Love was traded in increments. Subliminally, I now realize, I had pushed the issue until that final confrontation, just as I had done with my dad several years earlier. I needed to teach myself once again to believe in myself and to fight for what *I* wanted, not only in business but in my personal life as well. I still had issues with Alan over control and his relationship with my son. I still had to find peace with my stepchildren. Most important, I needed to find me; what I wanted; what I needed and what I felt. I didn't find it in my accomplishments. There was something empty in my success. I was not feeling worthy as a person. When would I feel, truly feel, that I belonged, that I had a right to "be"?

I wanted to find a deeper purpose. Chrissy wasn't enough. She was cute and pure and she helped me live a childhood that had been denied to me. But I wanted my life to have real meaning, and thus far nothing had filled the empty hole inside. Not all the success in the world could do it for me. So I had created my demise. I had pushed the envelope. I had to lose everything to get to a place in my soul that meant something to me.

As with all situations, when one door closes, another one will open if you want it to. When I first found myself kicked out the back door of that imaginary car, I felt consumed by the realization that I was suddenly powerless. I had never realized the power that starring in the number one show had given me. Overnight I was "old news," a "has-been," a "fallen sitcom star," a "whatever happened to?" kind of person. It changed my demeanor. I didn't walk quite so tall. Now, without anything to attach myself to, I had no identity. The glass was definitely half empty. I had fallen from grace. I lay on the ground in a pool of self-pity. I had lost my place in the hearts of Americans. I was still being written about, but as a person who had been "put in her place." I was perceived as "greedy" by the public and as "trouble" in the industry.

———

"You've got baggage," Bud Grant, president of CBS, told me. "We once thought we had a slam dunk with you but now I'm not so sure the public wants to see you."

No outside offers came in. No movies of the week, no guest-starring offers, no commercials, no nothing! All the doors slammed shut. Hollywood was "out to lunch" for me.

My Vegas offers diminished also. "Without the number one show in the country, Suzanne's not as valuable anymore," Bernie Rothkopf of the MGM Grand told Alan when Alan was trying to get more bookings at the hotel.

My mail changed also. The letters I had received formerly had been adoring. Now they were angry, disappointed. I stopped reading them. "Return to Sender" was stamped on all fan mail. Maniacally, I went about the business of trying to get "it" back. I had to "be" someone again. The network presidents' doors had closed. Now my meetings took place with guys with no authority to say "Yes." I didn't like it. It's hard to go backward.

Success means nothing if that's all there is. As the days passed from one to the next, a change slowly took place. I began to reexperience the pleasures inherent in my life and relationships. Alan and I had time to rekindle the passion and happiness that had been eclipsed by all the frenzy that surrounded my demise on the show. We took long walks along the Pacific Ocean, held hands, shopped for groceries, cooked glorious meals, and took long naps. It was a time of nurturing and repair. I finally had time to think again. Growth is difficult when you're riding full-speed down that highway of life. Suddenly I was able to look around and look forward.

I detached myself from the new *Three's Company*. I didn't want to look over my shoulder. I didn't want to wallow in "shoulda, woulda, coulda's." If fame was that fragile, why had I placed such importance on it? Maybe because back then, for the first time in my life, I had felt like "somebody." Finally I had felt as good as the others. As a child, I was always ashamed of myself and my family. I had no worth. In my mind I was unlovable.

My childhood fantasies about being a big star on the world's biggest stage were really about redemption. If I was famous, loved, and adored, people would admire me. They would see that my family wasn't worthless. We would no longer have to feel ashamed. I could redeem us.

That is a pretty heavy load to carry. Notice that this fantasy wasn't about me, but us. I felt I had to save the family. My needs and feelings were not important.

In many ways I achieved my childhood goal. My family's life did change with my success, and I believe for the better.

Shortly after my father had begun his recovery to sobriety, while I was still on *Three's Company*, I had felt safe in presenting him to the nation. We did a Life Savers commercial together.

We were awkward together off the set because I didn't really know him. I had only known my drunk father. I was used to cowering around him, and now we were working together as equals. We didn't know how to talk to each other. We had never touched each other except for his sloppy, drunken kisses, which I had abhorred. But the commercial required that we hold hands and act warmly together. I remember feeling proud that as a result of my success on *Three's Company*, people were interested in us as a family. In fact, we were being paid for giving the country a "look" at us.

Now, in my isolation, I felt rejected by the public and the industry. All my work, all my success, seemed meaningless. But really, it wasn't. In my grief and banishment, my life was finally about to begin. I decided I had to find a way to discover myself in all the confusion. The first step was looking at our blended family. I had been putting feelings aside for so long that I no longer was aware of the constant compromises I made in order to keep peace.

————

One night, after I had left *Three's Company*, Alan and I had just finished our dinner and were enjoying ourselves and the evening, with Vivaldi playing in the background. The telephone rang and the voice on the other end brought panic and a racing to my heart.

"Alan," I said, frightened. "It's Leslie's mother. Leslie's had a car accident."

Alan's face turned ashen as he grabbed the phone.

"Alan, I've got Leslie here," her mother said; she was very shaken up. "Leslie just crashed into a parked car in front of the house. No one was hurt, but I looked out the window to see what the noise was, and I saw Leslie get out of the car and walk away from it. I ran out to get her . . . she seems very drugged out."

"I'll be right there," Alan said, pained. He hung up the phone. His face was dazed.

"This has been coming for a long time," I said softly. "None of us wanted to see this, but we have to do something or she is going to die."

Up to this moment, every time I would mention that I thought Leslie was "using," Alan and I would have huge arguments. He didn't want to hear about it. He would insult me and lash out.

"You think because you come from your 'alky' family that you know everything. I've asked Leslie and she's told me over and over that she's not using drugs, and I believe her." His verbal lashings could be cruel like a sharp whip. They were so hurtful that I would usually retreat rather than be the victim of his viper-like tongue.

"I told you so" is pretty empty when reality is upon you. Alan had always been in control of himself and everything and every-body in his wake. Now his twenty-year-old daughter had ren-dered him powerless. For the first time he wasn't in control and he needed my help. I held his head against my chest as he sobbed silently into my breast. It was the first time I had ever seen Alan really cry. I called Leslie's mother back as Alan sat, his head in his hands, at the kitchen table. Both were distraught. It was the first time I could actually help any of them. And I wanted to.

"I can call Carol Burnett for advice," I suggested to Leslie's mother. Carol had recently gone through a painful and public drug experience with her daughter Carrie. Even though I hardly knew Carol, I had seen her a few times at CBS. Celebrities have a camaraderie. It is not so unusual to call someone you've never met and get a warm response.

"There's a doctor at a hospital in Orange County," Carol told me. "He's brilliant; he'll help you through this."

"Thank you," Leslie's mother told me when I passed the infor-mation along to her. "It makes me feel that you really care."

"I do! Truly, I do!"

We needed Leslie's cooperation to check her into the inpatient center. The only power we had was an ultimatum. Leslie's mother,

Alan, and I became a united front. Suddenly all the petty bickering that ping-pongs between former and present families dissipated. The stakes were much higher now. Leslie's life was on the line.

It was "tough love." Leslie had the choice of checking into the rehab hospital with all of our support or being financially cut off by the family. Money was the only thing that had any meaning to her at this time, and we hoped and prayed that she would find being cut adrift financially too frightening.

Alan and I went to Leslie's school to tell the dean what was going on. We were assured by the dean that Leslie would be able to return to school after getting treatment. Then he called her to his office as we waited.

"You know why we're here, Leslie. You have a problem and we all want to help. It's your choice," Alan told her seriously. "I can't make you do anything you don't want to do; but I'm giving you this option. Check yourself into the rehab center and we will support you emotionally and financially. We will be with you every step of the way. The other option leaves you on your own. We will love you, but you'll get no help from us."

Leslie put her head in her hands and started to cry. Finally she looked up, her face drenched with tears. "I want to get better," she said.

"Then let's go," Alan said softly.

Leslie entered the rehab filled with anger, shame, and sadness, a painful tug-of-war on her spirit. As we drove to see her at the end of the first week, I was overwhelmed with my own feelings of shame. Why hadn't I done something sooner? Her pain was so obvious. Every stolen item, every angry phone call, every family disruption was a masked scream for understanding. None of us were listening. I had been so caught up in my own feelings of anger and aggravation that I never saw the part I was playing in her rebellion. Now she had forced us into listening to her once and for all. Not one of us had had the courage to tell

Caroline and Bruce on their wedding day, in 1991. Leslie designed Caroline's dress.

Bruce and I share a laugh while dancing at his wedding.

Alan gives a heartfelt tribute at Bruce and Caroline's wedding.

With Regis and Kathie Lee,
who's wearing a ThighMaster
on her head.

Bruce, now a director,
and me working together.

My band today: Roger Ball, Greg Cunningham,
Doug Walter, Glenn Zottola, me, David Libman, and Kirk Smith.

Alan and I love to dance!

With my great *Step by Step*
husband, Patrick Duffy.

Performing at the
McCallum Theatre
in Palm Desert.

On the lecture circuit,
speaking out for
children of alcoholics.

WOMEN
INCORPORATED

My sister, Maureen, me, and my mother before she lost her sight.

Leslie's family today.

Me with two of
my grandchildren.

My granddaughter, Caroline, and Bruce.

Daisy and Leslie.

Bruce loves
being a father.

Sitting at the beach in St. Tropez, thinking about this book.

At home in the desert is where I feel most calm.

Monte Carlo, Monaco, where I performed for the royal family.

Stephen and me today,
dear friends.

Leslie and me wearing
her hand-painted jeans.

My aunt Helen, Maureen, Mom, my sister-in-law Mardi, and me
on our way to lunch for my mother's 81st birthday.

My family today: Bruce and
Caroline with their baby, Alan,
Leslie and Frank and their baby,
and Stephen and Olivia with their
baby. I'm taking the photograph.

Bruce and Alan now have
a deep, loving relationship.

Alan and me,
content and
happy, in 1998.

her the truth. No one ever explained the demise of her perfect world. One day it crumbled without explanation and she was expected to accept the situation.

No one had ever told Leslie why her parents divorced, so she had to guess; and in doing so, she must have become angry at each of us. She had to fill in the blanks and felt we had all let her down. And she was right. We had. We had let her down because we had all been too afraid or too ignorant to be honest.

After Leslie's second week of inpatient therapy, the doctor asked that all the important players in Leslie's life spend a week in intense family therapy at the recovery center. That included Leslie's mother, Alan, myself, Stephen, and Bruce.

The idea of such close contact with the past and the present was a frightening prospect. The doctor demanded we attend, explaining it was crucial to Leslie's recovery. I worried that because I was well known, our personal lives would become public. But there was no choice.

Alan, Stephen, Bruce, and I were silent as we drove the hour and a half to Orange County the first morning. We knew real feelings were going to be stirred up, and it was frightening. I had kept my feelings in check for so long, I feared losing control. Ignorantly, I saw this as something we were doing for Leslie. I did not initially see it as something we were doing to save ourselves as a family. We were driving toward our opportunity to rid ourselves of the negative and unsaid baggage of our lives together. We would be forced to confront our feelings, and each of us was terrified at what might be unleashed.

"We're all here today because we care about Leslie," the doctor said to our assembled group. We were seated in a plain but pleasant room, much like a therapist's office.

I looked around the room. We all sat in various positions of defensiveness—arms folded tightly, lips pursed, legs crossed, and eyes wandering.

"I'm sure you are all expecting Leslie to apologize for the problems she has brought to the family." The doctor continued, "Perhaps she might see it that way; perhaps not. Frankly, I've brought all of you here today to allow Leslie to tell you how angry she is with all of you."

We sat stunned as Leslie sat looking at her feet. This was a new concept. Hadn't we all been doing everything we could to be loving and understanding? Wasn't it Leslie who ruined every family situation? Wasn't it Leslie who was trying to drive a wedge between all of us?

"Leslie is very upset with all of you. She feels misunderstood; most of all, she feels left out. She feels like she doesn't belong. What we hope to accomplish this week is for everyone to reveal their true feelings. This is a safe room and I am a neutral arbitrator. I have no emotional stake in your differences. My job is to create a safe environment allowing each of you to clear away those things that cloud your abilities to think honestly. We are clearing the debris of anger and hurt in order to heal the damage that has been done by and to all of you."

One by one, each of us was asked to tell about our family experience as it related to Leslie—the anger, the pain, the confusion, and the sadness. What came out of each and every one of us was a compelling story of the events that had brought us to this point.

During this time, I was able to see a side of Leslie to which I had been blinded. She was so hurt. She became a vulnerable little girl before my eyes. I cried as her mother talked of her infancy; the joy she brought to her mother and father, her precociousness, her love of costumes even as a toddler. Visions of Leslie in high heels and Mummy's pearls appeared, and with it her humanness. Life had been so safe back then in her fairy-tale room with the canopy bed on the back side of their mansion. Her life had been perfect in every way. Then, as though a bomb had gone off, it shattered. And she never knew why.

I felt my own anger and hurt melt away. With each person's testimony, I saw their world from their point of view. Each day brought new healing. We were asked to sit opposite Leslie individually while we looked into her eyes and she into ours and told her of our feelings about our own pain. She was not allowed to talk during our turns, and we were not allowed to talk during her opportunity. We were forced to really listen to each other for the first time.

Stephen was not able to get angry on behalf of himself, but he was angry that Leslie had upset their mother. Emotional doors were opening. Each night we drove home in silence, lost in our individual thoughts. Confronting hurt and old wounds is aggravating. It stirs up the feelings we take such care to tuck away. Yet remembering is an important part of the "work." It is the gateway to healing; and that was the objective of this exercise.

Each day I saw a change come over Leslie. A light was coming back to her eyes. The shame that held her prisoner was disappearing. She was able to see for the first time why she had been acting out. She had been sad and didn't know how to express it.

"I never did this as a punishment to you or Daddy," she said to Alan and me. Then, looking around the room at all of us, she finally admitted, "I have a drug problem. I never understood that before."

These simple words of tremendous courage, and words which Leslie had harbored for years, had finally been released. We were all deeply moved by her honesty and her sincerity. And with this relinquishment, Leslie, Bruce, and Stephen watched Alan and me interact with his former wife. They saw that we were all communicating together. We weren't angry. Rather, Leslie's admission opened the door for each of us to allow the barrier of loyalty to the original family to crumble like the Berlin Wall. We could all get along together and help Leslie and one another on her path to recovery.

———

On the fourth day, after the silent drive home and dinner, I asked Alan, "Have you ever explained to Stephen what happened between you and his mother?"

"I guess I never did," Alan said, thinking.

"Why don't you go to his room and tell him the truth. Let all the skeletons out of the closet. He must think your breakup was because of me. I'll never be able to connect with him as long as he thinks I'm the reason for your divorce."

———

Nothing is more beautiful than love. Our week in therapy turned out to be the catalyst for the healing of our family. It saved us. Without it, I'm not sure if we could have found the road to love as a family. We still had more work to do, particularly Alan and Bruce, but now we were all on a new course. Finally we were starting to listen to one another.

Step by step, the barriers that stood in the way and prevented communication were dismantled. Piece by piece we put ourselves back together. The hurt was slowly being repaired; the anger, the misunderstanding, and the fear were dissipating. All the years of watching, adapting, and trying to please had only poured salt on the wounds. It was now apparent that truth was the only cure. Only truth would heal our lives.

TWENTY-SIX

⁂ As our personal lives improved with each passing day, my professional life was grinding to a halt. The nightclub business was drying up for me. Each inquiry was greeted with the same response: "Without a TV series, she really doesn't have much ability to sell tickets," promoters would tell Alan.

At least I still had my pilot commitment from CBS, which was in place from the deal Jay had made years earlier. Alan and I went into business with Norman Lear's company to produce my *Suzanne* pilot for CBS. I was looking for a series that was surefire, and the only thing I knew the public would accept was a continuation of the character to which they had grown accustomed. But we encountered obstacle after obstacle. There must have been a "mole" in Norman Lear's company, because every draft of my pilot script was met with a "Cease and Desist" lawsuit threat from the *Three's Company* group. I wasn't allowed to talk like Chrissy, walk like Chrissy, wear my hair like Chrissy, dress like Chrissy, or remind the viewers in any way of my former character.

Three's Company had given me outtakes several years earlier to be used in my nightclub act. They were the original TV "bloopers." It was John, Joyce, and me making mistakes that never got on the air—John tripping, each of us making dialogue goofs, John grabbing our butts. These clips were a consistent hit with the audience and allowed me to make a quick costume change and take a deep breath. Another "Cease and Desist" intent-to-sue letter arrived at our hotel in Las Vegas. The *Three's Company* group, headed by Mickey, insisted I stop doing my likeness of Chrissy onstage. I did not own the character, I was told, and from that moment on, I was prohibited from acting like her. It was a ridiculous suit, and one without any legal merit. We thought about a countersuit stating that no one could dictate how I "acted," how I dressed, or how I wore my hair; but in the end, Alan and I agreed that more legal entanglements with those people would only drain us of our energy. We did not feel like becoming embroiled in a legal battle, so we removed everything that had to do with *Three's Company*.

————

We were looking forward, not sliding backward. By the time the final shooting script of my CBS pilot was finished, it had been so watered down for fear of lawsuits that it had lost its punch. I was simply a stupid flight attendant who lived in an apartment with a female roommate. They always had trouble paying the rent. Sound familiar? But, there was no moral code, no back story, nothing to care about.

The night before we shot the pilot, I knew it was a lousy show. It never aired and I was given thirteen weeks' salary to walk away.

The further removed I became from my former life, the less I wanted to do with it. It was no longer positive for me. It dragged me down. I had new dreams. It would be hard work to change the public's perception of me, but I knew somewhere, somehow, I would find a perfect vehicle.

We decided to do my second special due CBS that same year. This time we were going to Germany to tape *Suzanne Somers and 50,000 GI's*. Most of my same troupe was rehired, with the exception of the choreographer. We hired Walter Painter, of Academy Award fame, who had choreographed for Shirley MacLaine, and I had always liked her act a lot.

Susan Anton, the Pointer Sisters, and Jonathan Winters agreed to be my guest stars. Again it was to be live with no stops, similar to the Bob Hope/USO shows. There was only one catch. The new vice president I was working with at CBS insisted that if we were taking all these people abroad, then Americans had to see the country. He insisted we shoot one number in a beer hall and do filmed pieces in different areas of Germany.

"Why?" I asked, sitting across from him in his office. "We killed in the ratings last time and the camera never left the deck of the ship! The show is about the soldiers and the entertainers onstage."

"No!" was the answer.

"If CBS is going to spend the money to send everyone there, we want to see it," he said emphatically. I was to do it his way or there would be no show. I had lost my power base. There wasn't much I could do but comply.

In order to have the cooperation of the U.S. Army, we made an "I'll scratch your back if you scratch mine" deal. I would have the use of one of the landing strips at Ramstein Air Force Base in return for a series of live USO shows with our dancers at ten different army bases in different parts of Germany over a two-week period. "Okay," I said. "No problem." I thought it would be exciting, like Marilyn Monroe in Korea in the '50s.

We rehearsed at KTLA-Metromedia, an L.A. studio, where Alan and I had our offices. Coincidentally, *Three's Company* was now taping their shows at the same studio. Even though we walked the same hallways, I never ran into one person connected with that show.

Only once, when Walter Painter was painstakingly teaching me a new tap dance hour after hour in the rehearsal hall next to theirs, did I hear from them.

Tap-a-tap-a-tap, I rehearsed. Suddenly their whole room tapped furiously on their floor in answer to my tap-a-tap-a-tap. I don't know what that response meant. It was a weird way for them to communicate with me. It didn't matter to me. I had moved on. I still didn't have resolution with my feelings toward them.

———

We arrived at Ramstein Air Force Base in October 1982 on a frosty gray day, tired, cold, and hungry.

Everyone was jet-lagged, so we agreed to get some sleep and start rehearsals first thing the following morning.

"Bad news," my director, Art Fisher, said.

"What?" I asked.

"The General just informed me that the show is to be taped *inside* an airplane hangar."

"That's ridiculous," I said incredulously.

"We don't have lights or a set for indoors," Alan protested.

Art said, "I told the General that, but he said 'negative.'"

We had planned on shooting the show outside with natural light with the exception of spotlights. The Air Force base, the airstrip, and the Black Forest in the background was to be our fabulous set. We had come with a crew to build a stage, but that was all. Suddenly an indoor set had to be conceptualized; and, somehow, we had to find enough lights to illuminate the equivalent of a baseball field. To add to the pressure, the show was due to be shot the following afternoon. If it wasn't, I would lose the Pointer Sisters and Jonathan Winters for sure. Also, Alan and I would incur all additional debt. We hadn't budgeted for these extras, so it would come out of our pockets personally.

Alan was up all night, along with Rene Lagler, our set designer, and Art Fisher, getting lights sent in by air from France, England, and other parts of Germany. Rene located five hundred American flags and two fighter-bombers. After moving the stage inside, which took hours, he and his team draped the hangar with the flags and set two airplanes in it. The finished result was the best we could come up with, but not really in keeping with the color schemes we had selected in our costuming.

Nonetheless, it was show business. You've got to do what you've got to do to put on the show. By 7:00 A.M. we had lights and a set.

The energy was crazy. I loved it. Lights, camera, action! Girls in tap shoes, cables, racks of costumes wheeling by.

At 10:00 A.M. I went in to get my makeup done by Bjorn, my dear and loyal friend. Regardless of my fatigue and lack of sleep, Bjorn could work wonders. He was incredibly talented, and if need be, he would just paint a face on me.

I could tell he'd been using drugs. Oh, God! I thought.

"Hi, baby doll," Bjorn said in his baby-boy voice. "Did you bring any hairpins?"

"Me?" I asked. "You're supposed to bring everything!" He'd forgotten pins, a hairbrush, and half of his makeup. Not to worry, I thought. He'll figure something out.

At 12:30 I was ready, dressed and looking good. The music started and out danced thirty of the most fabulous-looking dancers from Hollywood. The soldiers went wild. I had never heard the sound of fifty thousand screaming voices before. The adrenaline pumped through me with electric force. My feet were moving faster than my mind.

"He's a boogie-woogie bugle boy from Company B!" we were singing and tapping. The screams from the soldiers were deafening. Everything went great. Susan Anton and I sang a song about dumb blonds not being so dumb. The Pointer Sisters sang

"American Music" and "I'm So Excited." Jonathan Winters came out holding an airplane propeller and ad-libbed a bit with me about his plane coming down and this being all that was left. But then the Pointer Sisters and I were in the middle of doing "Bump It with a Trumpet," a burlesque comedy number from *Gypsy*, when suddenly the hangar went dark. I had been warned of a possible bomb scare before the show, but I hadn't thought much about it, because bomb-sniffing dogs were everywhere and sharpshooters were placed in the rafters with M-16s for our protection.

Suddenly we were all thrown to the floor, then scooted out of the hangar. I sat in a freezing room dressed in a large roll-away skirt, on wheels, with concertinas hanging from my breasts for six hours. (Concertinas are like small accordions.) I was afraid to take the costume off because I kept thinking that the power would come back on at any minute. I was sewn into a skintight corset that would have taken a half hour to take off and another half hour to be sewn back on. It was excruciatingly uncomfortable. I had stomach cramps and leg cramps and felt numb from the cold. The generators had blown, and Alan was now on the phone to France, England, and parts of Germany to fly in a new generator.

Our audience had evaporated, and the magic was gone from the air. While I sat in the icy room, a mirror fell off the wall and broke on my head and my back. Miraculously, it didn't hurt me or cut me; nonetheless, it added to the tension. The pressure of not finishing the show was enormous. This was a million-dollar show paid for by CBS. If we didn't deliver, we owed them.

At 10:00 P.M. the lights went back on. The Pointer Sisters were cranky and tired from sitting around so long in the cold and without decent food. I felt like a frozen Popsicle. We rounded up a ragtag group of a couple of hundred soldiers and kept moving them around to look like we still had a big audience.

I was exhausted. After finishing in the wee hours, I flopped into bed. The next day, we were scheduled to do a USO show in Baden-Baden.

———

The pressure continued. Every day another city, and every night another bomb threat. The Bader-Meinhof gang was on our tail.

The Bader-Meinhof gang was a faction of German right-wing ultranationalist terrorists looking to get publicity. If they could knock off a little blond American star who was entertaining the poor lonely U.S. soldiers, they could get a lot of attention.

So, I was their target of the moment. I had the protection of the U.S. Army, but nonetheless, changing cars in the middle of the Autobahn to throw them off was disconcerting and scary. I was a bundle of nerves and so tired I couldn't sleep. I had lost ten pounds. Ret Turner was frantically altering gowns.

By day we traveled, by night we performed. In every new city we were met by the bomb squad and given our instructions. I was worn out. The pressure was wearing all of us down. Art Fisher put his arms around Alan and cried from fatigue.

On the ninth day, we arrived late to Frankfurt. The hangar in which we were to perform was bulging with impatient soldiers. They had been waiting for hours and they wanted a show. Like puppies wanting the nipple, they were hungry. They demanded gratification.

"Miss Somers?"

"Yes," I said wearily.

"I'm from the antiterrorist bomb squad, and we have every reason to believe a bomb has been planted somewhere in this hangar tonight. We've searched with our trained bomb-sniffing dogs and haven't found it, but, Miss Somers, if the bomb goes off, I want you to look for any of us who are wearing these yellow tags." He pointed to his shirt pocket. "We'll get you out first. Have a good show."

"If the bomb goes off?" I repeated, in shock. There was no way to cancel. The soldiers were banging on the stage and hooting for the show to start.

"Let's not do the show," Alan said protectively. "It's not worth dying over."

"I can't cancel," I said, protesting. "It wouldn't be right." I was emphatic.

My legs felt wobbly as I walked onstage. It was surreal. I was "there," but I wasn't . . . it was like a floating sensation. The soldiers looked fake, grotesque, like characters in *Cabaret*. The scene looked like a mental asylum, or maybe I was just going crazy.

"I can't do any more shows," I cried to Alan after the performance. "I can't do the last show tomorrow."

"You don't have to," he said comfortingly. "I'll cancel and take you home." I loved him. He was always concerned about taking care of me.

The next evening as we were packing our things to leave Germany, we heard a flash news report. The Bader-Meinhof gang had claimed responsibility for a bomb that had gone off near a hangar at the U.S. Air Force base in Mainz. Luckily, the hangar was empty because we had canceled. We had been scheduled to do our show that afternoon in that hangar in Mainz! I was stunned. Somebody "up there" was obviously looking out for us.

Two weeks after we delivered the final edited show, CBS put it on the air. They had a slot to fill and my special would do the job. It gave me no time to set up any promotion. Before *Suzanne Somers and 6,000 Sailors*, I had been featured on the cover of *People*. Without promotion, the public wouldn't even know it was on. When the show aired two weeks later, it came and went, which was too bad, because it was a good show. But nobody knew it was on. Because it was not a ratings sensation, my next scheduled special was canceled. My star was fizzling. It was a big letdown.

———

For the next two years I sat around. Doors were closed everywhere. The money stopped also. Luckily, with Alan's good management, he had protected our remaining finances. He had invested wisely and we were getting good returns on our investments.

I took whatever jobs came my way. I was booked into the Holiday House outside of Pittsburgh. It was a real dump with a boozy clientele. My dressing room was boiling hot and was situated next to the kitchen, so the smell of garbage permeated the entire backstage area. It was a long way from the luxury to which I had grown accustomed, but it was work. I was learning and growing. I still had the visibility from *Three's Company*, which gave me entrée to headline at clubs, even if they were crummy.

The audience at the first show at the Holiday House consisted of a group of football players from the Pittsburgh Steelers. It was off-season and they were feeling no pain. The booze was flowing like water. I kept feeling a drip, drip, drip on my head and found out later that the toilet was directly above the stage; every time someone flushed, water would drip onto the stage. My dancer, Barry, slipped in the puddle and injured his ankle. Between shows there was a fight in the parking lot and someone was knifed. At the second show that evening, I walked out to twenty-five people. There were more people onstage than in the audience.

At another gig in Reno, my opening act was a greased-pig contest. A bunch of drunk guys chased after little piglets in the mud. I felt sorry for the little pigs. I thought the people cheering were the real pigs. But I had been hired to do a job, and I was a professional.

In Reno, another opening act I had was Bertha the dancing elephant. Every night before I went on, I would wait in the wings until Bertha finished "The Mexican Hat Dance" wearing a little sombrero. I would make eye contact with her while she was dancing, and this was not a happy elephant. She knew the sombrero was dumb. Two years later I read that she had killed her trainer.

It was a long, long way from Stavros Niarchos's yacht.

TWENTY-SEVEN

Alan and I started spending more and more time in the desert. There's something about the heat and the silence that is spiritual and healing. My feelings of love and commitment to Alan deepened; yet we still had issues looming around us that needed resolution.

Leslie was on track and back at Parsons School of Design at the top of her class. By now, the change in Leslie was amazing, and this change had a dramatic effect on Alan's temperament. A softness infiltrated his personality. Leslie's anger was also gone, and so was her resistance to me. A new person had emerged. I had never realized the depth of Leslie's humor. It was a quality I'd always enjoyed about her father—a take on human behavior that is rich with knowing. Leslie's humor isn't about jokes. It's her outlook on life. Her good heart emerged in her "well" state. Spending time with Leslie had once been a chore for me; now it was a joy. Our Sunday dinners were filled with laughter and ease. I looked forward to having her come to our home. The pain had been worth it for all of us. Because of Leslie's problems, the air had cleared in our family. We had been forced to face our feelings about one another. We had learned to listen; and we were able to hear the music in one another's hearts.

Leslie had always been an incredible artist. Even throughout her difficult period, it was obvious to her instructors at Parsons that she was exceptionally talented.

After her recovery, they welcomed her back with open arms. She immediately found her groove again. She began sketching the most amazing designs, the kinds of clothes and gowns you wish you could find when shopping for that one incredible thing. Two of her designs were featured in the annual school fashion show, which was hosted by Jean-Louis, the famous designer who had made Marilyn Monroe's gowns. I felt happy for Leslie when the room applauded enthusiastically as the models sashayed down the runway in her outfits. Alan had tears in his eyes; so did her mother. Leslie deserved it. She had come so far. We were all truly proud of her success, both personally and professionally.

We had all grown emotionally as a result of her experience. Leslie and I began to connect on a level that I doubt would have been possible had we not had this shared opportunity. A negative became a positive. It became clear that the elements of a truly loving relationship are listening and hearing. We were learning, but it's a skill that requires constant work. We needed to stay alert and not allow ourselves to revert to old behaviors. Without constant diligence, it would be easy to forget the progress that had been made. It was vital that we moved forward emotionally.

———

Despite the fact that I was not working and was still perceived as a "fallen sitcom star" soon to be on the "dinner theater circuit," I didn't see myself that way. I had this gnawing feeling that I had only passed through phase one of my career. In my mind I saw myself as someone entirely new. I couldn't quite explain the feeling, but a sense of positiveness was with me. It was almost as though, subliminally, I had given myself a time-out to rethink my career.

Until now my personal and professional success had been devoid of meaning. I wanted to find a way to put my learned information out and impact people positively. That I was thinking this way was a clue to my newfound strength. I survived a brutal childhood and I survived being publicly dumped from the number one show in America, and I was okay with it. Life went on. As a family, we were in various stages of healing, but we were healing. I had "picked myself up, dusted myself off," and was ready to start all over again. Thus far, my experiences forced me to grow. I had been kicked around, but I didn't despair. I was ready to try again; and, somehow, I knew I would figure out how.

———

In 1984 Alan got a call from the Las Vegas Hilton asking if I would star in their big stage extravaganza, "The Moulin Rouge." It was a six-month offer—overwhelming to imagine, and it was the first offer of substance I had had in a long time. I was working clubs here and there, but nothing steady. The Hilton was offering decent money, but not the kind of dollars floating around in the '70s. Unfortunately, there was a problem with "The Moulin Rouge." It was a big, fat, expensive flop. It was a great show that bombarded the senses with dancers, sets, incredible costumes, nudity, waterfalls, airplanes, jugglers, dog acts, and, of course, the big finale, "The Can Can." But nobody came. There was no focus. It needed a star, a recognizable name on the marquee to pull people in.

Henri Lewin, the president of the hotel, spent millions launching the show and he couldn't even give away tickets. It was a disaster, and his job was in jeopardy because of his error.

Alan and I flew to Las Vegas to meet with Henri. I wasn't sure this was a good move for me careerwise, but my options were slim. I was used to having my own stage show that we produced ourselves. How would I fit into a big production show?

We arrived at the Las Vegas Hilton on a hot, dusty midsummer afternoon and were immediately escorted by private elevator to Henri's office atop the hotel. Henri was a showy kind of man. He reminded me of Colonel Klink on *Hogan's Heroes*. He was six-tyish, tall with perfect posture, and immaculately dressed. His suit was cut to perfection. The French cuffs on his shirt had his initials embroidered on them. There was a yellow silk handker-chief stuffed just so in his upper suit pocket, which matched magnificently with his yellow-and-navy striped silk tie.

His office was large and impressive. Every tabletop was cov-ered with pictures featuring Henri with every famous person imaginable: Muhammad Ali, Sugar Ray Robinson, President Nixon, Elvis Presley, Barbra Streisand. The far walls were lined with lighted thick glass shelves featuring Henri's extensive col-lection of Baccarat and Lalique crystal.

Large picture windows overlooked the Las Vegas strip and the mountains beyond. It felt like the top of the world; and as the nation's largest hotel at that time, boasting five thousand rooms, it was awe-inspiring.

After a white-jacketed waiter asked what we would like to drink, we sat down to talk business. Henri was born in Germany, and although he had become American in every way, after twenty-five years in this country his accent had not left him. "Soosan," he called me. "I think you and I could be big assets to von anodder."

"Oh, yeah?" I said, not understanding.

He continued. "You haven't worked ze last couple of years, and I think ze people are veady to receive you again. Dey realize dat doze odder girls in ze apartment didn't click. I used to vatch ze show, but I don't vant to see it no more. I've got a great show dat no von is coming to because I have no bait!"

"Well, I feel like some kind of fish; like a trout or something," I said, laughing.

"See, dat's vat I like about you. You're funny. You should be in front of ze people."

We talked for over an hour, and then I said, "Let Alan and me go home and discuss your proposal, and we'll let you know in a day or two."

"Good," Henri said, smiling. "Dis could be very good." Then we left.

Later that night, as Alan and I lay in our bed, he said, "I think you should do it. If it succeeds, you'll be perceived as saving the showroom; and if you fail, it's a secret-service job, and no one will ever know you were even there."

"I know," I said, "but there's a lot to think about. What about the kids? We're going to have to move to Vegas for the next six months."

"Don't worry," Alan said assuredly. "We'll bring them there on weekends and vacations. They'll love it! It will be a great adventure. Besides, I think you'll succeed. It's a great format for you. We'll wrap this show around your talents until it fits like a glove," he said enthusiastically. "It'll be you and your eighty dancers. You'll have the biggest show in America." We decided to do it.

Rehearsals began almost immediately. Their original show was dismantled and rewritten to accommodate my personality. The Hilton stage crew built a huge locomotive train and a train station. The opening number was filled with people at the station dancing with anticipation.

"She's coming, she's coming, she's coming to-ni-i-i-i-i-i-te," they sang.

Then a big red caboose arrived and I was on the back deck, like all the presidents I had seen on the TV news, campaigning at whistle-stops. I waved to the excited crowd of onlookers, wearing a scrumptious white pin-striped suit with silver bugle beads. My platinum blond hair was piled under a big white pin-striped picture hat; I carried a white fox muff and showed legs for days. It was quite an entrance.

I had only one clause in my contract: No one would ever be topless or nude when I was onstage because I was afraid that would cheapen my performance. It was a personal decision that made me feel more comfortable.

Rehearsals were fun. I enjoyed being back onstage, and the rest of the cast hoped I would bring in the audiences. Their jobs were at stake. A lot of the dancers were single mothers working nights so they could give their children some semblance of a normal life. Most of them were young, but hard times and not enough sleep had aged them beyond their years. I remembered the loneliness and pressure of single motherhood and could relate.

After the opening number, I had only forty seconds to change into Ret Turner's gorgeous, "nude," beaded, skintight gown with a long flowing cape that blew behind me like a soft fluffy cloud.

"Heaven, I'm in heaven," I sang, while dancing down thirty-six stairs lined with thirty male dancers, fifteen on each side, in white top hats and tails.

The audience would be bombarded with one incredible number after another. Waterfalls, sacrificial virgins being burned at the altar, and mock airplanes would roll out in front of the astonished crowd. Just when they thought they'd seen it all, a huge volcano would erupt before them, blowing dancers out of its core. They would tumble down the sides of this make-believe mountain like human running lava.

Then it would be my time to do the "star turn"—thirty-five minutes in the middle of the two-hour production gave me a chance to connect with the audience.

Walter Painter helped me put this part together. "They'll be primed and ready," he said, "like foreplay. So far in the show it's been one big high-energy number after another. Now we'll roll back the volcano and bring down a crystal curtain, and simultaneously the live orchestra will come up from the basement on a hydraulic lift. We'll roll you out in your electric blue beaded gown lying on a huge grand piano singing Barry Manilow's 'I Was a Fool to Let You Go.' It'll create a complete mood change."

I love the creative challenge of keeping an audience entranced. In rehearsals I could almost feel the imagined audience relax and give in to their seats. It was a chance for them to take a deep breath, like a cigarette after sex. We dimmed the lights to soft and smoky. The brass section played in tight unison, smooth, silky sounds. The trombone slides went in and out like breath itself until the whole room caught the rhythm and sexiness of the mellow sounds. Then I slipped off the piano, with my gown caressing my ankles, and walked into the audience to choose a gentleman whom I could sing to.

Bringing a man from the audience onstage was my idea. It was a bit that always worked in my own act. "What is your name?" I'd ask. "What do you do? How long have you been married? How many kids do you have?" Inevitably the guy could never remember the answer to any of these questions. The audience would howl with laughter. They related to the man's nervousness and they connected with me for making him comfortable. Walter wasn't sure if it would work in this arena because the room was so big (eighteen hundred seats). He thought it brought too much reality to the fantasy. Luckily, I turned out to be right. They loved it.

For the big finale, I wore a long, red, beaded gown and a huge diamond headdress and rode out to take my bow on Tanya the dancing elephant.

———

Opening night brought the usual jitters, but Alan kept assuring me that no matter what, I couldn't lose. I hoped he was right.

"It's sold out!" screamed Henri as he ran into my dressing room. I was finishing getting ready for my opening. "Not only dat, dey're already lined up clear to ze back of ze casino for ze midnight show!"

It was exciting. Riding onto that football-field-sized stage opening night waving to the sold-out house from the mock caboose was a thrill I'll never forget. The audience would not stop applauding. It was as though they were saying, "Welcome back. We missed you." I was overcome with emotion. I thought I had been forgotten and that they had already moved on to the next blond. During the period between my leaving *Three's Company* and this night, I thought I had gotten what I deserved and that what my father had always told me was true—I was a worthless piece of shit. I had felt betrayed and abandoned by the public, but tonight they were saying otherwise. "Entertain us!" they were telling me by their continuing clapping. "Make us feel good!" In that moment, I realized many things. I was doing the job I was supposed to do, and never again would I allow myself to work in only one arena. When the television doors closed on me, I felt lost and abandoned. Tonight I realized that only I could create my future. Never again would I put myself at the mercy and whims of other people. I would branch out and diversify. I would be multidimensional. I would have many things going for me. If one area dried up, I would simply move on to the next. I would never feel sorry for myself again. From now on, I would always look at every negative as my opportunity for growth. In that applause, on that thrilling opening night, I grew up.

The audience loved the show. It was old-fashioned and wonderful, a big Busby Berkeley–type variety show like the ones they did in the '30s.

A STAR IS BORN declared the Las Vegas papers the next day. SUZANNE IS BACK said another. The reviewers loved it and there hadn't even been a single mention of *Three's Company*. I had moved beyond that show. I had shed the burden of my low self-esteem.

Night after night the house was full. Tony Orlando called me from the MGM one night. "What are you guys doing up there?" he asked. "Can't you share some of those audiences?" I laughed. I was having a ball. Every night for six months I did two two-hour shows. Henri asked me to sign on for another six months.

I hesitated for a moment, wondering if my health would hold up. I had already lost seventeen pounds. Once again Ret Turner was busy altering all the gowns to skintight perfection.

My reluctance made Henri nervous. He was pacing back and forth in his office. "I'll double your salary," he blurted, "and you can have unlimited use of ze Hilton jet anytime you vant."

"I can't continue working seven nights a week," I told Henri. "I feel exhausted all the time, and I've lost so much weight, I'm starting to wear pants under my gowns to make me look fatter. Fourteen shows a week is too much for anyone."

"I know, I know," Henri said hurriedly. "I figured you vould ask for a night off, so ve'll put ze understudy in ze Monday nights."

Done! We launched a whole new show. The Hilton put up ninety-two billboards in and around Las Vegas announcing my extended stay "By Popular Demand."

Most weekends we would fly Bruce, Stephen, and Leslie to Las Vegas. We all loved our Vegas experience. Besides having access to the Hilton jet, we had unlimited use of the Hilton yacht. It was a very large cabin cruiser with space for more than a hundred people. The hotel kept it moored on Lake Mead. As often as three times a week, we cruised the lake with lunches catered by a staff who was there solely to satisfy our every whim. Lake Mead, the entrance to the magnificent Grand Canyon, was a beautiful blue pool caught in a bowl of jagged red stone. Our kids dove from the side of the yacht into the clean, clear, midnight blue water of this gorgeous lake.

My life was taking form. I loved being together as a family. I loved the safety and security that we were all finally feeling. I had stopped being fake around both Leslie and Stephen, and I was astounded at the healing effect of not pretending.

As much as I enjoyed the show, it did not compare with the profound experience we were having as a blended family. Honesty and a lack of falseness put us on track. The barriers among us were slowly but surely evaporating. In my nightly prayers, I still asked that the final curtain between Alan and Bruce be lifted. Yet as I fell into sleep each night, I was sure I heard a reassuring whisper in my ear. "Have patience and faith," it seemed to say. "It will all come as you want when it is time."

I believed my prayers would eventually be answered and, as I wrapped my naked body into the form of my husband, I was thankful I could feel and be aware of such a deep and profound sense of peacefulness and hope.

———

The new show opened with rave reviews and the sold-out performances continued. The Hilton now opened the balcony for the first time since Elvis had appeared on the same stage. It had been used for storage in the interim.

Colonel Tom Parker, Elvis's manager, showed up at my dressing room one night during our seventh successful month, and from that night on, he became a permanent fixture. It was nostalgic for him, and he and Alan became good friends. They talked for hours every night. The Colonel was a sweet old guy who had been robbed of his power by the tragic and premature death of his one and only legendary client. Time had taken its toll on him. He walked with the aid of a cane, which was necessary to assist him in carrying around the hundred or so pounds of excess weight on knees that were no longer able to support him. I had Elvis's old dressing room, and I would wonder about him as I sat in the makeup chair turning myself into "her." He had sat in this same spot so many times before. I didn't have the room redecorated, which was offered, because I enjoyed the nostalgia of the '60s-looking decor and the thought that Elvis had hung out on this same furniture. I was aware that I was having a very different experience in this room than Elvis had had. What was it that had brought him such pain that neither sold-out adoring, screaming audiences nor legendary success could cure?

The messages of that dressing room were clear. If you are your accomplishments, and nothing else is meaningful in your life, it leaves an emptiness, a meaninglessness, a focus on everything other than your self. You fear that without all the trappings, you would be exposed and you wouldn't be enough. Elvis abused drugs to erase that pain. My dad abused alcohol. I abused the truth. I lied about my reality to make myself appear better than I thought I was. That was my drug. Lying took away my pain. It was the fear of exposure behind the pain, like the famous Peggy Lee song "Is That All There Is?"

This time around would be different for me. "I" was not this show. This show was only one small expression of myself. When it was over, I would move on. There would be something else. Alan and I were a real working team. Even though Henri ran the hotel, we produced my show. We decided on all the elements. I was no longer an appendage of *Three's Company*. We were in charge, and I was in control of my life, personally and professionally.

———

During this time, I became extremely attached to Tanya the elephant. She was the first animal to whom I had ever felt a spiritual connection. She was a friend. We worked together, played together between acts—she doing her various tricks, for which I would reward her with a loaf of bread, the equivalent of a cracker to us. We even walked to our vehicles together each night. She was also reliable. Like clockwork, she would appear at my dressing room door each night, dancing in place as if to say, "Come on, let's go!" I found myself talking to her as though having an elephant at the door was normal.

"Okay, Tanya," I'd say, "just a minute." Then we'd get into the oversize elevator, she in her jeweled headdress and I in my gown and matching jeweled headdress. Every night it was the same routine. We'd reach the stage, and while I chatted backstage with the dancers, Tanya would wait in the wings for our music cue. Five minutes before we were to go onstage, she would come over to me and get down on one knee so I could easily climb onto her back. If I didn't get on right away, she'd stand up and dance in place impatiently. I was supposed to give her a little tap with my foot when the music hit our cue, but it wasn't necessary. Tanya heard it before me. She'd strut onto the stage and prance around in a circle, and then at the edge of the stage, she'd rear back on her hind legs to receive her applause. Then, gently, gently, she'd come down on her front legs and tuck them underneath so I could easily slide off and take my bow.

After the show, I'd change into my street clothes, she'd change out of her jeweled headdress and velvet saddle, and together, like two old gypsies, we'd take the elevator to the back loading dock. Every night, before getting into her trainer's truck, she'd have one big hysterically happy run around the parking lot, like a kid at the end of the school day. She'd trumpet and gallop and then obediently walk to her truck and go home for a good night's rest.

It was through Tanya that I realized the incredible connection we all have with one another. I loved her as I have loved others in my life. At Christmas, Alan and I gave her a bottle of vodka, which she picked up with her trunk and drank in a few gulps. It had the same effect on her large body that a glass of wine would have on us; and she loved it. Often, she would pinch my breast or my butt with her trunk like a naughty little girl.

Whenever we had fruit left on the hospitality tray in my dressing room, we'd invite Tanya to finish it. Alan and I would laugh watching her wiggle her large body through the door. Sometimes on my day off, we'd go to her house, which was on the outskirts of Las Vegas, to watch her run and play with her tractor tires and outdoor shower. She was a great friend. I could count on her, and I knew she'd take care of me when I was in her presence. Tanya was a lesson in trust. The most important thing we have as human beings is trust, knowing we can count on those whom we love. If you can count on one hand those you know you can depend upon, you are lucky.

—

Henri tried unsuccessfully to get me back to seven nights a week. The Monday night show was dying. They got only a handful of unsuspecting audience members.

"Henri," I said, "it's very short-sighted of you to try to work me seven nights a week. I'll die of exhaustion and then what will you do?"

"I know, Soosan," he said. "I guess ve'll close ze showroom on Mondays."

The first year led to the second year and the audiences kept coming. Sunday night was the only night I would or could socialize. After my second show, we'd visit with the other performers who were in town. Frank Sinatra always had something going on. "Hello, baby," Frank would say when we walked into his dressing room. Jerry Lewis, Sammy Davis, Jr., Lionel Ritchie, Julio Iglesias, Rodney Dangerfield, Robert Goulet, and George Carlin were just a few of the entertainers whose paths we crossed during this time. I was one of the few women filling a showroom, and I loved being the toast of the town. We built a beautiful adobe ranch on the outskirts of Las Vegas, moved out of the Hilton Hotel, and settled in for a long stay.

Stephen and Bruce loved the new house. It was in the middle of a large, open, empty stretch of raw desert. We had chickens, ducks, rabbits (wild and domestic), and two pet geese named

Jake and Minnie. Jake and Alan became pals and Jake appointed himself official caretaker to Alan. Anyone who came near Alan had to earn Jake's trust first. Alan would sit out back on the little bridge over the pond pouring handfuls of water over Jake's head in the scorching desert heat. Jake loved it and would bob his head up and down in appreciation. Alan has always had a connection with animals. They love him. I loved looking out the back window and seeing Alan and Jake together. Every morning when we awoke, Jake would be standing at the glass doors of our bedroom looking at us, patiently waiting for us to wake up. You had to smile seeing his long neck and his bobbing head as if he were saying, "Get up! Get up! Let's play!"

In the winter, Bruce, Stephen, and Leslie skied regularly on Mount Charleston, which was a fifteen-minute drive up the mountain from our home. In the summer, they Jet-Skied on Lake Mead. They roamed the open desert and played with the animals on our property. The pool was always warm, thanks to solar heating, and the house was laid out in that Southwestern adobe fashion where everyone had a wing and a garden to themselves.

We filled the other bedrooms with weekend guests. Lunch became the focal point of our daily gatherings before my afternoon nap. The pace of two nightly two-hour shows six days a week required discipline on my part. I loved our desert life and its various facets—the home and family by day; and by night, a generous dose of glamour and excitement.

In 1986, several events happened that altered the course of my life forever. For starters, I was named "Female Entertainer of the Year." Frank Sinatra was named "Male Entertainer of the Year." It was an incredible moment for me. Five years earlier I had been dumped and labeled a "has-been." My roller-coaster ride seemed to be over. I had had my "place in the sun," and then a black cloud came over my life. As I received my award, I could feel the sun shining on me once again. I triumphed over adversity and had come out of it stronger and independent. I felt proud of myself. Awards really mean nothing. They come and are quickly forgotten. But the "work" it took to reach this moment when the statuette was placed in my hands was my triumph. I remembered when Frank Sinatra had once told me, "Don't despair." I hadn't! I took my adversity and I turned it around. I forced it to make me stronger; and inherent in my struggle, I found the joy of live performance. The absence of videotape and the lack of a safety net gave me focus and resolve night after night to give one hundred percent to a real, live audience.

The second event of the year was more profound. I told Henri I needed to take a month off. It had been almost three years of working nightly and flying our children to their new home base in Las Vegas on weekends to keep us operating as a family. Weekends, holidays, and summer vacations were mostly spent together at the ranch. I grew my own vegetables, plucked figs from our trees along with apricots and almonds, and gathered armloads of wildflowers to put in beautiful crocks around the house. We took long drives in the desert to watch for wild horses. It was always a thrill to see a herd gallop by, led by a magnificent stallion, his mane blowing in the wind. By day I lived a serene and calm life, and by night I would put on my stage makeup, crimp my blond hair into a wild yellow lioness mane, and become "her." I went to sleep at 4:00 A.M. and got up at 11:00 A.M., yet somehow I found a balance. My daily life was far removed from the "strip" and all its neon lights. Life at the ranch was shared with coyotes, desert burros, and the occasional rattler. The night brought costumes, music, excitement, and the occasional rattler of the human sort. But it was the days alone in the serenity of the desert when my mind began to calm itself and reflect.

That November, Alan and I took a two-week vacation in Santa Fe, New Mexico. Within an hour of our arrival, I felt connected to that part of the earth in a way I had never before experienced. I was amazed, having never been to Santa Fe, that the home Alan and I had built in Las Vegas mirrored those authentic adobes of the Southwest. Every day we put on our hiking boots to explore some new and wondrous part of this region—ruins, petroglyphs, shards of pottery, abandoned remains of a life that once was. It stirred up a new part of my soul. It was light-years away from my show at the Hilton. Being in New Mexico awakened a new part of me, as though from a deep, peaceful sleep. It was a wonderful place. The smell of mesquite filled the air; fajitas were cooking in the town square; Navajo, Hopi, and Apache mingled with Spanish and American sensibilities; a mélange of cultures, tastes, and smells, so pungent that the freshness of it all exhausted my senses.

One morning we decided to explore the cliff dwellings of Bandolier. They are the original "condos" built two thousand years ago by the Anasazi Indians as shelter and protection from weather, predators, and enemies. The caves were dug into the mountainside on top of one another, linked with an intricate series of paths and ladders.

Alan and I were all alone, not a soul to be seen. Alan went on ahead of me to explore, but I lingered on the ledge of a cave that attracted me deeply. There was a window and a doorway and the back wall of the cave was blackened by the fire that had once warmed the families who inhabited this same space. The front of the cave had a small ledge overlooking an untouched vista, and it was here my life was to take its most important turn.

I was deeply moved just being in this setting. Time seemed suspended. Cross-legged, I looked out at the beauty before me for what seemed like hours. The morning sun baked at the core of my being, and I felt connected to all those before me who had sat in this very same place looking at this very same sight.

That night I woke from a sound sleep at three o'clock in the morning, picked up a pen and paper, and began to write. I had never done this before, yet hours and pages passed with words gurgling out of me like a running brook. Five hours later, Alan awoke and groggily asked what I was doing. As though shaken from a deep sleep, I replied, "I don't know." I read him the words that flowed from my soul and began to "feel" all that I was and had been. With each page, heavy sobs of release came from a place so deep inside me that I had not known of its existence.

All the memories of my childhood flooded back like a book already written. The screaming, the yelling, the hiding in the closet, my mother's anguished cries coming from the other room, the violence, the craziness, the fear.

It was overwhelming fear I was witnessing—watching a little girl unprotected and unsafe, but it was me. All my life I had pushed the memories away. Yet all my life I had been driven by these memories, looking for whatever it was inside that needed filling. If I could just find the wound, I could start the healing. But it had remained deep and hidden; and like a festering wound, it had infected my life with the poisons and toxins of sorrow, guilt, shame, and low self-esteem.

I realized I was on a journey. I was being given the chance to make the corrections necessary to evolve to another level as a person. I was giving myself an opportunity to find "me" in all my glory—the good and the bad—the results of my choices. The only thing asked of me was complete and total honesty.

Upon returning home to Las Vegas, I started writing about my childhood ten hours a day for the next year. The book was to become *Keeping Secrets.* I'm sure I would have written twenty hours a day, but my nightly show demanded my presence.

I felt as though I were taking notes from someone; a presence on my shoulder was whispering gently yet emphatically, the truth welling up from deep inside me. At times, I wanted to stop because the memories became more and more painful, but the voice held me and comforted me until the fear passed and I found strength to go on.

The fear was more than facing myself. It also demanded that I face those I loved the most, and with that came risk. In telling the truth, I could lose everyone I loved.

When I was growing up, my family never discussed our awful reality. Night after night we were terrorized by my father's drunkenness. Yet every morning the memory of the previous night's events was put away so we could forget and pretend life wasn't really as it was. Each of us suffered in silence and guessed at the reasons for the lives we were living. I thought that if I could be better, smarter, prettier, or more talented, maybe I would deserve a happy life. But I knew I had been born bad.

As I wrote and felt the torture of this little girl's soul, I wanted to protect her. I wanted to tell her she had done nothing wrong. She had not been born bad. She was a beautiful person, born pure and innocent, and her life was a journey leading to opportunity. But patience was required.

In writing the book, clarity took its form. The puzzle was piecing itself together. Each day another breakthrough. Each day brought me another step closer to understanding. I was reliving my past in all its darkness, and with it came the light of understanding. All my choices—good and bad—were part of my makeup. My job was to correct that which I didn't like about myself. I was not a slave to an unfortunate childhood. My childhood was my opportunity to grow spiritually, intellectually, and emotionally. It had been a gift in disguise all along. Suddenly forgiveness was truly in my heart. How could I stay angry at the teacher who had presented me with my greatest opportunity to learn? How could I stay angry with myself now that I realized it wasn't my fault? How could I ever be afraid of truth again, now that it had set me free?

Finally I could emerge as the "me" that had been eluding me all my life. Finally I had found resolution and with it came peace.

Day after day, I completed my task. I was on a mission to exorcise all my old demons. Suddenly my past and present had meaning. The past was the lesson, and the present brought the opportunity to share the story so others might benefit. Without my success, I would not have had a loud enough voice or the kind of visibility to be heard.

With this breakthrough, I was able to embrace my fame. It had meaning; not as defined by others, but as defined by myself. I wanted to do something for humanity and my childhood gave me my opportunity. Now I was able to use my celebrity for something more useful than getting good tables at restaurants.

Producing and marketing myself didn't make me uncomfortable anymore. Instead, I saw celebrity as a privilege. The better known I became, the greater the opportunity to deliver the message. The pull and tug of fame dissipated. For the first time in my entire life, I felt good about me. It had nothing to do with anyone else. Now the past was "out of my way," and I felt excited at a future that was free and clear.

TWENTY-EIGHT

⁂ During my third year at the Las Vegas Hilton, television threw me its first bone since I had left *Three's Company.* The president of Lorimar Television, David Saltzman, called to say they wanted me to star in a new first-run syndicated series called *She's the Sheriff.* To my surprise, I had zero interest in returning to television. I had been very happy the last few years performing live, and this TV show seemed plagued with problems.

Three's Company had been a network show with a big budget and a time slot guaranteed to run every Tuesday at 9:00 P.M. in every city in America. The show being offered me was an experiment. First-run syndication meant that the show would run for the first time in syndication, meaning a different time and a different day in every city, much the way Oprah Winfrey airs her show. In New York, she's on at 4:00 on ABC. In Los Angeles, she's on at 3:00 on ABC, and so on. But everybody knows Oprah's show and knows what it delivers, so people will go out of their way to find out what time it is on. *She's the Sheriff* would be an unknown sitcom with no built-in viewer loyalty. The show would hang on me; and if it failed, it would appear that I had failed.

"No, thank you," I told David. But he was not about to take no for an answer. For weeks Lorimar pursued me. They kept increasing the salary. (When you're not desperate, the work comes.) They sent producers to flatter me, promise me the show would be to my liking, and entice me with extra perks—nice dressing room, a driver, etc.

Finally Alan said, "You need television to feed your personal appearance business. You've been off the air a long time. I think you should take this show. If it succeeds, you'll get the credit for carrying a show by yourself. It could prove valuable."

"And if it fails?" I asked.

"I don't think you will fail," Alan answered.

It meant saying good-bye to a home, a job, and a lifestyle I had come to love. It meant leaving Tanya, which was hardest of all. But after a lot of thought, I decided it was probably time to dive back into the rat race. My life was becoming too comfortable. I was starting to see myself living in this beautiful adobe wonderland with my animals and my best friend, the elephant, forever. Not that it would be a bad life, but creatively, I knew there was more out there for me. My book *Keeping Secrets* would soon be released and television was to be a big part of our promotional strategy. I wanted to be sure that all who needed to hear my story would know about it, and that would require countless public appearances on my part.

My personal growth was like a speeding bullet during this period, and I knew inherently it was time to push the creative envelope. My breakthrough in writing *Keeping Secrets* was rapidly changing me as a person. I realized I had to work at growing every day. It is not just something that happens and then is forgotten. Emotional growth is like a marriage. It needs nurturing, caring, concern, objectivity, and, most of all, honesty. I was surprised at the difficulty of honestly facing my every choice and decision. Do I take the highest thought in each situation? I asked myself. I didn't realize the ease with which I could be less than generous with my thoughts, deeds, and actions. How easily I could slip into gossip and conversation that was not generous. I had to make corrections on myself not only daily but moment by moment as well. But every time I succeeded, every time I took the "high road," I felt a glow, a beam of light that moved me forward. It was in my own best interest to work at being the best person I could be.

———

She's the Sheriff was not how I had wanted to reenter television. I played a single mom whose husband, the sheriff, had died (I never knew how) and somehow she took over his job. My character was Hildy Granger, a strong-willed survivor who accepted her responsibilities as a widow and mother of two. It was not the kind of character that got the laughs like Chrissy Snow; but given time, I felt the public would embrace her as a responsible and decent woman who wanted to do the right things in life. Pat Carroll played my mother and I liked that. She is one of those troupers who can do anything. Unfortunately, her character was never given a reason for being, so she was highly underused in the show. My costar was a wonderful actor named George Wyner, who played a whining, angry, conniving, jealous deputy.

It was 1987 and I was back in Los Angeles, back in the "loop." To the industry, I had disappeared, even though I had been working nonstop in clubs and in Las Vegas. The industry doesn't recognize nightclub success as career success.

It had been the better part of the decade since I was dumped from television, and all those who had been in charge back then were no longer around. Power shifts rapidly in Hollywood. That's why they always say, "Be nice to those you meet on your way up, because you're most likely to run into them on the way down." The street was littered with former executives. *Three's Company* was off the air, and Mickey Ross had tried unsuccessfully to create another hit; but *The Ropers* failed, and the show he created for John Ritter did not last long, either. Almost everyone who had been involved with the success of *Three's Company* was now unemployed, except me. I had let myself be dragged back to television, but if it failed, I would get myself booked on the next stage. Now I was multidimensional. I worked in three arenas—television, the stage, and publishing. I didn't know what *Keeping Secrets* would do for me, but I felt new doors would open as a result. I was happy knowing I had created a career that was not dependent upon waiting for the phone to ring.

Three years at the Hilton had been an exhilarating and, simultaneously, exhausting experience. I weighed ninety-two pounds at the end of the run. I was always cold because of the lack of fat on my body, and my skin and eyes looked drawn without makeup. One night, driving home from work, I said to Alan, "You've got to find a way for me to make a living that doesn't require my presence. I love doing this now; but as I look down the road twenty years from now, I don't think my body will be able to take this kind of punishment."

"I realize that," Alan said. "In fact, I've been thinking about the same thing lately. I'm worried about you. First, I think we need to take some time off, maybe a month or two, to take care of your health. In the meantime, I have an idea about creating a business for you in the fitness field. Let me go to work on it."

I smiled to myself. We were a good team. We were doing this together and I loved that.

Alan continued, "If we could branch out into direct-response marketing, it would further enhance our independence. I want to find a way that we can work for ourselves. I want us to be in control of our lives." I agreed.

She's the Sheriff launched its debut in the fall of 1987. I could tell by the tumultuous applause as I was introduced the night of the first show that the audience was expecting me to be Chrissy. I knew I was not going to give it to them. I hoped they would like me as a new character, but unfortunately they reacted coolly.

After the first few weeks of taping, I got a call from Joan Rivers to guest-host her late-night show while she was on another assignment. It was an incredible opportunity for me. I remembered the days when guest hosts filled in for Johnny Carson. He had recently named Jay Leno as his permanent guest host, so that door would now be closed forever. Filling in on Joan's show on Fox, *The Late Show*, was a thrilling opportunity.

Alan and I were asked to produce it ourselves, which was perfect. Alan is an excellent producer and had a vision as to the type of show we could wrap around my talents. In many ways, it was similar to so many of the programs Alan had starred in and produced in Canada years earlier.

What was frightening to other performers was a piece of cake for me. I had just come off a run of almost fifteen hundred stage shows over the past three years, so I felt comfortable filling in for Joan.

Instead of a monologue, I opened with a tiny baby monkey who was guesting on *She's the Sheriff* that week. He was the sweetest little thing, and while I was singing "It Had to Be You" to him, he kept trying to reach inside my cleavage to nurse. The audience laughed hysterically. I finally stopped the song and said, "The well is dry, honey," and he looked up at me with those big sad eyes. We were off to a good start.

Robin Leach, a good friend, was my first guest, so we had a great time together. It felt like a party in my own home. I was the host, and my job was to make people feel comfortable and have a good time. Perfect format for a "pleaser."

After the show, Barry Diller, the man who had created the Fox network, came to my dressing room and told me I was excellent. I began doing the show on a rotating basis throughout 1987.

Bruce and Leslie were in my dressing room, along with Bruce's new girlfriend, Caroline. I could tell she was important to Bruce. There is a look a son gets in his eye and you know this is the one. Caroline was a beauty—Italian in descent, with olive skin, gorgeous almond-shaped brown eyes, and fabulous wavy hair to her waist. A year earlier at Bruce's twenty-first birthday party, I had made a point of mentioning the beautiful girl with the long hair to Bruce. "We're just good friends," Bruce told me shyly; but I had seen a glimmer in Caroline's eyes that told me otherwise. The fact that he brought her to the taping was also an indicator. He wanted to show off his new girlfriend and, also, he was proud of my accomplishments.

Leslie was now having her first successes as a designer. Madonna had been photographed wearing Leslie's hand-painted Levi's that had been selling at various Los Angeles boutiques. The picture made the cover of *People*, and Leslie's jeans business had taken off. Leslie's adrenaline was running high. She glowed with satisfaction. She was creatively stimulated.

"Les," I said one day on the phone, "would you design something fabulous for me to wear to host Joan Rivers' show?"

"Sure," she said enthusiastically.

And it was a winner—a light sea green satin, spaghetti-strapped, short dress with a pale aqua satin jacket lined in pale pink satin. For the song, she made a crunched pale pink satin stovepipe hat. The next day the phone rang off the hook with people inquiring where they could buy the outfit.

"Great show, Mom," Bruce said.

"Thanks, honey." I was high with excitement. After Barry Diller left, Alan and I hugged each other, laughing. Then I grabbed Bruce and kissed him.

Late-night hosting is traditionally male territory. Joan had pioneered the way, and I had been able to pick up the ball. Alan and I talked excitedly about the possibilities. Maybe I could have a show like this myself. Maybe that's why we had been trudging around the country and staying up late for the past several years. Although Alan was no longer interested in being on camera, producing a show such as this was a good fit for him.

Alan had picked up Bruce and Caroline at the airport earlier that day, but I had not seen Bruce before the show. He seemed quieter than usual, and I figured it was because he was bringing his girlfriend to meet us. "Are you okay?" I asked Bruce. "You seem kind of quiet."

He said, "Fine," but as he answered, his eyes wandered over to Alan. I surmised something must have been said in the car. In all the years Alan and I had been together, the last missing piece was his inability to completely embrace Bruce. It was a source of continuing pain for both Bruce and me. How do you explain to your kid that your husband doesn't like him? I'd given up trying to patch things between them. Bruce had hardened to Alan; but, underneath, he was terribly hurt. He didn't know what he had done. Everyone always liked Bruce. His beautiful smile and his infectious laugh won over the most jaded of people. Yet in his own home, the man I loved, my husband, was not able to see Bruce's beautiful qualities. It came up often in our arguments. In itself it was an argument starter. The subject could ruin an evening. I had tried for years to walk in Alan's shoes in an attempt to understand his indifference to my child. With Bruce away at college, things were easier. We could pretend everything was fine. But his return always provoked something between Alan and me because of Alan's attitude. Then Alan would retreat into silence. To ask him if something was wrong would only make things worse. "Nothing's wrong," he would say tersely. "But if you keep asking me, something will be wrong!" He might as well have said, "Shut up!" In my anger, I would favor Bruce, which only fueled the fire.

Couldn't he see that the progress I had made with Leslie and Stephen had moved us forward as a family, as a couple, as lovers? I was connecting with his children. We were no longer angry; we were learning to respect one another. The closer I got to Alan's children, the closer Alan and I became as husband and wife. Alan appreciated my efforts to make peace with his kids, but he wasn't able to piece the puzzle together for himself. He couldn't open up to Bruce. What was it? I often wondered. Would he fear alienating his own son? I couldn't know, because this one area was closed to my questioning. A perfect and happy time was always subject to ruin if the question came up. I hated being controlled like this. I felt as though I were living in a house divided. Once again, I was running from one side to the other, trying to keep everyone happy. Would it ever end? Maybe I had to accept this as one of the parts of my life over which I had no control. But it was hard not to get angry.

———

Later that evening, after *The Late Show*, Bruce, Caroline, Alan, and I were in the kitchen of our beach house. It had sat empty during the Vegas years, but now we were back, and I wanted to make a great dinner for us and make Caroline feel welcome.

I started boiling water for pasta and took out some fresh garlic, parsley, and pancetta, a salty thin-sliced Italian ham. I was making pasta *a* olio with sautéed pancetta and a green salad.

"Alan, could you go to the wine cellar and bring up a nice bottle of red?" I asked.

When Alan left the room, I questioned Bruce. "Come on, honey. I'm your mother. I know you well. What's the matter?"

"He's an asshole!" Bruce blurted out.

"Why? What happened?" I asked. I was surprised by his volatility.

"I can deal with him treating me badly, but I can't take it if he's rude to Caroline."

I asked him to explain.

"We were in the car and Caroline was trying to be nice and asked how *She's the Sheriff* was doing. Alan said almost like he was irritated, 'What do you mean? The ratings or the critics?' 'Either,' Caroline said. 'Well, the ratings aren't in yet, and who gives a shit what the critics say.' But it was his tone, Mom. Alan spoke to her like she was a fool; like the way he speaks to me most of the time." Bruce continued angrily, "I can't stand it."

I knew that tone of Alan's. I knew how infuriating it could be. So many times in our earlier arguments, I would say to him, "Don't talk to me like I'm a fool. I'm your wife!" It was a controlling device of Alan's. It put him in charge if you let him get away with it.

By the time Alan came back to the kitchen, the mood was tense. I didn't know Caroline well enough to risk having an argument in front of her, so I was rendered mute. This situation recalled all the previous feelings of years gone by. I had done so much work to emerge as my own person, yet I still didn't have a handle on this one.

I sliced the garlic paper-thin, immersing myself in the task. Alan opened the wine, and as he poured glasses for Bruce and Caroline, who also seemed quiet and uncomfortable, he mentioned that Stephen had just sold a building we owned and had earned a commission.

Bruce said sarcastically, "Just for referring a buyer. That's all he had to do?" Bruce was obviously jealous.

Stephen had sold it to his best friend's father and had known up front that the friend's father wanted the building, but he had left out that information when he asked Alan, "If I can find a buyer, could I get the commission?" Bruce's lack of appreciation for Stephen's cleverness irked Alan.

I was sautéing the garlic in olive oil, just until it browned so it wouldn't become bitter.

"If I had done that, you would have been all over me," Bruce shot back.

The pancetta was sizzling in the pan. "I think you're jealous that you didn't think of it," Alan said angrily.

"Maybe I am," Bruce said defensively. "But I know you'd never let me get away with that! Of course, I'm *not* your real son."

"Oh come on; grow up," Alan shouted back, completely denying Bruce's feelings.

"Fuck you! Asshole," Bruce yelled.

It had escalated so quickly. Then Bruce reared back, and as if in slow motion, I watched his closed right fist come from behind his head with the full intent to punch Alan in the face. In an instant Alan grabbed Bruce's trembling fist and held it tight.

"I hate your fucking guts," Bruce yelled in a voice so deep and penetrating I did not even recognize it as my son's.

I stood watching as Alan's hand tightly gripped Bruce's fist. The two people I loved most in the world and I was impotent. I couldn't help either of them. This was a moment they had both created and only they could complete it. I held my hand over my shocked mouth. That moment seemed like an eternity.

"All my life you've treated me like shit. All my life I've felt like dirt in my own house. I hate you. I hate your guts!" Bruce screamed.

"I know," Alan said. "I know."

Bruce now had tears streaming down his face. His fist was still trembling. My own face was wet with tears and so was Caroline's. I felt agony for all of us.

Then Alan released Bruce's fist. "Hit me," he said sincerely. "Hit me if you need to."

Bruce started to cry even more and Alan took him in his arms and held him tightly.

Alan walked Bruce into the living room with his arms tightly wrapped around him.

The pancetta was burnt.

"I'm sorry, Caroline," I said. "I just can't finish cooking dinner." I was shaking.

I went to my room. Caroline went to hers.

Bruce and Alan spent most of the night in the living room releasing a shared lifetime of anger, frustration, and hate. Bruce told Alan all the ways he hated him and how much he hated him. Every wrong done to Bruce by Alan was now thrown back in Alan's face. From the back room of the house, I could hear their heated voices. My heart was pounding with anxiety, but this was between the two of them.

"The problem with us," Alan said hotly to Bruce, "is that we have nothing in common. I hear you on the phone for hours at a time talking to your mother about your English paper. Well, I don't give a shit about your fucking English paper. Nor do I give a fuck about baseball or your fucking bike or your fucking hobbies."

"Fine," Bruce shot back angrily. "So let's not bullshit each other anymore. Let's not even say hello if we don't want to. Let's not try at all. We don't care about each other, so let's stop faking it."

I had prayed they would find resolution that night. Instead, they created a pact. They were not anything to each other any longer. They had only one thing in common, and that was me. Because of that, they agreed to tolerate each other's existence.

It was not the tidy resolution I had wanted. Real life is not necessarily about living happily ever after. I felt let down. The tension was gone, and in its place there was nothing. Nothing.

I didn't understand what they inherently knew. There had been so much anger, agitation, frustration, resentment, and hate between them, the only way to begin again was with a bare slate.

But now, Bruce felt freed, liberated from his pain. He didn't have any relationship with Alan and he felt better. Suddenly, Bruce didn't have Alan thrust upon him.

"We began our relationship by living together, and within a short period I was supposed to think of him as my stepfather?" Bruce explained to me. "We never had a chance."

Their relationship remained in this suspended state for the next few months. In the spring, Bruce had to file a tax return for the first time in his life. He needed advice, so he called Alan.

"It was the first time Alan ever talked to me as a friend," Bruce recalled. "He gave me constructive advice. As silly as it sounds, the first time Alan and I ever bonded was over taxes."

After that, Bruce began asking Alan for business advice. Bruce was setting up his first production company and needed guidance. Alan was there for him every step of the way. Bruce had graduated from Berkeley and was in his second year at the legendary UCLA Film School.

"I have an extra camera you might want," Alan told Bruce one afternoon. "It might help in your directing pursuit."

"It was the respect with which he said it," Bruce told me. "It showed respect for the direction my career was taking. It was very mythical to me," Bruce said. "In that way, gifts are important."

After that, Alan hired Bruce to do several projects for our company. Alan admired Bruce's creativity and professionalism. As I watched the two of them interact, I remembered all the prayers I had said throughout our lives together hoping that Alan and Bruce would find a way to get along.

———

One weekend Bruce and Caroline came to visit us in Palm Springs. It was a wonderful three days, calm and relaxed. We laughed a lot. No one was trying to be anything except comfortable.

That Sunday night, Bruce was in the stone cottage on our property packing his things. Caroline was in the kitchen with me. Unbeknownst to me, Alan had gone to Bruce's cottage to speak with him.

Bruce looked up from his packing and saw Alan standing at the door. "Come in," Bruce said warmly.

Alan was silent for a moment and then said, "This is long overdue, Bruce, but I owe you an apology. I'm very sorry for how I treated you."

Bruce was taken aback. He stood looking at Alan for a moment. Then, with tears in his eyes, he put his arms around Alan and hugged him. "Thank you," Bruce said softly. "Apology accepted."

From that point on, they started loving each other. It came easily. They said so each time they hung up the phone with each other.

"My whole life was validated when Alan came to me in the stone house," Bruce told me. "I didn't know I needed that apology. But I did. It helped me to know that I hadn't been crazy all my life. I had always wondered what I had done. Alan volunteering to apologize was incredibly healing. Finally, we were speaking eye to eye. I felt total respect from him, which meant everything. Growing up, I never had Alan's respect. Because of that, I had always lacked confidence. I didn't know where I stood. When I was able to accept his apology, forgiveness came easily. The man who represented the greatest source of pain in my life has ironically given me the greatest gift.

"I grew up as a result. Today I don't walk on eggshells. Not with him; not with anyone. I went from knowing Alan as someone in whom I would never confide anything to someone who is now an incredibly important role model and confidant.

"Today he is one of my greatest friends. I love him. He is a father to me. Our ability to overcome our differences gives me faith in humanity. We went from hate to love by following an honest path. Because of that night in the kitchen when I told him I hated him, I now know I can face anything perilous in life. I know that if something is worth it, I can find a way to work it out. By going from hate to love with Alan, I now believe that nothing is impossible."

It was the final resolution to our blended family. The last missing link. All my adult life I had been trying to patch the quilt together but the more I tried, the worse it became. Every time I would feel Bruce had been slighted in any way, I would run to him . . . and away from Alan. Instead of soothing and bringing us together, I was pushing the family into enemy camps—my son on one side, my husband on the other. The only solution would have been to choose. But how could I? How can you choose between two such great, yet different, loves? I did not want to live without either of them.

———

I had not been able to comprehend my lack of control. It was another of those situations in life I could not fix. If I had tried to interfere when Alan held Bruce's fist so tightly, I would have taken away their opportunity to resolve the problems in their relationship. It was not for me to solve. Only the two of them could.

And they did.

TWENTY-NINE

Keeping Secrets hit *The New York Times* Best-Seller List immediately.

Our growth as human beings is measured in passages. The author Gail Sheehy regards passages in terms of seven to ten years. Every ten years, we "pass" through another phase of our growth. We change, mature, gain perspective, and move forward as people.

My first ten years were filled with fear. I cowered from everything because of it. I was afraid of vacuum cleaners, marching bands, and my father's driving.

My teen years were filled with sadness and hopelessness.

My twenties were about my low self-esteem and feeling that I was not as good as others.

My thirties brought growth and a desire to be emotionally well.

And my forties brought an unraveling of the confusion along with the realization that the route to wellness is through forgiveness and compassion.

Now as I begin my fifties, I anticipate continued growth, peace, and serenity.

Keeping Secrets definitely signaled the beginning of an important new passage for me. It would completely change my direction as a person and alter the course of my life. Through this experience, I began to realize the importance of turning the arrows of ego away from me.

Publishing *Keeping Secrets* was the most difficult choice I had ever made. Weeks before publication, I had a recurring nightmare that woke me, night after night. I dreamed my father read the book, had a heart attack, and died. In the dream, I arrived at his funeral dressed in black, and as I walked to his coffin, the whole congregation hissed at me. At this point, I always seemed to wake myself up from the incessant, apologetic thrashing.

What astounds me is how drastically I had underestimated my father. He not only allowed me to publicly tell our story, he even gave me his blessing. In many ways, I believe that was his way of making amends. He was not a verbal guy when it came to expressing his feelings.

If I could have found a way to tell my story without mentioning any of my family members, I would have. I was on a personal journey of truth. I wanted to discover how I had been affected by growing up within this disease. I wanted understanding and resolution. I wanted to forgive myself for all the stupid and wrong choices of my life. In finding understanding of myself, I hoped to be able to find forgiveness for my father. Through my writing, I was able to find compassion, not only for my father but for myself as well.

Forgiveness allowed me to let go of the hurt and release the past. Not to forget it, but to allow it to fall into its proper place. I realized that by not forgiving, I was not able to live my life in the moment. I was still expecting my father to make payment for the injuries he had inflicted. I was still bearing a grudge.

In writing about my feelings, I taught myself the importance of having them. They were real and they defined me. In this process, I also learned to believe in myself. I could now find all that I loved in life and follow it. My life had always been about suffering. I now realized life is about joy. The suffering came from not paying attention to the hurt. I had to go back and relive my life to find the hurt and resolve it. I let it go and forgave. I realized that everything is and was exactly as it was meant to be. The greatest gift of all was finding those other people across this country and eventually throughout the world who were starving for clarity, waiting for the answers that would help them unravel the puzzle of their own lives.

I started this next journey of self-discovery on the talk-show circuit. I chose Phil Donahue's show to launch the book tour. I felt that perhaps Phil, being Irish, would have a keen understanding of alcoholism. Somewhere in his family, maybe even in his own life, he might have been exposed to this disease, which some people call "the Irish flu." It seems to run rampant among the Irish and Native Americans. There is some X factor inherent in the genes that creates an allergic condition. Alcoholics are allergic to alcohol. Yet it is the substance they crave the most.

Three weeks before the program, Phil called me and said, "I'd like to have your whole family on my show."

I hesitated. "I don't know, Phil," I answered nervously. "I'm not sure they could take it, but I'll ask them."

After I hung up the phone, I sat staring out the window of my office, trying to imagine what it would be like. What was I afraid of? For sure, I was afraid of the awkwardness between us. It was one thing to read about our family problems, but somehow we could delude ourselves into thinking our story would remain private. Phil Donahue had the number one talk show on the air in 1988, and once the family went on television, it would no longer be private. Would they get hurt? Would my father be chastised? Would I? Would he have that heart attack and die right on television? Would the whole country hiss at me for putting him through the ordeal?

And then the presence, the voice on my shoulder, came through as it always does, asking me what right I had to make choices on their behalf. What gave me that kind of power? I realized it wasn't up to me. How long would it take for me to absorb the lessons I had been learning? It was as if I would take three steps forward and two back.

My only job in life was and is to be honest with myself, to face myself and tell the truth. I was trying to do a good thing with *Keeping Secrets*. I was trying in my small way to create change. Change always involves risk. I had risked my family's love, so far, through the writing and I hadn't lost them. They had given me permission to write. I had interviewed all of them. They were grown-up people with their own right to choose. Why was I still trying to control things by protecting them? "Let it go! Let it go!" I heard the voice say. "Stop trying to control others." The voice was right.

"Hi, Dad," I said on the telephone. "How would you like to be on *Donahue* and talk about the book and our family problems?"

"Oh boy!" he replied; and I feared that he was upset with me. "Wait until I tell my friends at the Senior Center," he finished excitedly.

One by one, each member of my family embraced the idea enthusiastically.

Two weeks later I met my family at Rockefeller Center in New York City. They were calm. I was a wreck. "I want to talk to Phil before the show," I told his assistant nervously.

Moments later, Phil walked into our dressing room. My mother gushed and blushed a beautiful shade of pink. My father greeted him Irishman to Irishman. My sister, Maureen, and my brother Dan were gracious and composed as always. My brother Mike was unable to make eye contact. Everything about this experience was overwhelming to him.

"May I speak to you alone, Phil?" I asked. We went into the hallway. I looked him in the eye and said, "Remember, this is my family."

"I know," he said, understanding.

To my knowledge no celebrities had ever written a book such as mine about people they loved who were still alive. Usually autobiographies are written long after everyone involved is dead, and then the writers are free to call them sons of bitches. I always felt that would have been unfair. The dead have no voice. If I was going to expose us, I wanted to do it this way. If my family didn't like it, they each had the right to say so publicly and make corrections.

"I mean it, Phil! This is my family. Don't mess with them."

"Don't worry," he said gently. "I want their stories and yours. This is not going to be about attack. This is going to be a show about courage and admiration and recovery. Don't worry," he repeated. "I'll take care of everything."

"Thanks," I said softly. I had tears in my eyes as I walked back to our dressing room. I was very nervous.

———

Moments before the program started, we sat together on the dais in those famous chairs in front of a large studio audience with an unimaginably larger audience watching from home. We all held hands, and the energy and love passed among us. Silently I asked God to stay with us and protect us. The audience had no idea why we were there. I sat next to my dad.

"So," Phil began, looking my father right in the eye. "Your name bein' Mahoney might have something to do with your drinking problem, huh?"

Quick as a wink, my dad answered, "Yeah, and my grandmother's name was Donahue!" That was him. That was what kept me loving him through all the bad times. I loved his quick wit. It took a few minutes for the audience laughter to calm down.

Each member of my family had a unique point of view. Each of us had carried our pain differently throughout our lives. It was an opportunity to cleanse and purge. There was still hurt, yet joy, in the recovery not only of my father but of my two brothers and my sister as well. The family had been ravaged by the disease; and although my father and my siblings were sober now, the pain had been stuffed so deeply for so long that emotions were easily triggered.

My brother Dan, who had become sober in 1980, cried when he recalled the violent nights with Dad, and the additional knowledge that his own drinking had disappointed his daughter. My sister cried knowing how close she had come to losing everything, including her life. My mother cried over the wasted years. But it was my brother Mike who broke my heart. He couldn't talk. The tears were so close to his gut that trying to release them choked him. And in the aching silence, his story was told. His posture, his lack of eye contact, his overwhelming grief said everything.

One woman called in and said to my father, "I know who you are. You're the little guy who gets away with all of it because you're funny. Well, I've known men like you, and I don't think you're funny at all."

My dad just sat there looking down at his feet. I wanted to crawl over the chairs and create a barricade of protection around him. My heart ached with the pain of responsibility; but it was Phil who took over.

"Listen," he said to the caller, "how many of us could have a book written with all the negative parts of our lives highlighted and then allow that to be the subject upon which others pass judgment? What we are witnessing here today is a family of integrity and great courage. By their example, they have laid themselves bare so others might be helped. I admire Mr. Mahoney and Suzanne and the whole Mahoney family. They've been to the bowels of life, and they've worked their way back."

At that, the audience applauded for a long time, and as in my childhood fantasy, we were redeemed.

After that, the requests for me to appear on other shows poured in. The *Today* show, *Sally Jessy Raphael*, *The Tonight Show*, and *Good Morning America* asked me to be a guest. While on Larry King's radio show, I had my first opportunity to talk with the public. I realized my story was not unique. The pain and sadness that came back at me through the radio receiver gave me a heartache. As a family, we had not been alone. The common thread in all their stories was unbearable pain and feelings of worthlessness, hopelessness, nothingness. The inability to understand their feelings kept them trapped in their pain.

Letters came in by the thousands. Sackloads of letters. We had a small room that was filled floor to ceiling with nothing but bags of mail. I started the impossible task of trying to answer each one, to tell each writer of my path to happiness. Maybe, by example, they would want to get help.

One night around 3:00 A.M. Alan walked into my office and rubbed my shoulders as I continued to answer letter after letter, each one more painful than the last. "You can't do this," Alan said gently. "This will take all of your time, and you still won't finish. You can do more good by speaking to large groups of people and passing the word that way. You'll kill yourself doing this." He was right.

Finally I realized that each letter represented a person's fourth step as set forth in the Alcoholics Anonymous handbook: a deep, fearless moral and personal inventory of themselves. My book had opened the door for them to release their feelings.

I had already done my part. They now knew that by doing the "work," they could have happiness also. Their letters to me were opportunities to put their feelings on paper, to relive the pain so they could begin to understand how it had ruled their lives. With this understanding and a lot of work, they would find resolution and peace.

I began to receive lecture requests. I had never spoken to large groups of people before. I wasn't sure I could do it. I didn't know if I had enough to say. "Do it," Alan urged. He still supported me in every way. And ever since that awful night when Bruce and Alan had almost come to blows, our lives had changed drastically. I reveled in the joy I now felt at seeing Bruce and Alan interact on a new loving level. They joked and touched and looked into each other's eyes, as if to reassure themselves that the war was really over. It was the answer to my prayers. Gradually, step by step, the obstacles to happiness were evaporating. My personal life was on track. I had realized my dream of a magical union of woman and man, a union of respect and collaboration; of happiness, contented children, and passion. Work was my bonus; but without work, I would still be okay. The freedom of personal happiness allowed me to enjoy the simple things. I found great joy in my herb garden, picking fresh basil to sprinkle over vine-ripened homegrown tomatoes, garden roses dripping over a trellised arbor, gardenias fragrant in the spring; staying home and luxuriating in our nakedness on Saturday mornings, watching tiny wrens and doves fight for space on the feeders outside our bedroom window and the symphony of song that they gave back in return for their breakfast. Life became glorious. Not fame, not work, but life. I had faced the demons and, like bullies, they had backed off and faded away with confrontation. I was finally able to be grateful for all of life's experiences, good and bad.

THIRTY

Along with my glorious new sense of peace and serenity came work . . . by the truckload. *She's the Sheriff* was canceled after two seasons, which was okay. It was not the right show for me, and for the moment, it was in my way—an obstacle to the other work I was drawn to as a result of *Keeping Secrets.*

More and more hospitals, rehab centers, women's groups, large corporations, and universities were inviting me to be their guest speaker. The first speaking engagement was the hardest. I allowed fear to undermine my abilities to deliver my message. I had been asked to speak at the opening of a new drug and alcohol rehab center in San Diego for an audience of eight hundred people. The public was invited by the hospital to "Listen to Suzanne Somers' inspirational story of recovery." I didn't feel I would be able to inspire them. For days preceding the event, I read and reread my book, making index cards of bullet points and highlights. I made myself sick with worry. My thinking was clouded. I couldn't remember anything. What was the book about, anyway? Armed with this lack of confidence, I walked onstage to "inspire" people. One hour and thirty-six index cards later, along with a lot of yawning from the audience, I realized I was bombing big time. Not only had I not inspired, but I had also bored them to death.

After that first lecture, I realized I had approached the engagement incorrectly. Why did I have to try to remember my story? I asked myself. I could not forget what I already knew. I remembered the line from AA: "Keep it simple, stupid!" All I had to do was tell the truth.

My next speaking request was from another drug and alcohol rehab center in Mission Viejo, California. This time I would be speaking before a group of over a thousand community leaders, interested members of the public, and recovering substance abusers. My approach was completely different. I meditated before the lecture, asking God to be with me and resolving that if one person was helped by my story, it would be a success.

I had a beginning, an end, and some idea of where I wanted to be around the middle of my speech. As I walked through the large crowd toward the dais, I was overwhelmed by the reaction. The audience rose to their feet and clapped until I was settled on the stage and I asked them to please be seated. I stood quietly before them for a moment, and in that space of time, I picked up all the emotion in the room. A lump formed in my throat, making it hard for me to speak. These people were friends. I could feel they had already read my book or had seen me on *Donahue* and were hoping I could move them forward in their recovery or in their understanding of those around them afflicted with the disease. I was not alone. I would be okay.

"I am a grateful child of an alcoholic," I began. "Let me repeat that. I am a grateful child of an alcoholic . . ."

Speaking became the most powerful creative force I had ever experienced. When you tell the truth, it's mesmerizing for all involved, including yourself. When the audience realized I was speaking without notes, without any safety net, they became still and rapt. Interestingly, the freedom of extemporaneous speaking took away all stage fright. I believed I would be given the words, and that belief did not let me down.

Each time I stood before a new congregation, my message became more powerful. The message was of forgiveness and of the peace that accompanies it. When you tell the truth, you can't trip up. I felt tremendous responsibility to my audiences. I appreciated the energy it took to get themselves to this auditorium, and I didn't care if the audience was large or small. I only cared to deliver a message of hope. My job was not to advise but to tell them of my experience in the hope that they would see bits and pieces of their own lives. By my example, they might want to change their lives. I spoke as a person who had been to the bottom and found my way up by facing myself with complete honesty. I told them to see pain as a gift. Adversity teaches us; but often, when people experience pain, they look for things or substances to take it away. I had dealt with the pain of my childhood by closing off my feelings. I told them, "I pretended the pain didn't exist. I numbed myself just as the alcoholic does. If I could believe it wasn't happening, I could live in denial. It just wasn't there. Yet," I told them, "I always had this emptiness inside, like a hole in my chest that I was unable to fill, a constant unhappy cavern. I didn't allow myself to 'feel' unless there was violence. Then I couldn't avoid feeling. It was a crazy cycle."

After each speech, I would ride away from the venue and watch the people running after my car with books or pieces of paper, but I had nothing left to give them. My autograph was not going to change their lives. Only my truth and my example would have any meaning.

While riding away, I would usually cry from the exhaustion of taking myself back to a past I had left so long ago. This was now my work. It was a gift and a privilege, and I cried from the joy of being given this great assignment. My life had meaning, and I was grateful.

During these times, I also realized the tremendous opportunity I had been given on *Three's Company*. The pettiness of my departure seemed insignificant compared with the platform I had been given as a result of the exposure and fame I had won during my years on the show. Chrissy had made me lovable and trusted. That is who my audiences thought they would meet. Instead, they met the real me; and to my good fortune, they were not disappointed.

THIRTY-ONE

We resumed our lives in Los Angeles and it felt like the right place to be. We were back in the action, the creative vortex of the entertainment business.

"I've been thinking about that conversation we had in Las Vegas about passive income, and I have an idea," Alan said one night. "I keep getting calls from people who want you to represent their products. So far, nothing has impressed me. But there's a guy who wants to present his piece of fitness equipment, and he's willing to drive to the desert to meet with us. I've seen it already. I think we could really make something of it. You could inspire women by telling them that it is possible to stay in shape with a minimum of effort."

"I don't want to do one of those exercise videos," I told him. "Everyone has done them. Besides, that's Jane Fonda's territory."

"Yes," Alan said, "but this is a great piece of equipment, not a video. You like to keep in shape, but you're not fanatical. Most women feel that way. This device might be perfect for you."

"It's a V-Toner," the man explained, sitting in the gazebo of our desert home. "It's for the upper body, shoulders, biceps, et cetera."

I looked at the device. It looked like a large V with a steel coiled spring at the base. I studied it for a while and asked, "Will this thing work for the inner thighs?"

"Oh, sure," he said. "It's great for that area. I just thought if we highlighted the shoulder area, we might attract more interest."

Alan and I played with the V-Toner, looking at it from every angle, and we both decided that very day it should be renamed "ThighMaster."

Things happened quickly after that. The V-Toner had been around for more than twenty years. The man who presented it to us had been one of its inventors. None of them understood anything about marketing and promotion. They had taken the V-Toner to a company called Ovation for financing, and Ovation said they would be interested in manufacturing it if they could find a well-known celebrity to front the product. This is where I came in. After testing it for a few weeks, I noticed that my thighs had tightened to their youthful firmness; best of all, I had been able to use the device while lying in bed watching television.

"This is great!" I told Alan.

"Okay, let's go with it," he said enthusiastically. "I think it's a winner."

Neither Alan nor I wanted me to merely "front" an item. Alan met with Ovation and told them what we wanted if we were to be involved. "Suzanne will do the commercials, which we'll write, and her picture will be used on the box and in advertisements. Suzanne's image will be linked with the item and we'll do all the marketing and promotion. For that, we want equal ownership."

Ovation was a new company backed by a wealthy divorcée and needed a "hit" to jump-start the company. They recognized Alan's keen sense of marketing and my value with the public. I had a following and had never lied to the public. So if the product worked for me (and it did), they would believe it.

We began the process of starting a new business. Ovation was involved with the manufacturing. We did the photo layouts for the box, and chose the blue and red color for the ThighMaster. We felt it looked very American. Then we created the television commercial.

One night, while getting ready for bed, I decided to show Alan the new pair of luxurious Manolo Blahnik satin high-heeled shoes I had recently purchased. I put them on and walked into our bathroom in my bra, panties, and the new shoes. Alan gave me "that look" that I love and said in his sexiest voice, "Great legs!"

"Thank you," I said, smiling coyly. At that moment we both realized that the best advertising always comes from real life.

"That should be the commercial," Alan said excitedly.

I enthusiastically agreed.

One month later, I walked onto the set of the studio in a leotard and my high-heeled Manolos. The camera started at my feet and worked its way up, while off-camera Alan said, "Great legs!"

"Thank you," I replied, and the ThighMaster was off and running.

I had been worried that doing a fitness commercial might look cheesy, but Alan said, with his usual insight, "If it succeeds, you'll be perceived as brilliant; and if it fails, it'll come and go and no one will remember it."

Within the first week, sales were skyrocketing. The 1-800 number was operating twenty-four hours a day. Big national stores such as Target and Kmart were making large areas of floor space available for the ThighMaster. It became the number one Christmas gift. Everyone had to have one, even if they bought it as a joke. It was under $20, so everybody could afford it.

Alan continued to use every available opportunity for free advertising. He booked me on *Oprah*, *The Tonight Show* with Jay Leno, David Letterman, *Geraldo*, Larry King, and *Live with*

Regis and Kathie Lee. We gave a ThighMaster to everyone in the audience on *Maury Povich* and *Jenny Jones.* Every national and local talk show in America eventually had me on their program promoting the ThighMaster.

Mel Gibson's company called. They wanted to use the commercial in his next movie, *Forever Young.* In it, his character had been cryonically frozen for twenty years; when he woke up, the first thing he saw was me on TV doing a ThighMaster commercial! We also got a request from Universal Pictures to use the ThighMaster in their production of *The Nutty Professor,* starring Eddie Murphy, as well as a request from Warner Bros. to use it in their movie *Heat,* starring Robert DeNiro and Al Pacino. *Saturday Night Live* did skits using the ThighMaster. Then the late-night hosts began referring to it in their monologues. Weekly (sometimes nightly), Jay Leno would wisecrack about the ThighMaster. He did demos using it as an orange juice squeezer. It was on David Letterman's Top Ten List so many times I lost count, and Keenan Ivory Wayans used it as a story line for his half-hour sitcom. So did *Murphy Brown* and *Designing Women.* I turned on the TV set one afternoon and Phil Donahue was wearing a ThighMaster on his head. But the topper was watching the President of the United States, George Bush, on CNN speaking to a black-tie audience. He said, "The reason Marlon Fitzwater can't be here tonight is because he busted his ThighMaster." I screamed with laughter. CNN ran that piece over and over for days.

ThighMaster became ingrained in the American consciousness. It was an answer in the game Trivial Pursuit and was put into the dictionary. It became the highest-selling piece of fitness equipment in history at that time. We had done it.

"You wanted passive income, you got it!" Alan said, smiling.

We were on a roll and having a ball. ThighMaster had sold millions of units, and to this day shows no signs of slowing down.

In 1991 Alan received a phone call from Tom Miller and Bob Boyett, megaproducers of such smash television hits as *Happy Days*, *Laverne and Shirley*, *Perfect Strangers*, and *Family Matters*. "We'd like to talk to Suzanne about starring in a new sitcom called *Step by Step* with Patrick Duffy."

The timing was perfect, and within days I had entered into negotiations to costar in this new fall entry for ABC Television. ABC had an entirely new management and executive team since I had starred on *Three's Company*. I felt like I was returning from exile. I wanted to tackle television again, and this company seemed to be the right fit for me. Tom and Bob were perfect gentlemen from the beginning. They conveyed an attitude of respect in the very first meeting, a willingness to be flexible with my now-busy schedule, and they were completely honest about their intentions.

"We want to be up front with you from the start," Bob explained. "We're hoping one of the kids will 'break out' from the show the same way the Fonz did on *Happy Days*."

They understood how television worked. If one of the kids "broke out," it would make the situation better for the show and in turn for me as a profit participant. A "breakout" character elevates ratings and adds to the longevity of the show.

I couldn't help but think of Mickey Ross and his lack of understanding when my Chrissy Snow character broke out and went beyond the show. Mickey had seen the situation as threatening. Tom and Bob saw it as good business. I was going to enjoy working with these guys.

The only unknown for me was Patrick Duffy. I had met him once before, at a Lorimar benefit for David Saltzman. He was the master of ceremonies, and I provided the musical portion of the evening. I had talked with Patrick for only a moment, and other than noticing his devastatingly good looks, I couldn't pick up anything about his personality. I hoped the chemistry would be right between us.

What a pleasant surprise Patrick was! From the moment we met on that first day to read the script, I felt as though I had known him all my life. He was gentle, kind, generous, and giving; he was and is the most selfless person I have ever met in this business. Best of all, he was funny and extremely mischievous. I loved him instantly and decided that no matter what happened regarding the success or failure of *Step by Step*, I had made a friend for life.

Patrick was "Frank" and I was "Carol," a married couple with a blended family of six children. My three children hated sharing their house with his three kids. Parallels of my own life emerged. Putting blended families together is difficult at best. Fifty percent of all the children in America are children of divorce, and the success of the show was guaranteed by a Friday-night time slot geared to the kids across the country who were allowed to watch TV on ABC's "TGIF." A large quotient of these kids were experiencing blending families in their own lives.

Within that first year of *Step by Step*, I was honored with another People's Choice Award. It was the same award I had won when I played Chrissy Snow on *Three's Company*, as Favorite Actress in a New Television Series. It felt good. The public hadn't forgotten me.

———

The difficult part of doing a sitcom was lack of time to do all the other things in which Alan and I were now involved. Poor management by Ovation caused the company to go bankrupt. They had wasted money right and left, while Alan and I had managed our half separately. The wealthy divorcée was in over her head and had not been paying proper attention to "the store." As a result, Alan and I assumed total ownership of ThighMaster and decided to use this opportunity to branch out.

Inventors lined up outside Alan's office to present their inventions; and out of every couple of hundred, someone would come in with a great idea. Soon we were in the manufacturing business with everything from billion-code garage door openers to Ozonators (an air-cleansing device) to heated cat pillows, and, of course, additional fitness equipment, including our new ButtMaster. The ThighMaster continued selling by the millions, and soon other celebrities were coming to Alan to have him match a product to their image.

I was still overwhelmed with the sacks of mail from *Keeping Secrets* and the flood of lecture requests. In addition, I had started the Suzanne Somers Collection, a line of jewelry for the Home Shopping Network, which was very time consuming. Both Alan and I realized that electronic shopping was the wave of the future and we wanted to be in on it at the outset. From the beginning, I clicked with the seventy-million-plus audience of mostly women. I chatted with them every few weeks for three hours on Saturday and again on Sunday. We talked about their lives and problems and jewelry and laughed together. It was in essence the first real interactive talk show, and over the years, these women have become my friends. I was able to bring them jewelry that up until then had been out of their grasp. Because we sold such a huge volume, we were able to give them classy necklaces, bracelets, rings, and earrings for an affordable $35 to $99.

Then the Suzanne Somers Institute ... for the Effects of Addictions on Families was formed by myself, Alan, and Gerry Myers, the former director of NaCOA (National Organization for Children of Alcoholics). I wanted to use my celebrity to lure the best and brightest minds in this area from all over America. Together we gathered a traveling team of experts who created a medical protocol specifically designed for those people surviving in the hell that is created by living with an alcoholic, addict, or abuser.

I needed to be able to send the readers of my book to a place
to find help. Every letter I received asked me where to go, and
up until this time I hadn't known where to send them. I figured
if we had a program, my team of experts could travel to whatever city requested our services and hold workshops, while
training the professionals who would run the centers. It was
instantly successful. On weekends away from *Step by Step*, I
traveled to various cities to lecture and hold press conferences
there, talked with reporters, and appeared on the local news to
let the community know that this service was now going to be
available to help them.

Somehow, Alan and I kept a balance. We scheduled rest and
vacation times and had an agreement that we would treat these
as sacred. During these times, we often stayed at our desert
home and luxuriated in the magical dry air. Something about the
weather and the silence of that region rejuvenated my soul. I
would watch the many birds I lured to our home with dozens of
feeders. I would cook incredible meals for the two of us. All of
Alan's favorites—Honey-Vanilla Duck, chocolate soufflés, and
fresh fig tarts. We loved having friends over for dinner.

Some days I would spend my time doing simple things like
sun-drying Roma tomatoes, then packing them in olive oil with
sprigs of rosemary and cloves of garlic. Or if the peaches were
ripe, I'd make peach sorbet and peach ice cream, peach pies and
peach confiture.

Alan would always be somewhere on the property. I would
call his name, and from his answer, I could tell the direction his
voice was coming from, usually from some rock high atop a
mountain.

———

In September 1991, Bruce married Caroline. We set up a beautiful huge white tent in front of our beach house, the same house
in which Alan and I had been married years before. I never knew

I could be as happy as I was when I watched Bruce escort Caroline to the altar and commit his life to her.

At the reception, we had a sixteen-piece orchestra on a five-foot-high platform inside the tent. The two hundred and fifty guests danced the night away, occasionally stopping to nibble on spit-roasted baby lamb with a yogurt-cucumber sauce, grilled salmon, rosemary potatoes, grilled vegetables, and wedding cake. One of the big highlights for me was Alan's twenty-minute toast to Bruce and Caroline. He told the assembled guests what it meant to have Bruce as his son and how grateful he was for their relationship. There wasn't a dry eye in the room.

I surveyed the room. Leslie looked fabulous. She had designed Caroline's incredibly beautiful wedding dress as a gift to both of them, as well as designing my dress.

Stephen had come all the way from Europe to attend Bruce's wedding. It meant a lot to all of us, especially Bruce. It was the first time we had met Olivia.

"Is this getting serious?" Alan asked Stephen.

"Getting?" Stephen replied. "I'm going to marry her."

Olivia is a delicate wistful beauty, much like a young Genevieve Bujold—with elegant features and skin like a rose petal. We all loved her immediately. She had grace and passion coupled with a thoughtful intellect.

"We're very happy for both of you," I told Stephen honestly. It was our way now. I only acted or said things that I felt to be true. As a result, Stephen and I began to connect. I realized I had never needed to pretend my feelings. It was honesty that bonded us. Acting false had kept us disconnected.

All the pieces had fallen into place.

To my right I watched my parents, Maureen and Bill, Dan and Mardi, Michael, my nephews, nieces, cousins, aunts, and uncles, all the people I loved, sober and happy, enjoying the celebration. Bruce's father was there also; and I knew that somewhere down the road Bruce would deal with the issues between them. For now it was a joyous occasion. It was the beginning of another passage for all of us. But this time we didn't enter kicking and screaming, but gently, softly, and lovingly.

———

Our desert house became a family haven. Bruce and Caroline would often come for weekends, as would Leslie and her new husband, Frank. Born in a small village near Marseilles, France, Frank had dreamed of coming to America when he grew up to become rich or famous or successful, or all three. He had pursued a career in bodybuilding while still living in France and had sculpted his physique to male perfection. A year before leaving for America he had won the title of Monsieur France ("Mr. France"), and he hoped he could parlay this success into a career similar to Arnold Schwarzenegger's. When she met Frank, Leslie fell in love and lust simultaneously. Four years later they married. We were happy that Leslie had found what she wanted in life. A year before the wedding, Leslie had given birth to a beautiful flower of a little girl, whom she and Frank named Daisy.

During this time Stephen had moved to Paris to follow his artistic dreams of writing and directing films. Stephen is still very private, like his father and sister, and needs to live in an environment that does not smother him. Maybe our commercial success made him feel uncomfortable. Whatever the reason, we understood and accepted his choice. Fame should be chosen. No one can ever understand the absence of anonymity unless they've lived it. I chose it. I love it. Stephen does not.

We all gave him our blessing; and within a very short time, Stephen created a life for himself that finally fit his personality. He liked the privacy and culture that France offered. Shortly after arriving, he met Olivia, and one year later, in November

1991, they were married, shortly after Bruce and Caroline's wedding.

Today we manage to see Stephen and Olivia often, particularly in May, when we take our annual trek to France.

———

The only area of my life not getting the proper attention at that time was my nightclub act. The nightclub business had changed. The crowds had thinned; the hotels were no longer paying enough money for big acts to survive unless they were subsidized by a record company. My act required semi trucks, a twenty-six-piece orchestra, ten dancers, wardrobe assistants, lighting designers, sound equipment and operators, and a musical director.

By the early '90s, many of my dancers had died of AIDS. My "ace" dance captain, Michael Empero, had been ravaged by the disease, and Bjorn, my sweet, darling makeup artist, died of it as well. The fellow who replaced Bjorn, Steve Reilly, also died of the disease; and in that same year, we lost our cousin David the same way.

———

Back in August 1988, we had been rehearsing a Latin number for my opening at Caesars Palace. It was a big extravaganza. I would be wearing a rhumba skirt with a twenty-foot train of brightly colored ruffles and a big fruit hat of melons, pineapple, bananas, and grapes (all designed by Leslie). I asked my youngest dancer (he was seventeen) why he seemed so glum.

"I've just been diagnosed as HIV positive," he said with tears in his eyes.

I was stunned. I hugged him tightly while he wept. There was nothing to say.

I had been attached to these beautiful people. The dancers were like my children. The illness and each death took something from me. By the time Michael had passed away, I had lost my interest in dancing. It wasn't fun anymore. I wanted to try something different.

———

We decided to scale down the act and make it simpler. "I feel differently now than when we first started," I told Alan. "I've danced and leaped and kicked and tapped and bounced basketballs while tapping and jumping rope. I rode an elephant for three years! It's time to get in touch with the woman in me. I feel 'her' trying to bust out. Something sexier. I'd like to concentrate on singing and let my feet move their own way. I'd like to put together my own band."

We held auditions and gathered together Doug Walter, a great jazz keyboard player; Kirk Smith on stand-up bass; and David Libman, a Juilliard graduate, who is an incredible drummer. On the first day of rehearsal, a horn player showed up unannounced and I felt a little perturbed.

"Who are you and why are you here?" I asked, confused.

"I'm Glenn Zottola, and I heard you were putting this group together through the musicians network. Would you mind if I just listened for a while?"

"Well," I said, "it's a little rough. We're just getting started, and I'm not sure what we're doing; but, okay, you can stay. If it gets uncomfortable, though, you'll have to leave, all right? No hard feelings?"

"No problem," Glenn said.

I loved singing jazz. I had always loved the music of the female jazz pop artists—Nancy Wilson, Sarah Vaughn, Peggy Lee, and Ella Fitzgerald. Having the opportunity to sing jazz moved my insides around in a way I'd never experienced.

"Can I sit in on this one?" Glenn asked after about three hours.

"Like I said, I hadn't really planned on a horn." I felt a little irritated. Who was this guy anyway?

"I think I could add something you'll like," he said.

"Okay," I said reluctantly. "Let's try 'But Beautiful.'"

Glenn took his alto saxophone from its case. He touched it with a reverence and a respect that softened my feelings. Then he started to play the most beautiful sounds I had ever heard. His playing seemed to actually get inside me and sounds came out of me I had never heard; deep, breathless, soulful, and sexual. When the song was over, I almost felt embarrassed because it had seemed so intimate.

"Let's try 'Misty,'" I said.

Again, piercing, haunting, beautiful music.

"Hey," I said to Glenn, "I'm sorry if I've been unfriendly. You're great! Do you want to work with me? I think we could do something very special together."

It was with this new act that I found my musical heart. Our first club date together was a month later in Las Vegas. The reviews came out from the *Las Vegas Sun* and *Variety*. One reviewer asked where I had been hiding this part of me.

When I walked onstage that first night, there were no nerves, there was no anxiety. This was my stage, my time. I wasn't singing to please anyone but myself; and because of that, honesty filtered through the notes. I had worked out the act myself and only talked about real-life experiences and how they related to the music. Sometimes it was funny and self-deprecating. Sometimes it was poignant and meaningful. I could feel truth moving this audience in the same way my lecture audiences had been moved. I was one of them. We'd all been through events that had changed us and helped us grow. We connected; and when it was over, I took their standing ovation with pleasure. I had given them "me," and they had accepted it.

A few weeks later we were back in Vegas. After the show one night, I said to Alan, "Why don't we go over to the Hilton and visit Tanya? I wonder if she'll remember us?"

Wonderful memories flooded back as I descended the stairs under the great Hilton stage to the underground holding space where all the dancers, musicians, and various acts waited in their dressing areas until it was time for their performances.

I said hello to familiar faces, but my focus was Tanya. As I got closer, I could hear her special snorts and wheezes. I wanted her to know me.

"Tanya?" I said as I slowly walked toward her.

She looked up at me for a moment.

"Hi, Tanya, sweetheart. I've missed you." I began to rub that spot under her neck that used to make her purr like my cat. As I petted, the purring became stronger and Tanya rubbed her head next to mine and started to gently trumpet and flap her ears with excitement. "Oh, Tanya, you remember!" I hugged her. She nuzzled as a dear friend would do. Tears came to my eyes; and as I looked up at Alan, I noticed his face was also wet with emotion.

THIRTY-TWO

Today we are a happy family. Friendship has turned into love. My feelings are parental toward my stepchildren, but I am not their mother. I am their father's wife; and in that definition, I have found comfort. We know who we are to each other, and everyone feels secure in that knowledge.

Watching Bruce and Alan interact today is another joy in my life. When Bruce finally found the inner strength to stand up to Alan and demand to be treated the way he wanted, he took the first necessary step in his evolution. As a result, they are as close as father and son, dear friends and coworkers.

Recently Alan asked Bruce to come work with him full time. "I can teach you a lot, and I know how quickly you'll catch on," Alan said.

Bruce thought about it but declined because he is running his own successful production company with Caroline and did not want to interfere with its momentum. He also worried it would take too much time away from his beautiful baby daughter. Bruce later told me how he felt about Alan's offer. "Do you realize how far Alan and I have come? We share ideas with each other. We learn from each other. We talk on the phone several times a day. He's important to me."

"I know," I said softly. "I feel happy when I see the two of you arm in arm or hugging each other. You made it, Bruce. I'm proud of you. You have your relationship on your terms. Was it worth the effort?"

"Absolutely," Bruce answered. "I love Alan. There would be a big void in my life if he wasn't there."

The path to total love with my husband was to love his children. I always knew if Alan were to embrace Bruce as a loving part of his life, I would hold nothing back in my devotion for him. As long as he withheld love and treated Bruce as someone he had to endure, I stayed angry.

Back then, I did not comprehend life's lessons as I do today. With this knowledge, I can only imagine the joys of future wisdom. Clarity is an unbelievable gift. I do not see anything as "wrong" today. All wrongs are opportunities. It is evident to me now that Bruce, whom I love so completely and with such focus, learned a lot about rejection, loneliness, exclusion, and even cruelty from Alan. We all have a purpose in one another's lives. As I chose Alan to learn about control and the choices I needed to make (which in turn would help me create an equal partnership), Bruce learned that all love does not come easily. The love he received from me was unconditional. The love he eventually received from Alan took work. And he is better prepared for life as a result of it.

As a family, what we were simultaneously teaching ourselves and learning during our difficult time was that it's up to each one of us to make our lives exactly what we want them to be. Lessons are painful. They agitate, they stir up feelings. Most of us would prefer to push our feelings down and not deal with them; but is that the stuff of life? I never wanted to have a polite relationship. I wanted a relationship with guts and passion—the good, the bad, and the ugly.

Raising kids is much like nurturing the hummingbirds I watched this spring at my home in the desert. Every day I observed the parents building the nest with spider webbing. They flew back and forth bringing the necessary ingredients to build the strongest and most perfect nest. They chose a location that was safe from predators. Finally two flawless, beautiful, tiny eggs were in the nest. Day after day the mother sat patiently keeping those eggs at the correct temperature, while the father brought her tasty morsels of food—nectar from honeysuckle, jasmine, bougainvillea—all her favorites. They were in this together. Then the baby birds broke through their beautiful blue eggshells; and day after day, the parents traded places, keeping the babies warm, flying off to get good nourishing food. The mother would digest it first, making sure their first baby food was of a consistency just right for their delicate new systems. After the appropriate amount of time, the parents left the nest more and more frequently, giving the babies the confidence to get used to life without them. Then one day, while I was resting on a wicker lounge in my gazebo, I witnessed something remarkable. One of the babies lifted himself up on the side of the nest and, through sheer instinct, attempted to move his wings. They fluttered, then stopped. It frightened him. He jumped back into the safety of the nest. Once again, he pulled himself up and fluttered. This time he was a little better at it. I watched most of the day. Over and over he tried until finally he got up his nerve. He revved his wings and took off. Wobbly, unsure, he flew not up but down. He caught himself on the banister of the gazebo, and in an instant he was off again. Like a mother bird, I watched anxiously. Flap! Flap! I was saying to myself, You can do it. Be safe. Be well. Have a wonderful life.

For me, that nest was a metaphor for life and child rearing. Our job as parents is to guide, not own. Our children are not ours. We give them life. We keep them safe. We nurture, we guide, and then we must let go and let them live and learn and make their lives what they want them to be. As they leave the nest, our only hope is that they learn to fly before they hit the ground.

As a blended family, we did not have the luxury of instinct. We were all learning from one another to determine our roles; testing, watching, initially not trusting. The roles were not clear-cut. We had to work our way through uncharted territory. We didn't come together with unconditional love. We had to learn it and work for it. It's easy to cut off your feelings and say, "Screw it"; but is that the highest purpose of being together? I don't think so.

Some blended families never really make it. Along the way, one or all give up doing the "work" and they learn to merely tolerate one another. As years go by, the pain lessens because the children grow up and move away. But deep down inside, there is a resentment at having had to share part of a life with someone you didn't care about. Those small eruptions in public that we have all witnessed are never really about the matter at hand. They are about "stuffed" feelings that eat away inside; about lack of control in your life; about being unable to have your life exactly on your terms. It's about wasted years, unresolved conflict. Feelings are our truth. They don't go away, they just get buried deeper and deeper as life goes on, until that inner darkness is such a part of us that we don't realize what it's about anymore. You've seen those people. They are the short-tempered ones, filled with unresolved conflict. That is, in fact, what a short temper is—unresolved conflict. Those people never know peace or serenity; you can see it on their faces—mouths that turn down rather than up. We wear our pain externally and internally.

Today my blended family, which had once been a source of intense anger and frustration, is the base of my life.

Recently I was talking with Leslie, who is now not only a mother but a stepmother as well. As we discussed the difficulties of blending families, I experienced déjà vu. All the frustration Leslie was feeling was an exact mirror of what I had experienced years before when Leslie, Stephen, and Bruce were acting out their rebellion and fear in our blended family. "Don't give up," I advised her. "It's worth it. Look what we have today."

"I know," Leslie said, "but it's different with my stepchild."

"No, it's not, really," I told her. "I can't imagine not having you in my life; and sometimes, when we're together laughing and enjoying ourselves, I think about the old days and how easy it would have been to give up. I would have missed so much. My relationship with your father could not have been as rich and full if I had not hung in there."

My family is one of my biggest assets. Leslie is lovable and a dear friend. I adore her and love her daughter, my granddaughter, as if they were my own blood. Leslie is one of my favorite people to hang out with. She is sweet and kind, loving and honest. I learn from her constantly, as she does from me. She succeeds at anything she attempts to do creatively.

I feel the same about Stephen. He is living a wonderful life with his family in France and is getting ready to direct his first feature film. We are great friends; and because we have been together so long, there is a shorthand to our conversation—a nod of the head or a look in each other's eyes—and our conversation picks up where we last left off. He maintains his mystery and privacy, and I accept that.

Stephen, Olivia, and our darling grandson, whom I adore, are my family. The lack of a blood connection doesn't enter into my thinking. I trust them with my secrets and my love. I would fiercely protect all of them if they were in danger.

Yet there was a time long ago when, on a daily basis, I thought about walking away from the whole experience. It didn't seem worth it. They didn't like me, and I didn't like them. Nothing good comes easily in life. You have to work for it. My initial approach had been wrong. I tried to be another mother to Leslie and Stephen, so naturally they rebelled. They already had a mother and did not need or want another one. From my perspective today, I agree with them. No one could ever replace my mother, and I would resent anyone trying to do so.

What I realize today is that the role of stepparent must be earned. In France there is no word for stepparent. In speaking with Stephen's mother-in-law, Mizou, in Paris one day, I asked her, if there isn't any word in the French language for *stepmother*, then what am I? She thought for a moment and then gently said, "You are his father's wife!"

That was profound to me. Of course, just because I married his father does not make me a mother to him on any level. I think all of us who become stepparents go into our marriages to be parents to the other's children. The goal at first should be to be a friend. It is a privilege to become a friend to your spouse's child. As time and events go by and it is earned, then, perhaps, we can be given the title of stepparent.

The role of stepparent is a delicate one. Nevertheless, initially I tried too hard with them, and then when I was rejected, I became hurt. Because I didn't have the wisdom back then to express my hurt, it built inside me and turned into anger, and I could no longer clearly understand my feelings. My anger made me feel ashamed and it confused me. Sometimes just seeing my stepchildren would trigger my emotional buttons, but I didn't understand why. We were all reading one another's faces, and what we saw created a tension between us before a word was spoken.

None of us understood how feelings work. If I had been able to express my hurt to Alan, Stephen, and Leslie, it would have created a safe environment for all of us to vent our feelings. Because we did not do this, and we resented being hurt, we were angry about it. The more we held in that anger, the more confusing it became.

But as a family, we didn't give up. We stayed with it—with all the hurt, anger, and anxiety. Finally it was honesty that healed us.

My father died a few years ago, and I felt grateful that I was filled with love and happiness that he was my father. His death did not bring up old unresolved angers and hurt, because we had repaired our relationship. I felt nothing but love as I held his hand while he lay dying. After having a massive stroke on the operating table, he was lucid for only one moment in intensive care. In that short space of time, he was able to articulate four words before another stroke took away his ability to speak forever. Only my nephew Billy was present at that moment when my dad spoke his last words: "Tell Mommy I'm sorry." He had not forgiven himself. When my nephew told me what my dad had said, I anguished over his pain.

She knows, Dad, she knows, I thought when I looked into his frightened eyes, as he was drifting away.

Amends are never too late. My mother needed these words in order to be free of her own anger in her last years.

My mother awakened one morning not long ago, and she could not see. Overnight, she had been afflicted with incurable macular degeneration, which took away ninety-eight percent of her sight. For so many years she had not allowed herself to "see" her circumstance as it really was. Denial of her painful existence with her alcoholic abusive husband, was her means of survival. You've heard the saying "You make me crazy" or "You make me sick." Maybe these statements carry with them more truth than we realize. When feelings are not dealt with, they will manifest themselves in other ways. Yet we continue to pretend that life is something other than it truly is. All because of fear. What are we afraid of? I believe we are afraid of truth. Because once we face the naked truth about ourselves and our feelings, we will have to act on these feelings, which brings change. Change is difficult because it is unknown, and the unknown is not safe. There is risk. Maybe it won't be better. So rather than take the risk, it is easier and safer to stick with the status quo. We create little uncomfortable boxes for ourselves to live in. While in these boxes we are depressed, angry, unfulfilled, controlled, abused, creatively stifled, loveless, sexually deprived, unhappy, or lonely, but at least we feel safe. We didn't have to take a chance; we never had to live our lives with all the dangers. Avoiding feelings puts a safety net on life. You can't fall, but you also can't fly. Is this our purpose?

Recently, in a conversation I had with my mother, she quietly said, "Today is the second anniversary of Dad's death."

"How do you feel?" I asked.

She thought for a moment and then said, "A little sad."

"Really, why?"

"Because I think of all the time we wasted together. We didn't bring out the best in each other, and now it's too late."

Messages come to us all the time. Think of the wisdom she passed on to me at that moment. Don't waste your life. It is a precious gift. Each moment is an opportunity to grow, learn, and find resolution. Strangely, since my mother could no longer see, she saw more than she ever did in the life that preceded her blindness. At the end of her life, she saw the truth of it all. It's never too late to grow. In my mother's twilight years, she finally faced her feelings and her truth. She learned to express herself. So was the time of denial wasted? I don't think so. It was as it was meant to be. It wasn't "wrong."

The gift of knowing is useful only if it is shared. By sharing, we all grow, learn, and move forward. My work today is about seeing; looking at my life's choices, with all their joy and all their shame; and then sharing that knowledge.

———

As I look back over the past twenty years, I realize that life's lessons presented themselves to me and will continue to do so. My opportunities came from the growth of learning. We are all in the School of Life. Today I am concerned only with being the best student.

Getting knocked down several times along the way made me stronger and gave me clarity. If I didn't change and grow, I'd be living a pathetic, sorry life. If I didn't choose to learn from each knockdown, my life wouldn't be my own. I'd still be that sad little child of the alcoholic, controlled by men and people in positions of authority. Thank you to everyone in my life who was presented before me as an obstacle to my growth.

Dad, you were my greatest teacher. I wouldn't change a thing about my childhood. Every event of that time was a disguised lesson. Through you I learned forgiveness. I remember reciting memorized prayers in grammar school that held no meaning, just a mantra I was forced to say over and over at Mass. "Forgive us our trespasses as we forgive those who trespass against us." I said the words to escape into a more beautiful place in my mind. A life of beauty, peace, and happiness. But the mantra transported my thinking to the possibilities of the life I now have.

Only now, though, do I hear the words I had actually been saying. I have made many mistakes in my life, I have made many bad choices, and I have asked forgiveness from all those whom I have hurt. I have tried with all my being to make up for my mistakes as a mother. I wish I could have done a better job of protecting Bruce from all the hurt. But that hurt is now his opportunity. I did my best to keep him safe and I hope one day he will truly understand.

Forgiveness is a gift you give yourself. I know that I never made choices to be bad or cruel or evil. My mistakes were

always based in fear. I can finally let myself off the hook. I've forgiven myself, and in doing so, I realized I had to forgive the mistakes of my father. He had a terrible disease. It made him do
horrible things. But they weren't rooted in evil or malice. The
drink made him act in an unacceptable way and the guilt made
him continue to nourish his disease. His fear of facing himself
made him continue drinking. He did the best he could. He didn't
plan to abuse any of us. He loved us but was too guilty to show
it. He didn't feel worthy. His last apology revealed his feelings
about himself. I have deep compassion and forgiveness for him.
I wish I could have understood the vicious cycle of guilt and sorrow in which he was living. Dad, I remember and love you with
all my heart. You were my opportunity.

Mickey Ross gave me opportunities to have an inspiring
career. He taught me to act, and he also unwittingly taught me
about control and accepting the consequences of my choices.
He pushed me to the edge and from there I taught myself to
value what was really important in life. Through him, I learned
that I was not my accomplishments. That was a great gift.

John Ritter and Joyce DeWitt were also teachers for me, and
I'm sorry if I was self-absorbed and insensitive during those
years. I'm pleased to say that John and I have recently begun to
rekindle our relationship.

At the premiere party of *Victor/Victoria* in New York, I felt a
tap on my shoulder and heard a familiar sweet voice say, "Hello,
darlin'." I turned around and it was John. The moment was very
emotional. It had been so many years since I had seen or talked
with him.

I tried to bring up the past, but John softly waved it away, saying, "There was no problem." I believe he was right. We were all
learning in those years and everyone was doing their best to fit
into a new existence. The familiarity of the lives we had known

had dissipated and we had all been wandering in the jungles of fame. I was happy to look into his sparkling eyes again.

As I was finishing this book I ran into him once again at my doctor's office. I told him I had written a book about our experience mainly to find the part I had played in the drama of my demise on *Three's Company*. A self-examination of sorts. John handed me his phone number and said if I wanted to talk, to please call him. I sensed a maturity about him that made him even more appealing than the John I used to know. We all grow. We have no choice. The lucky ones grow up.

I have never seen or heard from Joyce since the day I left the show, nor have I made any real attempt to contact her. But if we were to find ourselves face to face in some situation in the future, maybe we would hug each other. That would be nice.

———

Jay Bernstein introduced me to the country and the rest of the world. He opened the door to give me the privileged gift of fame. I've tried to use it well. He is the Starmaker! He offers hope to every little girl who's ever dreamed of being a star. I am grateful to him for seeing my potential and for keeping his promise to me.

Jay and I are friends today. I interviewed him several times for this book. Recently I met with him and he immediately slipped back into his old mind-messing self. "If you'd have stayed with me, you know, I'd have made you into a Goldie Hawn," he said manipulatively.

"Oh, I see. Would that have been a good thing?" I asked mischievously. "Do you really think she's happier than I am?"

"Well," he said, "it's just that you fired me at the wrong time. You still desperately needed me, but you didn't know it."

"I can't believe you're still upset," I said. "It's been almost twenty years."

"No, I'm just frustrated because I felt I had a purpose with you. It wasn't about making you rich. I wanted to make you a

role model. You offered hope to the average little girl. Through
you, they thought they could make it too. I wanted to push your
good heart. You have the biggest heart of anyone I've ever represented. Farrah only pushed people's heads. I guess you never
knew this, but I loved you more than I ever loved anyone in my
own family and I wanted to make America love you because you
were a good person who made it.

"I know Alan copied my style," he continued, "but I liked Alan!
He's a good person, but because of his background, he had a dis-
trust of people. After you and I split up, I missed my friendship
with Alan. He was never a people person. He was a strong business person. I didn't like that he cut me out. I was hurt. I felt like
I had been adopted, then neglected. But now I understand what
happened. I was in your life, but as time went by I realized that
you were going to have to make a choice between Alan and me.
It came down to marriage or career."

"Wait a minute," I asked, annoyed, "don't you think Alan's
done a good job?"

"That's my problem," Jay said. "The two of you worked it out.
The ThighMaster was good for women, your message is good
for women. You created a second turn for yourself in the business. People like you again and you made it happen. The two
of you have done it. You've gone on to do what I wanted to do
for you.

"Don't you understand?" Jay asked emotionally. "I don't have
a life. You and Farrah were my life and now I'm alone. When I
met you, I realized that if I could fall in love with you as a person, then I could make America fall in love with you. I was the
camera and you were the subject. When I put the spotlight on
you, you bloomed like petals on a flower. The spotlight was like
sunlight on a plant. Before you met me, there hadn't been any
sun on you. Through me you grew into a beautiful flower. To me
you were a gardenia; the most beautiful, fragrant, and delicate
of all flowers."

I stared at Jay, not knowing what to say. Was he being dramatic? Was he living a melancholy existence dreaming of what could have been? I felt sad, yet at the same time warm and loving toward him. No one had loved him enough as a child, I thought, and that had shaped his entire life.

"What now, Jay?" I asked, concerned. He thought for a while and said, "I'd like someone to do a movie of my life. *Starmaker* would be the title. You see, I'm an egomaniac and this would affirm to me that I accomplished my goal."

"Who would play you?" I asked, amused.

"John Wayne, if he were alive. But Harrison Ford or Kurt Russell. Maybe even Jack Nicholson or Michael Douglas. Lately people have been telling me it should be Kevin Spacey but that worries me. I know I'm more handsome than he is."

I laughed. So did Jay.

"I love you, Jay," I said sincerely. "You're weird and impossible, but I'm glad you're in my life. You did a good job for me."

"Thanks," Jay said as he looked softly into my eyes.

He paused, then he picked up his cane and walked away.

———

The book *Conversations With God* says we get our messages in mysterious ways—perhaps in a lyric of a song, or the words of a stranger, or maybe a passing remark on television. I hear the messages more often now. Not all the time, but more than ever before. It causes me to pay attention to and value others in a way I might not have in the first part of my life. Each person before me might be the carrier of information I need to move forward in my evolutionary growth. We are all connected in this way. That's the beauty and joy of the life we have been given and the reason to value all living things. By abusing or ignoring life in any of its forms, we might possibly push away important information relative to our growth.

What have I learned over the past twenty years? What was the point of these experiences? These questions were going through my mind one night while watching a segment of *Dateline NBC*. The show featured a woman who had adopted two little girls into her serene life. Because of the children's prior abuse, which she had not known about, they brought chaos and misery to her orderly and idyllic existence. They acted out, had tantrums, exhibited personality disorders, and were unable to accept love in any form. It went on for years, and all the while the woman was trying to change the girls, trying to make them conform to her idea of normal. She was never successful, and when finally, twenty years later, they angrily moved out of her home, the woman felt relieved. At last she could have her normal life back. But to her surprise, she found herself missing them. In the twenty years they had lived together, they had subliminally taught one another things they needed to know about themselves. The woman realized she had spent her life trying to change these children rather than accepting them as unique individuals. This kept her from giving love, which she now realized was the only thing they craved and wanted from her and the one thing she had wanted to give.

This made me think about my stepchildren. In the early years of my life with them, I was always trying to fit them into a mold of what I understood. I wanted them to act the same way as my child. I wanted them to conform to my ideal of children. No wonder they acted out in their different ways. I never accepted them for who and what they were. I never allowed myself to see their free and beautiful spirits. I wanted them to be like me. I now realize I was ignorant and close-minded.

But along the way, love grew. In spite of ourselves. It's not the same love I feel for my own son, Bruce. It can't be, no matter how much I might will it. It's a different kind of love, but it is love. I would miss them terribly if they were not in my life; they are now a part of me. They are my family and the love I now feel for my stepchildren is as deep and as important as that which I feel for my own child. My stepchildren have been gifts in disguise. They have taught me about patience and control. I am always putting myself in situations to teach myself about control. It comes from a childhood where everything was out of control. As a result, in my adult life, I've always tried to control everything. But that thinking has limited me, not helped me. The time has come to be open to new thoughts, new ideas, and new ways. My stepchildren were and are a big part of my learning. Today I love and admire their differences. I constantly learn from their unconventional attitudes. They approach life from another angle than I do, but now I enjoy it and am expanded as a person because of it.

The biggest surprise has been the growth we've all experienced as a family through our grandchildren. They have taught the family about love and acceptance. They don't know about blood connections or family divisions, they simply react to love. As I watch my stepchildren interact with their own children, I see what it would have been like to be loved by them without all the baggage we brought to one another's lives. I see their patience and attentiveness; their kindness, joy, and boundless capacity to love. In watching my stepchildren, I am able to imagine what it would have been like to have accepted one another earlier on, and I find great satisfaction in realizing how wrong I had been about them. This knowledge allows me to love them without working at it.

We've all changed and grown through the tangled webs of our making. Bruce and Stephen have finally found a natural way to connect, which brings me great joy. It is through their mutual respect for each other as fathers and husbands. Stephen is an incredibly caring and loving father, as is Bruce. Bruce respects the way Stephen takes care of his family. There is a calmness and maturity that comes with marriage and parenting. Both Stephen and Bruce are responsible men who love their families deeply. I admire that quality.

In turn, my relationships with our grandchildren have taught our children, including my son- and daughter-in-law, about me. Through the babies, my stepchildren see what kind of mother I could have been. They watch me love their offspring without agenda, and as I love their children, it allows them to love me. Of course, Bruce always knew me as a loving parent, but now he can watch my mothering skills objectively. Through observing, he becomes more and more appreciative of the life we shared together when he was a child. My daughter-in-law Caroline sees me as a mother figure while observing me interact with her daughter, rather than knowing me only as her husband's mother.

Who would have thought that these three beautiful little beings were sent to us as our most important teachers? Yet the true gifts are in our ability to be open to learn from them.

All the experiences we had together have been important. It is through problems and mistakes that we learn and grow. That is the point of life . . . to keep moving forward as people.

———

Today I realize that love takes time and patience and that growth takes desire and work. All events have purpose. The job in my life is to understand the meaning. Why else would I feel the need to walk back through the hills and valleys of my life? The details really aren't all that important, yet there is no way I could understand the lessons without looking back at my teachers. This part of my life and my choices were lessons granted in the greatest classroom, observing myself. As a family we were like a sea of ants trapped in a maze among the obstacles with which we were living. When an ant in an ant farm comes upon a blockade, it backs up, goes around, or crawls over it, always rerouting itself until it reaches its destination. Like the ant, I too learned to crawl around and reroute myself on this journey.

Now I am happier than I have ever been in my life. Sometimes I feel I could burst with joy. My relationship with Alan has become exquisite. After thirty years together, we are connected, joined at the hip, our lives intertwined like branches on a vine. What we have together is holy. He is my greatest friend and my most trusted ally. My respect for him is infinite, and as it was the very first time, so is our passion. My marriage is everything I ever imagined in my fantasies. Our bodies breathe together night after night as one, in peace and tranquillity.

We watch our children and grandchildren grow with pride and also with the same fear as the mother bird who watches her babies fly from the nest. What matters is their ability to flap their wings and soar, rather than fall to the ground.

But my happiness comes from a place deeper than all of this, because I am now happy with myself and who I am. I love my life. I love my work; but my work does not define me. I am just as happy putting a bouquet of my homegrown roses on a table or floating a gardenia from my garden in a beautiful dish as I am singing in front of thousands of people.

Lecturing to groups starved for clarity in their own lives gives me purpose. I don't know what tomorrow will bring, but today I am aware that forgiveness heals, that blame is wasted energy, that awareness of each moment of life is precious. I don't want to waste any of it. I want to be present, in the moment, and accept all that happens to me as the gift that it is and to grow and evolve into the best person I can be.

———

Truth is the goal. It has set me free. I try to look for it, speak it, and live it every day, not only with myself but with every person I encounter. Everything seems clearer because it is the truth.

At this moment as I finish writing my book, I am in my dressing room backstage sitting on a stool facing a large mirror surrounded by lights that allows me to put on my makeup and transform myself into "her." It is a process that takes two hours to complete. It starts with a long hot bath with lavender oils. Then I wash my hair and stand under the shower to rinse. While drying my hair, I start to think about what I want to accomplish while performing this show. I want to make the people feel something. Somewhere in a song and somewhere in my talk, it must be so raw and so honest that the intimacy of the words or lyrics makes all of us squirm with that private kind of discomfort. That is my job.

When my hair is dry, I brush it all up high on the back of my head, twist it from left to right into a mop on the top, and anchor it with a pin or two. While I highlight my lashes with mascara and brush my cheeks with pink, I am thinking about accountability, caring, decency, and love. If we all were accountable and were the best people we could be, our example would inspire the next generation. There is so much anger and misunderstanding in families today. Not just families like mine who have worked through the entanglements of blending, but all those connected by blood who keep up their defensive walls of noncommunication. They never get to know one another because they never know themselves. But interacting with total honesty is the most tremendous personal gift we share. The reward is contentment. The work it has taken to have a better understanding of who I am allows me to relax and enjoy. There are no more demons now. Life seems simpler. There is no competition. There is no race to win. I'm just living my life my way and loving it. Because I'm aware, I'm able to truly enjoy each day and every event big or small; the smell of my husband's skin, the twinkle in Bruce's eye, the way Leslie makes me laugh, when Stephen lets down his guard—all these precious moments add up to peace and satisfaction.

Yes, this is what I'll tell my audience, I say to myself as I finish putting on "her" lips, big, red, and full. I push one diamond earring into my right earlobe and the other into my left. I reach for my gown—black satin, long and tight.

Nothing is really bad, I think to myself, so all of life's experiences are lessons from which to learn and grow. We each have a choice. To be a victim? To say why me? Why do bad things happen to me? Or to look at it from another point of reference. How can I grow? What can I learn? What is the opportunity being presented?

I pull on one white opera-length glove and button five small pearls at the wrist. Then I pull the left glove on and button it.

As I look at myself, front and back, in the floor-length mirror in the dressing room, I can see that I am ready. I am now "her," the part of myself that gives me such enjoyment. You go out there, I say to myself, and tell them these things; let them see the possibilities. Where you come from is not where you have to stay. It's our only life right now. Make it the best. Be the best. Live your dreams and know yourself. Be happy.

I spray myself with Chanel No. 5, behind my ears, in my cleavage.

"Let's go, Alan. I'm ready."

I walk down the long hallway; there are people lining the sides, but I don't see them right now. I'm in focus. My heart is beating with excitement and privilege. I continue across the open courtyard; the air is fresh. I like the feel of the black satin against my skin. I go up the six steps to the stage level. I hear musicians warming up. I'm saying hello to people, but I am still in focus. The backstage is dark. Alan steadies me in my high-heeled black satin Manolos to keep me from tripping on the floor cables. My eyes adjust to the dark. I hear the buzz, a low roar, from behind the curtain. This is a good audience, I think to myself. I can tell by their tone. I meditate behind curtain ropes.

I speak to the voice within. "Together we can do anything," I say to someplace deep within me. I visualize my body filling with liquid gold, entering through a cavity at the top of my head. It fills my limbs, my torso, my neck, my face, my entire head. I feel strength. I am not alone; I can feel it. I see Glenn pick up his horn. I smile at him. My band swells with sounds of music.

"Go get 'em," Alan whispers into my ear.

"Ladies and gentlemen . . . Universal Amphitheater presents . . . MISS SUZANNE SOMERS!"

Photograph Credits